790.01922
P22p

**Parents' magazine & better homemaking.**

Parents' magazine's Family fun book. Compiled and edited by Frances Fielding-Jones. Illustrated by Lewis Parker. [New York] Parents' Magazine Press [1965]

254 p.   illus.   24 cm.

1. Family recreation.   I. Fielding-Jones, Frances, ed.   II. Title: Family fun book.

GV182.8.P293                    790.01922                    64-66134

Library of Congress            [5]                    RBP

Parents' Magazine's

# FAMILY
# FUN
# BOOK

Compiled and Edited by
Frances Fielding-Jones
*Associate Editor, Parents' Magazine*

Illustrated by Lewis Parker

Published by Parents' Magazine Press
a division of Parents' Magazine Enterprises, Inc.

# ACKNOWLEDGEMENTS

Most of the material in this book has appeared previously in PARENTS' MAGAZINE and we are grateful to the authors for the use of their material. We thank, too, the National Recreation Association, the U.S. Children's Bureau and other organizations from whose publications we have adapted material.

PARENTS' MAGAZINE PRESS
*a division of Parents' Magazine Enterprises, Inc.*
52 Vanderbilt Avenue, New York, N.Y.

# CONTENTS

6992

# INTRODUCTION

Begin with the essential ingredient: family fun; add a dash of imagination, a pinch of planning; season with laughter, and stir well. Result: a fun feast with something for everyone to enjoy.

Selected from the pages of Parents' Magazine, here are ideas for play and playthings for every member of the family, year round, indoors and out.

At home, there are games to play alone, with a friend or two, in a small group or at a neighborhood get-together; diversions for the convalescing child; simple, inexpensive things for youngsters to make and do; a workshop plan for all who have ever dreamed of a chance to "do-it-yourself"; hundreds of hobbies; songfests; party ideas; dramatic play; music lessons, and endless new toys to build on.

For outdoor fun, there are races to run, pets to play with, science to study, backyards to barbecue in. There are suggestions for water play; pointers for picnics—large and small; guides for gardening; clues for successful family camping, for exploring the world of nature, for car games that take the travail out of traveling.

Beyond the fun and games, you'll discover, too, *why* children play as they do, which activities they prefer at different ages, how their creativity can be developed—all kinds of helpful hints, in fact, on how to encourage youngsters to grow into fun-loving, pleasure-giving adults themselves.

This book is, of course, a wonderful reference source. Dip into it frequently for specific suggestions on rainy days, when you plan a special party, when a child asks, "What can I do now?" It's also a book to browse through—for future activity ideas, for insight into the ways and means of enriching family life. Basically, it's a book for all seasons, for all ages, for all occasions. Have fun!

—*Frances Fielding-Jones*

7

# PLAY

# IS CHILD'S

# WORK

*PLAYLAND IS A WONDERFUL WORLD in miniature, more bountifully and beautifully populated than ever these days with toys and games—versions of everything that walks, talks, rolls, slides, sails or flies. Whether it's an imaginary, exciting trip to the moon, a colorful old-time circus, a ship to command or a doll that talks back or kisses, your child will find it in the wonderland of play . . . to enhance his fun, his growth, his confidence.*

9

# WHAT
# CHILDREN
# LEARN FROM PLAY

Play can be a powerful educator in many important ways. What are some of the things play actually teaches children?

**Play helps youngsters to be part of the group.**   Watch the youngster of three, four and five who wants to join a group of other children. Perhaps he offers a child a toy, or asks about a fancy gadget dangling from another child's belt. Sometimes he asks directly, "Can I play with you?" Such interchange helps him to belong. And the most comfortable age to learn how to become a joiner is at three, four and five.

**Play teaches teamwork.**   Good play requires give and take, sharing, waiting and a sense of honest exchange. "Three swings and a jump" were the turn-taking orders agreed on by the group. When George took four he met a vigorous reprimand. "You took more than your share," the other children shouted.

Many such rules are made up and enforced within a group of children at play. Instead of having grownups tell them how to manage and why rules are needed, they sense a need of regulation, make rules and often rigorously enforce them. What a force for the development of good law-abiding citizens!

As children grow older and play organized games with standard rules, these early learnings are reinforced. To a play-experienced youngster, rules make sense and are accepted—no fussing, complaining or cheating. "Good sports" in the play sense have learned a fundamental need of life, namely, to accept and obey regulations and laws that groups and communities must establish to make life safe and comfortable.

**Children discover their own limits and strengths through play.**
"Pete, you're good at clay. I'm lousy," said Andy, age seven.

Children tend not only to understand their own unique strengths but also to accept their limits while according credit to their more able friends. Such understandings are more readily developed when youngsters play with only enough supervision to protect them.

Of course, once in a while an adult must interfere to see that a young manager does not browbeat the weaker members of the group. But in day-after-day play most youngsters get a superb lesson in where they stand in skills. Montie expressed it perfectly when he said, "When it comes to running bases I'm O.K., but when it comes to batting I've got a lot of practicing to do." Although not all children can face up to themselves as honestly as this, many do because they are helped to do so in play, games and juvenile sports.

**Play provides a chance to test out ideas.** There is learning—actual knowledge—that youngsters acquire through play. In the early years, through much imitating of adults in housekeeping, policing and baby tending, they learn how to propose ideas and then try them out, often improvising as they go along. So much of a child's life is lived in a family, school and neighborhood where he has to fit into established ways of behaving that play may give him the only chance he has to test out his own ideas.

**Play increases energy.** Today we are growing in understanding not only of how important play is to the child and what a valuable set of social and technical skills he learns through play, but in addition we are seeing the deeper, harder-to-define values which he acquires chiefly through play. For example, we have an opportunity to see him grow in his ability to put forth energy, to stick at games tenaciously and to love the feeling of zip, action—and fatigue.

Without play many a child would not have a chance to experience such vigor and punch.

**Play is preparation for living.** Of course, not all play is sweet harmony. Perhaps too often we may idealize play. What a mistaken idea! Play often is cruel, full of quarrels and an occasional crisis. This is fortunate because youngsters need to learn to manage themselves in turbulent waters as well as in calm. Often, if adults do not interfere, the children settle arguments and acute differences so successfully that play is quickly resumed. Sometimes a brief armistice is declared until heads cool off. All of this

**11**

adds up to good education in living. Via such rugged experience children are learning how to meet clash and dissension in home, school and later life.

**Play can teach respect for others** from different backgrounds and with different customs. The ability to disagree and yet get along together and the willingness to see worth in friends because of their qualities at play, these are powers we adults may strive for and envy; yet children, if not warped by poor guidance, seem rather naturally to acquire them.

**Play develops good sports.** From the specific skills and social techniques he learns as well as from the more general attitudes learned at play, a boy or girl can get that wonderful sense of being "all right" or "adequate." As Carol and Jane put it, "We weren't so hot but we had a swell time and we played a good game. We did O.K."

It would be comforting to think that for each blow life deals a child he could have another experience about which he could say, "I did O.K." He could then go more surely through life without being fearful or apologetic. Play offers him this chance to find out that one can't win all the time. Neither should one always fail. The good sport is the one who picks himself up and carries on. And this is one more of the all-important lessons our children learn from play.—*Roma Gans*

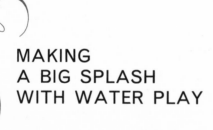

## MAKING
## A BIG SPLASH
## WITH WATER PLAY

**Water, water everywhere.** Whether a child is at the sea, bay, lake, pond, brook, pool, creek, stream, puddle—water enchants. Wading's good for splashing, toe-squishing, the surprise of little jets cast up on tummy, tail or chest. Pouring's good from pail to cup to hand to toe. Sieve the water. Yes. This time perhaps it'll stay in. Even if it won't, a person can shake it and make it into a rainstorm!

**Foam.** Can foam be caught, can bubbles be kept, can pokey wondering fingers be deft enough to catch delight and put it in a pail?

The joys of water play don't have to be confined to summer's bright weather. Indoor days aren't hard—faucets, too, provide a flow, sinks and tubs a basin to catch and hold the wonder and the pleasure of water.

**Too messy?** Not if you take the time—five meager minutes—to cover the floor with newspapers, cover the plumpness of his or her person, if necessary, with plastic or oilcloth or any water-repellent fabric. You can make a poncho-style apron for water play out of any of these materials. For a usual size three or four-year-old, you'll need a piece of material about 45 inches long. Fold it in half, cut an opening for the neck, bind the opening with tape—the press-on kind of tape will do. If you cut the apron's outer edges with pinking shears, you won't need to bind or sew them. The smallest size person can slip it over his head without help.

**Back to the sink.** Back to your bathtub sailor in his poncho, intent on his navy. Are there toy boats sailing his sea, bits of wood he can pretend are anything? Plastic cups and containers for the fun of their different colors and forms? Add a spoon or ladle to his equipment—and let him scoop! Add a funnel—and he channels the water from one cup to another. Add soap flakes, a dash of detergent—and give him the rapture of mountains of bubbling foam!

He'll set to, scooping, pouring, channelling, gauging the gush from the faucet, kneading gossamer soapy mass, stirring it up, stirring it down. He's having fun, yes—but he's also doing what a scientist does when, having perceived wonder, he explores an element, learns its power, its limits. And he's also acting like an artist—in love with his medium, aware of its wonder, playing with its possibilities.

So heave to, and let him do more. Soapy water can be used for washing small cups and teapots, for bathing and shampooing dolls. Dolls aren't for boys, or teacups either? Watch a three or four-year-old male and see for yourself as he scrubs away intently. Filled with a sense of their achievement, too, are these pint-sized scrubbers as they "help" Mommy with the washing of whatever unbreakable objects she gives into their chubby hands.

**There's water in pails, too.** Give your child a small pail and sponge and let him wash table tops and chairs, part of the kitchen or bathroom floor if you will. The porch? An outdoor flagstone? A spot of insufferable

**13**

woodwork? How helpful this bucket-and-sponge brigade feels.

Give your helper a bowl of water, some cleanser and a small piece of sponge. (Spread newspapers first, of course, over the area he'll inhabit.) Then give him what you will for polishing—brass bowls and candlesticks, pewter plates, spoons and metal trays. Turn him loose. See him go—dipping his sponge into the water, from the water to the cleanser, then round and round over the metal with zeal. Water will trickle down small fingers onto the newspapers. Will leave smudged trails on wrists and arms. Will drip off elbows. Do these drawbacks deter The Polishers? A thousand times no!

**Bubble-blowing** hardly ever loses its charms. A bowl to hold water, soap flakes or detergent, some kind of blowpipe and perhaps newspapers over the blowing area are all you need. Puff through the pipe stem, send magical, shimmery-shiny multi-colored spheres floating around the room. They rise, curve slowly in the air, glowing with light—until exploring fingers burst them into spray! Discovery! Endlessly repeated.

Small wire forms dipped into the suds give variety to this fascinating play. When your child blows directly on the film of liquid on the wire, the rainbow colored bubbles again float before his fascinated eyes.

A whole group of blowers can blow at the same time. Give each child a plastic tumbler or two paper cups, one inside the other to last longer. Pour each receptacle half-full of sudsy water and hand out straws—plastic ones for firmness, colored ones for interest. Result: mounds of varicolored bubbles in all sizes that build up, run over the cups, spread their sparkle for puffy cheeked blowers.

**Water play outdoors.** "Washing" is the simplest form of outdoor water play. Again, a pail of water and a sponge. One child may fill the sponge with water and drip it to the place where it's to be used. Another child may press and squeeze the water from the sponge to make it easier to handle. Each child plays and works at his own level of discovery and development. Doors and steps and railings may be washed. Wagons, slides and swings may be washed. Fences, gates and floors. Over and over again, eager hands dip into the water, sturdy feet trudge back and forth to complete the task. Or maybe not to complete the task. Maybe to spill the pail over! No harm done—pails can be filled again—"work" and play merge once more.

Take the sponges away, and this time give your child a fairly wide, flexible paint brush with his filled pail. All things that need "washing" also need "painting." With one exciting addition: sidewalks! Invariably, children will go down on their knees to "paint" the sidewalk. And no

**14**

wonder. For magical designs can be traced with brush and water. One minute there they are—then, presto, chango, they disappear as the air and sun get to work on them! More discovery—again undiminished by endless repetition.

**A sandbox** of any size, shape or condition should be part of the equipment of any upstanding preschooler. For mish-mashing with sand and water is also a universal delight of childhood. Sifting, pouring, patting, shaping, feeling, molding add up to unparalleled pleasure. Some children like to add just enough water so the sand holds its shape and is easily moldable into forms. Others add more and more and MORE water till the sandbox becomes a gritty, flowing pond—to be explored with hands or feet or stirred with wooden spoons.

Don't overlook the garden hose. The spray of water lifts, like a fountain, into the air—a challenge. Which child will be first to brave the jetting water? It takes courage to try that first breakthrough into the squirt, the jet—but oh, the joy of it once it's done . . . and hoses can be used to fill the garden wheelbarrow, to add "rivers" to the sandbox.

Small, plastic pools, too, are treasures for outdoor water play. Lucky the child who on an extra warm late spring day or a balmy Indian summer one, plays in his pool and savors the first or the last feel of water, sun and air.

Heave to with the buckets, the basins, the pails, the sponges, the brushes! For there's wonder in water for your child.—*Jeanette Guillaume*

# PLAYTHINGS

*A toy should be appropriate to the child's present interests and capacities; at the same time, it should have possibilities for play which encourage his further development. And toys—especially for younger children—should be capable of being played with in many ways, as the child's imagination directs. Complicated toys of limited use may be attractive, but they don't encourage imagination.*

*The best over-all guide to a child's taste and needs in toys is the child himself—not necessarily what he says but what he does. Watch him when he's at play, and you'll see what he likes to do and what he'll soon be able to do.*

## Choosing the Right Toy

**Toys for infants and toddlers.** Very young babies like to grasp and reach for nearby things; they need to bite on objects when they're teething; and they like to find out how different things feel and smell. The more stimulating a toy is to the child's senses, the more welcome it will be.

Even before a baby can focus his eyes, a smooth-feeling object which makes a pleasant sound can amuse and soothe him. When he can follow objects with his gaze, brightly colored hangings or slowly moving toys, such as mobiles, make good gifts.

As soon as a baby sits up by himself, simple building toys, such as blocks, rings and boxes to pile one on top of another, will entertain him and help him to improve muscular coordination and control. As he begins to move about, his toys should move with him—or ahead of him, so that he can follow. The need to get a toy which has rolled away has helped many a youngster start crawling, and pull-toys are favorite companions for babies just beginning to walk.

Between eighteen months and two years of age, most children begin to show an interest in colorful picture books. Choose ones with simple illustrations of familiar objects, without confusing background and details. At about this age, too, soft bedtime toys become great favorites.

**For preschoolers.** Among children of this age, building materials, blocks, modeling clay and paint sets are the most popular toys. After two years of age or so, the interests of boys and girls begin to differ. Dolls, crayons and scissors may be a girl's favorites, while boys tend to prefer mechanical toys. As a child's interests broaden, toys which are miniature replicas of familiar people and objects—policemen, mailmen, trucks, fire engines and buses, gas stations and other buildings—can help him play-act his ideas about the world.

Three and four-year-olds enjoy impersonating animals, and the discarded Teddy bear often comes into its own again at this time. Stories with animal characters—those you read or those you make up—usually delight children of this age.

This is the time when many children begin to limit their violent impulses to (more or less) socially acceptable actions. Play helps them do this. Suitable toys for this play-acting kind of aggression are the traditional toy guns, rubber knives, rubber tomahawks, as well as various kinds of blocks and pegs with which children put together—and boldly destroy—towns, buildings and objects.

**For young school-agers.** With the beginning of school, children's play interests and toy preferences change. They like games which can be played with friends, and toys which can be used by more than one child at a time. As school learning increases, number games and word puzzles become popular. Girls will show new interests in dolls and doll houses, treating them more gently and taking increasing pleasure in dressing them.

**For the middle school years.** At about eight, children frequently enter a dramatic stage. Their own behavior becomes somewhat theatrical at times and they adore to dress up and be other people, and things. Puppets through which they can speak, or various disguises in which they can dress themselves, make good gifts. By the age of ten, they begin to enjoy games of skill, both manual and mental.

More and more, of course, as a child grows older and develops specific skills and interests, the choice of his toys will directly depend on his own personal taste. In general, the preteen and young teen years are the time of the model airplane, miniature sewing machine, complex metal construction set, chemistry set, craft outfits, athletic equipment, inexpensive cameras, books and records.

Some children start stamp or coin collections at about this age; some like terrariums and aquariums.—*Alan O. Ross, Ph.D.*

# Children's Toy Guide

**The newcomer.**

- rattles of different sizes, shapes, tones
- squeaky rubber and plastic animals and dolls
- soft stuffed animals and dolls
- floating toys
- exercise toys for playpen and crib
- string of very large brightly colored beads
- small rubber, plastic or wooden blocks

- nested boxes, beakers, cups
- books with pictures, rhymes, jingles
- records with light rhythmic music
- brightly colored balloons
- dolls that child can handle easily
- small light doll carriage

- nursery mobiles
- animals on wheels
- push-pull toys
- small light wagon
- simple take-apart toys
- simple musical toys
- squeeze toys
- shoo-fly

### The doer.

- low tricycle—to fit child
- trucks big enough to straddle and ride
- small low gym and slide
- balls—big and little—balloons
- inflatable figures
- sandbox and sand toys
- play table and chairs
- dishes and cooking utensils
- toy telephone
- sturdy wagon
- play furniture, child-size range, bed, chest of drawers
- play house
- stuffed animals
- stick horse

- simple dress-up clothes
- laundry and cleaning outfits
- dolls and doll furniture
- take-apart and put-together toys
- puzzles with few pieces
- dough clay
- finger paints and easel paints
- crayons, chalk, blackboard
- musical toys (chime, tom-tom, tambourine, swiss bells, etc.)
- various blocks
- water toys
- pounding toys
- books, phonograph and records
- hobby horse
- push-pull toys

### The learner.

- additional dress-up clothes (police, fireman, nurse, airline hostess, cowboy outfits)
- doctor and nurse kits
- hand puppets
- greater variety of stuffed animals and dolls
- additional housekeeping toys (ironing board and iron)
- pegboards

- set of farm animals and equipment
- store keeping toys, scales, cash register, working telephone
- more blocks for large buildings
- counting frame
- small trucks, boats, autos, planes, doll families
- trains small and large (not electric)

- village sets
- greater variety of large trucks (road grader, milk, dump, fire, etc.)
- easy construction sets
- puzzles with more pieces and shapes
- larger tricycle, wagon, doll carriage (or 2 wheeler with auxiliary wheels

- wheelbarrow
- sled
- swing, teeter, slide, large gym
- simple carpentry tools and sturdy work bench
- wading pool
- garden sets (tools, lawn mower)
- crayons and paints
- books and records

## The worker.

- more housekeeping toys that really work (iron heats, mixer works, etc.)
- more doll accessories
- doll house and furniture and small dolls with lots of accurate detail
- paper doll sets
- more store play items
- simple word and number games
- board games
- toy typewriter
- printing outfit
- masks and joker items
- jack stones, jump rope, marbles, tops, kites, balls
- pogo-sticks, hoops, stilts
- baseball, football, hand ball equipment
- bicycle, sturdy wagon, scooter, skates, Irish Mail, skis

- simple gym equipment (parallel bars, ladders, etc.)
- more complex puzzles (the jigsaw type)
- musical instruments (accordion and harmonica)
- metal construction sets
- work bench and tool chest
- blackboard
- first electric train (add on later!)
- simple sewing and embroidery sets
- simple weaving materials and equipment
- dominoes, lotto
- gun and holster sets
- good-grooming sets
- garden sets with seeds, etc.
- interlocking building blocks in addition to others mentioned
- books and records

## The member of society.

- handicraft sets of all kinds (jewelry, beads, leather, etc.)
- model kits for boats, airplanes
- magic sets

- hobby kits (old cars, minerals, flowers, etc.)
- archery, target shooting, dart games, table tennis, ping pong, etc.

- make-up and good-grooming sets
- telegraph, sound effect sets
- card and board games
- anagrams, lotto, dominoes, checkers, chess, cribbage
- more intricate construction sets
- jig-saw puzzles

- character dolls in addition to others
- sculpturing materials in addition to clay, plastics, wax, etc.
- punching bag
- marionettes
- science toys
- books and records

# SPECIAL TOYS FOR MAKING AND BUILDING THINGS

In a world where so much is ready-made, the experience of building things yourself has special meaning. It gives the child practice in solving technical problems and in carrying a job through to completion. It also gives him a chance to reproduce and understand things he has encountered —a bridge, a tower—and use his imagination in designing structures of his own. In the process he will develop manual skills, learn elementary facts about mechanics, and explore the properties of different materials such as wood, plastics, cardboard and steel.

**The beginning year, 1-3:** Before the child can actually construct things, he must learn to manipulate objects of different shapes and sizes, and coordinate hand with eye. By the age of three, he will be building nameless block structures, and will be able to copy simple towers or houses.

Playthings: Interlocking plastic rings, rubber cubes, nesting blocks, kindergarten blocks, large hollow blocks, interlocking block train.

**Early childhood, 3-6:** He will gradually learn to make complex structures, using all the blocks in a kit—but don't keep asking him what he is making! Very large cardboard box blocks and plastic panels will give him a chance to make tunnels or houses he can crawl into. He can learn to use large wooden tools and put interlocking logs or plastic bricks together.

**Playthings:** Structural building blocks, wooden construction kit, wood models (plane, car, truck, etc.), Lincoln Logs, wooden road system, Tinker Toys, wooden hammer and screwdriver.

**Middle childhood, 6-9:** Time to introduce steel and plastic construction sets—beginning with simple shapes, then adding more complicated components, such as gears, pulleys and motors. Show him how to use tools correctly and help him follow printed instructions for building models or structures that can be used with a train set or other toys.

**Playthings:** Erector set, Lego System set; simple airplane, boat and car models, helicopter kit, hydrodynamic building set, fix-it tool belt, train equipment and put-together village.

**Later childhood, 9-12:** This is the peak of the construction period. Children build larger and more complex objects, although ambition often exceeds skill. They may make whole series of planes, cars, boats, etc. Girls as well as boys like to make articles that can be used: shelves, bookends, boxes.

**Playthings:** Planes that fly, cars with motors, schooner kit, plastic car kits, antique cars, dragster kit, auto chassis kit, auto engine kit, Kart with or without engine, tool chest, work bench.—*Robert M. Goldenson, Ph.D.*

# TAKING CARE OF TOYS

From the day the first rattle comes into the house until the last bicycle's scrapped, toys and mothers seem to be at odds. Where to store them, how to protect them, how to keep track of them! Perhaps these five general rules, and a cooperative child, will help:

**1. Buy the Right Toy.** A successful start means buying toys of good quality which are suitable for the child. A toy too advanced may be misused. A toy outgrown may be abused.

Look over toys before you buy them with an eye to repairability. Bolts are replaceable. Rivets are not. Wooden toys can be glued but flimsy ones can't. Some wagons have inherent weaknesses in the tongue. Some wheelbarrows are rickety on their stands from the beginning. Using such a yardstick for toy-buying will eliminate most of the shoddy things that break.

Having bought the right toy, a toy suitable, sturdy, well made and repairable, how can you help your child keep it in good condition?

**2. Account For It.** Parents have to train and help children to straighten up their play areas daily. Quite apart from the benefits of teaching children to be orderly, the playroom which is ready for today's new play will be more fun than the one which is the aftermath of yesterday's game.

A daily pick-up time—which with preschool children, at least, should have Mother in the picture—is the time when missing wheels will be discovered and broken toys put aside for mending. This is the time when blocks go back into their box and puzzle parts are collected.

Of course, a daily pick-up isn't going to rout every colored peg out from under the bed or stretch out long enough to find every wooden bead. Those come to light on cleaning day and a smart mother keeps a small box on the dresser top into which she can drop such items before vacuuming.

Out-of-doors toys should have the same daily attention. Wagons, wheelbarrows, trikes and tractors should certainly be in the stable by dark. Even the most expensive pieces of model truck equipment will rust if they spend all their time outside. They do better under cover every night. If you've no outdoor shelter, they can be taken to the garage or house. One family tells us that they leave out all the plastic trucks, buckets and sand toys, but put all the metal things into the barbecue shelter or tool shed at sundown.

**3. Store It.** Toy storage is something for every architect, housebuilder and furniture-maker to chew over, but usually each household has to come up with its own custom-designed storage.

Most families use open shelves for trucks and cars, dolls and stuffed animals and books. Some families have removed bedroom closet doors and

**22**

fitted shelves into the recess. Others settle for planks resting on bricks.

But stowing toys means more than just shelving. Some households add perforated hardboard with hooks for items like scissors and jump ropes. They save small boxes for trading cards and "collections." (A picture is a good label for the child too young to read.) They hoard shoe boxes for crayons, chalk, erasers; big baskets for assorted balls, bats and mitts; mesh vegetable sacks for wooden beads. They fit orange crates and apple boxes with casters for blocks and train equipment. They prefer vertical storage for records, a rack that holds records on edge to prevent warping. They put art supplies all on one open shelf. Young children's powder paints belong way up high. For very young children, in fact, it also seems best to keep the games of many parts on an out-of-reach shelf to be brought down upon request. This minimizes the underfoot problems and keeps the games safe from exploratory dumping by visitors.

**4. Mend It.**   In spite of all this, of course, toys get broken. Find a place to keep broken toys out of play until they're mended.

Usually an ordinary screw or bolt, friction tape and household tools (wrench, pliers, screwdriver) are all the repair takes. There's more than just "saving a toy" to get out of repair work. A father and son together tightening bolts on trikes aren't just fixing something.

Mother's place in the fix-it department more usually involves the sewing basket-cellophane tape-plastic-household glue routine. Heads come off toy monkeys; buttons come off clown suits; doll clothes are ripped.

Washing and iron doll clothes occasionally is a good joint project for mothers and daughters. Dolls also need new wigs or legs sometimes. Doll hospitals restore such maimed creatures if you can't, and a trip to a doll hospital is a wonderful excursion.

**5. Get Rid of It.**   You might store your outgrown toys somewhere for guests to use or a young sibling to grow into. You might give them away to other children. But don't clutter up the daily-use storage space with toys that are no longer used or usable. There are organizations which accept used toys for children and various institutions in any community will welcome them.—*Ronnie Welch*

# THERE IS
# NOTHING LIKE
# A GAME

*IT WOULD BE HARD TO FIND a single aspect of a child's personality that cannot be cultivated by one game or another. Physical faculties? There are games that sharpen the eye, perfect the sense of balance, quicken reaction time, promote coordination. Intellectual abilities? Some games require logical thinking; others enhance vocabulary, observation, memory, imagination— and practically all games develop concentration. Social skills? In varying degrees, games are a stimulus for teamwork, poise and conversational ability.*

*In fact, so great is the versatility of games that we even use them to meet the special needs of our children— charades for the timid, anagrams for the poor speller, number games for the weak in arithmetic. And best of all, every one of these benefits can be achieved in a spirit of fun.—Robert M. Goldenson, Ph.D.*

**25**

# THE RIGHT GAME
# AT THE RIGHT TIME

**The beginning years, 1-3:** One-year-olds who have been given plenty of chance to squeeze, cuddle and bang will probably be ready to place wooden rings on a post, put pegs in a board, and throw beanbags somewhere near a target. Between two and three, they will enjoy hammering pegs and putting simple wooden puzzles together.

**Playthings:** Puzzle placques, beanbags, Ring-It, mailbox game, peg board, hammer board.

**Early childhood, 3-6:** At three, children usually possess the small muscle skills needed for games that involve sorting, buttoning or inserting; and they are equally ready for large muscle group games such as Ring-around-the-Rosie and Farmer in the Dell. At four, they like different kinds of Lotto, in which they match food, animals, flowers, etc. with pictures. By five, they are ready for simple table games in which a spinner determines the moves: Peter Rabbit, Puss in Corner; and many children can also play games that require recognition of numbers and letters.

**Playthings:** Simple jigsaw puzzles, Picture Lotto, button-sorting, buttoning strips, ten pins, Ring Toss, simplified Bingo, number blocks, alphabet blocks, dice and spinner games, play money, cash register, blackboard and chalk, ABC card game, simple anagrams.

**Middle childhood, 6-9:** The youngsters are increasingly interested in developing and displaying manual skills in games like darts or tricks like jumping a spoon into a glass. They begin to enjoy games with rules, including such card games as Cowboy and Indians, Menagerie and Hearts, and are intrigued by games that give them practice with numbers and letters.

**Playthings:** Pickup sticks, jack straws, jacks, electric fish pond, spinning

**26**

top game, dominoes, Chinese checkers, lotto, playing cards, arithmetic lotto, more complex jigsaw puzzles, Bingo, checkers, Spill and Spell, quoits, horse shoe pitching game, magnetic darts, magic kit, mirror-drawing game, simple puzzles (wire, block and match puzzles).

**Later childhood, 9-12:** This is the peak of the game period, for many reasons. Their abilities and personalities are expanding and they like to test their skills and measure themselves against others. They'll try anything that looks like fun: card tricks, word and vocabulary games, observation games (e.g., finding small objects, such as paper clips and rubber bands), number games (Fizz-Buzz), memory games (When I go to California), information games (quizzes, geography), dexterity games (pool, ping pong), reasoning games (20 Questions, puzzles, strategy and detection games).

**Playthings:** Tiddly-Winks, pickup sticks, wire puzzle set, magic kit, table basketball, table soccer, electric football, electric baseball, Golferino, Nok-Hockey, Puff Pool, Puff Billiards, pinball machine, Pufferino, pool table, Kikit, Labyrinth game, Tennis Tenball, putting practice game, ping ball, ping pong, jungle hunt, electric car-racing game, battle game, bowling game, Polly-Shoot, Parchesi, The Winning Touch, Tic Tac Toe, jigsaw puzzles, Puzzle Chest, Mandalay Puzzle, Risk, Monopoly, Clue, Diplomacy, Smarty, Bali, Scrabble, Stock Market, Backgammon, Strategy.

*—Robert M. Goldenson, Ph.D.*

# TRICKS
# AND MAGIC

As a well-known saying runs—"It's fun to be fooled but it's more fun to know." Tricks and mystery stunts are entertaining to watch, but it is more fun to perform them yourself. The tricks which follow are simple to master. They are not the kind that will qualify you as an amateur Houdini but they are guaranteed to impress even your most skeptical friends. It's a good idea to practice first by yourself before performing for others.

**27**

**The Knife Bridge.** Place three glasses upside down on the table in the corners of a triangle and three knives of the same length between them, forming the sides of the triangle. Be sure that the glasses are one-half inch away from the knife ends. The problem is to form a bridge with the knives, using the glasses as bases, without moving the glasses from their present position.

*Solution: Place the flexible blade tips together, under one knife and over the other, so that they remain firmly together. Then place each knife handle on a glass.*

**Mysterious Fork.** Prick the tines of a fork with the thumb and index finger of your right hand. Now with great ceremony place the fingertips of your free hand on a glass, vase or some other object and draw from it—to the bewilderment of the onlookers—a ringing musical note. Can you discover the trick?

*Solution: Placing your free hand on some object—and perhaps giving a talk on magic while you are doing so—is only for effect. The trick is done with your other hand. Lower the fork to the table as soon as the tines have been pricked. The table acts as a sounding board and allows the note from the makeshift tuning fork to be heard.*

**Card Magic.** From a deck of cards place five or six Jacks, Kings or Queens on a table in an orderly row. Ask someone to turn some of the cards around while you are out of the room, and when you return you will tell them which cards have been reversed.

*Solution: Notice that the cards have a wider margin at one end. When you place them on the table, have all the wide margins nearest you. Then when you return to the room it is a simple matter to see which cards now have narrow margins nearest you.*

**Magic with a Watch.** Have a player mentally select a number from one through twelve. Tell him to start with the number above the number he selected, and count to himself the taps you make on a watch until he reaches 20, when he tells you to stop. Now if you know how to do the trick you can announce to the assembled audience the number he selected, and show those near by that the match stick or pencil which you used for tapping is pointing to that number. Can you figure out how it is done?

*Solution: You tap at random for seven taps, but on the eighth tap touch 12 on the watch, on the ninth tap touch 11 and so on, going around the watch face backwards. When the player stops you, your pointer will be touching the number he had selected mentally.*

**How to Tell a Person's Age.**  Let the person whose age is to be discovered do the figuring. Suppose, for example, that his age is 15 and that he was born in August. Ask him to put down the number of the month in which he was born and proceed as follows:

Number of the month . . . . . . . .    8
Multiply by two  . . . . . . . . . . . .   16
Add five  . . . . . . . . . . . . . . . . .   21
Multiply by fifty . . . . . . . . . . . . 1050
Add the age 15 . . . . . . . . . . . . . 1065
Subtract 365, leaving . . . . . . . . .  700
Add 115, making  . . . . . . . . . . .  815

The first two figures on the right will always indicate the age and the remaining the month the birthday falls in.

## MYSTERY GAMES

In these games you need a confederate who knows the trick or system used in each one.

The confederate then leaves the room, and while he is out the group decides upon some object. When he returns he tells what object was selected without any apparent signal from you or the others. The other players try to guess how the confederate learns which object to pick. When a person thinks he has discovered the trick, he takes the confederate's place. Frequently it develops that the person's idea is all wrong. The confederate then goes out again. If the person is right, however, he may take the confederate's place until someone else guesses the trick.

**Telepathy.** Place four objects on the floor or table or mark 4 rectangles on the blackboard. While the confederate is out of the room, the group selects one of the four objects. The leader then calls the confederate back to tell which object was chosen. He may pretend to take great care, studying each object in detail first. Later he may give the correct one from some distance, even from outside the room, or blindfolded. The trick is simple. Actually, the signal is given by the leader in re-calling the confederate. Both players have memorized a word or phrase in connection with each article as follows:

|          |           |
|----------|-----------|
| O.K.     | All Ready |
| All Right | Come In   |

Therefore if the group selects the upper right article, the leader would call "all ready" and the confederate upon returning would point to or name the upper right hand object. Don't play this game too many times in a row, or the spectators may catch on.

**Tom Thumb.** Three objects are placed in front of the leader, one of which is selected by the group while the confederate is out of the room. Upon returning the latter pretends to make a difficult decision, and then names the correct article. The leader has signalled him with his thumbs. His hands are folded in his lap and very quietly he crosses his right thumb over his left to indicate the article on the right; his left thumb over the right one to indicate the article on the left; and his thumbs parallel and together to indicate the center article.

**Mind Your Questions.** Place four objects in front of you. Before the game starts, you and your confederate number the articles mentally from one to four. As the game begins, the confederate leaves the room as in the previous game. When the group has selected one of the objects, and the confederate returns, give him the signal by asking any question, starting with a one-letter word if the first object was selected, a two-letter word for the second, a three-letter word for the third, and four-letter word for the fourth.

**30**

# FUN
# WITH WORDS

**Guggenheim.** Each player draws a square, divided into 16 boxes. Any name may be used across the top, and four or more nouns are put in the spaces at the left. The purpose of the game is to fill in the spaces with words that begin with the letter at the top of the column and are in the class of nouns indicated at the left. For example, if M A R Y is used as in the illustration, the first line might be filled in with the words "Mushroom, artichoke, radish, yam," and the second with the words "Mississippi, Arno, Red, Yangtse." Four points are scored for each entry selected by no one else, and one point for each entry used by other players.

**Word Lightning.** The leader calls out any letter in the alphabet other than J, Q, X, or Z, and points to one of the players who, in sixty seconds, must name just as many words as he can think of that start with this letter. Another name for this game is "Stammer, Jammer," which is what the victim usually does. The average number of words named is between 15 and 25, although with practice as many as 50 and 60 words can be given in one minute. The game continues until each player has had a turn.

# LET'S ALL
# BE ARTISTS

**Drawing in the Dark.** Give each player a pencil and a piece of paper. Turn out the lights and ask them to draw a picture of a house. They will undoubtedly be very careful the first time, expecting you to turn on the lights as soon as the house is completed. But not yet! When they have finished their houses—and lost their places on their papers—ask them to put a tree in the yard, then a path up to the door, and then a fence around the yard. As a final touch, have them draw a bird sitting in a tree, and the moon shining down on the whole peaceful scene. When the lights go on, exhibit the masterpieces, and page the surrealists! The artists in your group will probably have a bird sitting on the moon, a lane over the house, and a tree growing out of the fence. Next time vary the subject, making the picture more complicated, and you'll get even funnier results.

**Blot Drawing Game.**   Each person writes his name in ink on a slip of paper and folds the paper while the ink is still wet. The papers are then passed to the right, and from the blots each player draws some object mentioned by the leader—a horse, automobile, a house, or even the portrait of one of the guests. Display the drawings and award a prize for the best likeness, or the worst!

# GUESSING GAMES

**Hunting Trip.**   Tell the group of some proposed adventure and explain that you will take certain articles with you. However, you are limited to articles of a definite type. The players are to guess what kind of things you can take. You mention the first thing. The next person names something else. If it starts with his initials, the leader accepts the article. Sam Smith might take a pair of sharp scissors, for instance. If he does not mention an article starting with his initials, he must sit on the floor or some other place of "dishonor" until his next turn. If by that time he has guessed the trick he may join the others. If not he remains where he is until the next round. The game will be more fun if several people besides the leader know how to play it.

**"I've a Bright Idea."** One person leaves the room while the rest of the players decide upon some object. It should be in plain sight for children. Any object may be selected for adults. When the player returns and stands in the middle of the room this dialogue is heard:

Seated Player: "I've a bright idea."
Standing Player: "What's it like?"
Seated Player: "It's like you."
Standing Player: "How so?"
Seated Player: "It's very green" (or all wet, or full of air, or anything describing a characteristic of the object selected).

Continue playing until the player guesses the article; then the person who gave the last clue leaves the room, while the others select a new object.

# GAMES FOR LARGER GROUPS

**Spelling Bee.** Even if your friends think spelling bees dull, try these words on them and see their egos deflate. The words seem easy, but few people can spell them all correctly.

| | |
|---|---|
| Repellent | Gaseous |
| Colossal | Naphtha |
| Supersede | Embarrass |
| Inoculate | Kimono |
| Vilify | Rarefy |
| Shellac | Manageable |
| Picnicking | Harass |

In very large groups, select two teams of eight players each to compete before the rest of the group. Line up the teams facing each other. Give a word to the first player on Team A. If he spells it correctly, give another word to the first player on Team B. When a word is spelled incorrectly, the player is eliminated and the word given to the next player on the opposing team. Play 2 rounds. The team with most players at the end of 2 rounds is the winner. Players who are eliminated do not resume their seats until the

Spelling Bee is over. When the winning team has been determined, the losers each select a person to take their place, and the contest is resumed with new words. In this type of contest the words should not be too difficult, although there should always be a few "sticklers"—words that sound easy to spell, but aren't.

**The Trial.** This is really the game "20 Questions," modified for larger groups. Several teams are formed, the number depending on how many people take part. The size of individual groups may vary from five to ten.

Each group selects some object, the more difficult to guess the better. It also selects a representative. At a signal from the leader, all the representatives move to some other group. Here they are questioned by all the players in that group, who try to guess the object chosen by the representative's home team. The group which first guesses the object correctly is awarded a point. When a score has been made, the representatives return to their original groups, and the procedure is repeated. The group which first scores five points wins the game.

**Intellectual Baseball.** Place chairs for nine players of a team in regular baseball formation with an extra chair at each base for batter and runners, and also one for the umpire back of the pitcher. The other team sits on the sidelines. The player who is to be the first batter takes his place beside the catcher. The pitcher fires a question at the batter who answers it if he can. If correct, the batter goes to the first base; if incorrect, he is out. If the batter cannot answer the question, he fires it to any member of the team in the field, by calling the position, i.e., "Right Field." That player must answer correctly to put the batter out. If incorrect, the batter goes to the first base. No prompting or delaying is permitted by the umpire. Runs can be made only by moving from base to base. No stealing is allowed. Play as a regular baseball game for three, five or seven innings. Use any subjects for the questions—history, geography, nature, or current events.

**Charades.** Charades are as old as Grandmother, and then some. But the game is still fun. Usually players are separated into two groups no matter how many there are. The groups go into adjoining rooms where they decide on a word to act out for the other side to guess. When each has chosen a word the groups come together and take turns acting out their word while the other side plays audience. The game is most successful if you choose words which can be pantomimed effectively, such as:

**34**

| | |
|---|---|
| workmanship | upbraid |
| booklet | bandage |
| gangster | infancy |
| handbook | feline |
| ingratiate | spinster |

*—from "GAMES—For Quiet Hours and Small Spaces," a publication of the National Recreation Association*

## A GAME
## OF A DIFFERENT
## VARIETY

**Candle Bowling.** Set up ten candles in regular bowling formation, arranging the candles in a triangle with one candle in the front row, two in the second, three in the third and four in the last row. Mark a starting line at a distance suited to the age and sex of the players. The object is to blow out the candles, each player having two attempts for each frame or set of ten candles as in regular bowling. Score as in bowling. If you want simpler rules give a point for each candle blown out, a score of 20 if all the candles are blown out on the first attempt and a score of 15 if all are blown out on the second try.

## GAMES
## THAT MAKE
## CHILDREN THINK

If you introduce your child to a wide variety of intellectual games, you will stimulate him to think logically, use imagination, develop concentration

**35**

and perseverance. You will help to bridge the gap between generations since mental play can be equally enjoyed by parent, grandparent and child. You will provide an effective counterbalance to the passivity of spectator sports and, at the same time, you will show your child that racking his brain can be fun—a lesson that will apply to work as it does to play.

How? To illustrate, here are a number of examples.

**Observation Games.** To aid quick thinking, keen observation is important, and there is no better way to develop it than through games like these:

Typo. Type out a number of short paragraphs from books or articles, but deliberatly make several typographical errors. Give these paragraphs to your child or to a group of children and see how many errors they can find in, say, three minutes. (Did you notice the typo in this paragraph?)

What's Wrong? Make drawings of some common scenes, no matter how crude, but in each case leave out one essential detail. Examples: A house with a tree on the lawn and the sun behind; a shadow falls from the house, but not from the tree. . . A road curving to the left, with a sign that warns of a right-hand curve. Your child will get as much pleasure and benefit from making up pictures like these as from solving the ones you create.

Find It! Place ten small objects at various points in the room, all in plain sight—for example, a rubber band around a vase, a one-dollar bill in a plant, a paper clip on a curtain. Give the child a list of these objects and challenge him to locate all he can within five minutes. .

**Stimulating Imagination.** Children should learn to let their minds roam far afield, for this kind of imaginative wandering has given rise to the greatest stories and the most important scientific discoveries. Here are two types of activity to stimulate imagination.

Brain-Storming. Advertising men sometimes gather around a table to dream up new slogans or names for products. At these brain-storming sessions, they are encouraged to say whatever comes into their minds, and an exciting chain-reaction of ideas soon gets started. Try this one at a party for older children. Company X is about to market a new dictating machine which will transfer the spoken word directly into type. What would you name this machine?

In about five minutes the girls of one group came up with: Talkwriter, Dictype, Autosteno, Teltype, Dictoprint, Audiograph, Parlograph, Talkatype, and—the name that won the most applause—Speakeasy.

Limerick Game. No better example of disciplined imagination can be found than the poet's flight of fantasy—even in that questionable type of rhyme called the limerick. One rainy evening two teen-agers made up the first four lines of the following limerick, and the rest were challenged to add the final line:

There was a young fellow named Dryer
Who was a most terrible liar
He said he could fly
Without wings in the sky
. . . . . . . . . . . . . . . . . . . . . . . . . . . . . . . .

Here are a few of the last lines: (What can your child come up with?)
He was killed by his foolish desire.
But he rose just three feet and no higher.
Yes, he flew, but straight down in the mire.
He was dropped from a plane—on a spire.
Now he's flying in angel's attire.


**Problems of Reasoning.** Many board games, such as checkers, Gettysburg, chess and bridge, cultivate logical thinking—but here are a few problems that do not require special materials:

Logic. A child can often solve simple logic problems even before he knows the meaning of premise, inference or syllogism. Example: "Tennis players are usually good athletes; Andy is a tennis player; therefore Andy is a good athlete." If your child does not discover for himself that the conclusion does not follow, point out that we did not say that tennis players are always good athletes. Here is an example that will help to make the important point that an argument can be logical but at the same time untrue: "Swedes are tall; Hendrika is a Swede; therefore Hendrika is tall."

Process of Elimination. Tell your child that we can sometimes arrive at the right answer by eliminating the wrong solution.

This one will show your older child how useful it can be to make a chart or diagram. "Dave, Stan and Nick are married to Sally, Jean and Cathy—but not necessarily in that order. Each couple has one child: Billy, Teddy and Jill. Name the three families from the following facts. Two of the children, Cathy's and Dave's, are Boy Scouts. Stan's wife is not Jean. Nick's son is not Teddy." One girl solved it in two minutes, ten seconds, but the average time for a group of teen-agers was approximately six minutes.

If your child is intrigued by problems of this sort, you might resurrect this ancient but honorable one: "Three missionaries and three cannibals must cross a river. The missionaries must never be outnumbered by the cannibals. The one rowboat available holds only three persons, but only the missionaries can row. How can they all get across the river alive?"

**Mind-Stretchers.** Most of our thinking follows customary channels. How can we get our children to break through habit barriers in trying to find solutions to problems? One good way is to pose brain-busters that require flexibility of thinking. Here are some cases in point.

"A taxi driver named Jones turned into a one-way street going the wrong way. Two policemen were standing at the corner, looking directly his way, yet neither one stopped him. Why?"

**Fun with Memory.** One of the simplest but most flexible memory games is Following Instructions. The instructions can be easy enough for a four-year-old to follow, or hard enough to amuse a group of teen-agers— especially if they are required to do several ridiculous things in the right order, such as "Walk three steps backwards with your eyes closed, then kiss the nearest person on the tip of the nose, then recite the first stanza of *America* backwards."

When I Go to California. This is as good a game as ever. The first contestant says, "When I go to California, I will take a toothbrush." (Californians, of course, can pick another state.) Each person in the group has to repeat all preceding items in the right order, and add a new one. Those who make a mistake must drop out of the game, until there is a single winner.

What's There? This, too, is a game that can be played by children of different ages. Place from three to twenty articles on a table—an ash tray, a pencil, a saucer, et cetera—and allow the child or the group to look at them for exactly one minute. Then, cover the table with a cloth and see how many articles they can list on pieces of paper.

**Enhancing Verbal Skills.** Games with words are probably the most popular. For the very young there is "Word Bingo," in which simple words are used instead of numbers; "Word Fishing," in which slips of paper containing words are fished out of a bowl and read; and "What Happens Next?" in which an adult starts a simple story and each child is required to add an event of his own creation. "Word Blocks" provides good practice for beginning readers. Paste selected common nouns on the six sides of one block; pronouns, verbs and articles on other blocks. The blocks are then

**38**

rolled, as in dice, and the child tries to make a sentence out of the words that show on top—for example, "He hit the ball" and "The ball hit him."

All of these games can provide practice in reading and verbal expression, but care should be taken to use words that fit into the child's school work.

Mid-school-aged children like anagrams, word dominoes, simple cross-word puzzles and derivations. (How many words can you make from "dread"?) Many older games are worth reviving—for instance, Guggenheim. Select a master word, such as RATE, and also choose two or three categories, such as countries and flowers. Then see who can write down a word in each category beginning with each letter of the master word—for example, Russia, Algeria, Thailand, England; rose, azalea, tulip, Easter lily.

Youngsters also enjoy a game in which they write down as many words as possible for a common action. In one case ask them to name different ways a person could get from one place to another without assistance. They can come up with a total of over 50 different verbs, including not only the usual walk, run and jump, but roll, tumble, slide, sprint, slouch, amble, tip-toe, dive, stumble and slink.

**I.Q. Problems.** Practically all school children have taken intelligence tests, and an absorbing game can be created by simply asking them to construct their own I.Q. problems. Here are some of the problems which one half the group can pose for the other half.

If North and South are reversed and East and West are reversed, which way would you be facing, if East is on your left?

What number is next in the series 3, 9, 4, 8, 5?

Rearrange the following words to form a sentence as quickly as you can: shake-up place the took government biggest in yesterday the.

Which of the following does not belong with the others: oil, molasses, buttermilk, clay, gasoline.

### Answers to Problems:

*The typo in the paragraph under Observation Games is in the word "deliberately."*

*Family Problem. Answer: The three families are: Nick, Cathy, Billy; Dave, Jean, Teddy; Stan, Sally, Jill.*

*Cannibal Problem. Answer: Missionary takes one cannibal across and returns. Three missionaries cross, two return. Two missionaries, one cannibal cross, one missionary returns. Missionary, remaining cannibal cross.*

*Taxi Driver Problem. Answer: Jones, the taxi driver, was walking.*

*North-South Problem. Answer: South.*

*Number Series Problem. Answer: 7 (Explanation: The following decreasing series is added to the given numbers: plus 6, minus 5, plus 4, minus 3, plus 2.)*

*Word Rearrangement Problem. Answer: The biggest shake-up took place in the government yesterday. Or, Yesterday the biggest shake-up took place in the government.*

*Oil and Molasses Problem. Answer: Clay (It is a solid; the others are liquids.)—Robert M. Goldenson, Ph.D.*

# QUICK TESTS OF MENTAL SKILL

**Dictionary.** A player challenges another to say in one minute all the words he can think of that start with a given letter of the alphabet. When time is called, the score is given. The accepter may then select the initial letter his challenger is to use. This may be made more difficult by giving the letters with which the words are to start and also to end.

**Alphabet Speeches.** A challenge to an alphabet speech means that the accepter must try to make a more impressive-sounding speech than the challenger, reciting the letters of the alphabet instead of words and saying them with great feeling.

**Musical Memories.** The challenger may hum a line or two of a song for the accepter to guess, or he may clap the time of a song. It is well to limit the field to old songs, popular songs, or well known hymns.

**Wrong Capitals.** The challenger names a state capital, placing it in the wrong state. The accepter must place it correctly before he takes his turn. For example, the challenger may say, "Montpelier is the capital of Kentucky." The accepter replies, "Wrong! Montpelier is the capital of Vermont.

Sacramento is the capital of Illinois." The challenger must then locate Sacramento correctly, and so the game goes on. One of the players may occasionally trip the other by placing the capital in the right state, in which case he scores a point if his opponent starts to correct his statement. This shouldn't be done too frequently though.

**Mixed Dates.** The first player mentions a well-known event but gives with it the date of some other event. The accepter must correct the date before he offers his own challenge. For example, the first player may say, "Columbus discovered America in 1492. Shakespeare died in 1812." Neither player may name an event for which he cannot himself give the date. One may trip the other occasionally by giving the right date instead of a wrong one for the event he names.

**"U Auto Know" and Other Riddle Contests.** Riddles make good challenge material. There should be no one challenger or accepter, but any player who gives a riddle that is not guessed may score a point for his side or team, and the player who guesses a riddle scores a point. Individual players or the whole group may offer solutions.

A popular class of riddles may be announced as "U Auto Know," this title furnishing the hint for the answers, all of which are names of automobiles. The phrases in the following list suggest various automobiles, some being suitable for repeated challenges because they describe more than one kind of automobile:

| | |
|---|---|
| A man's nickname, plus to vend | (Edsel) |
| Ancient, plus able to move | (Oldsmobile) |
| To boil, plus a letter of the alphabet, plus an occupation | (Studebaker) |
| An Indian chief | (Pontiac) |
| A crossing | (Ford) |
| A famous rock | (Plymouth) |
| An explorer | (Chevrolet) |
| A president | (Lincoln) |
| To avoid | (Dodge) |
| Found on the golf course, plus to be without | (Cadillac) |
| A Roman god | (Mercury) |
| To weep, plus to blur or slip over | (Chrysler) |
| An incline, plus a male | (Hillman) |
| A big cat | (Jaguar) |
| German for people, plus a means of transportation | (Volkswagen) |

Another popular guessing game consists in giving advertising slogans. The challenger recites the phrase or question that has become familiar through widespread use in advertising, and the accepter or the opposing team or group names the article meant.

In still another type of riddle the name of a famous character may be the answer required. The challenger mentions something that will bring to mind a noted person or familiar mythological character. For example, "Give me liberty or give me death" would be answered "Patrick Henry." "A glass slipper" would be answered "Cinderella." *—from Handbook for Recreation, a publication of the U. S. Children's Bureau*

# FOR FAMILY EVENINGS

**Give A Shadow Show.** Shadow pictures are loads of fun and everyone can learn how to make them. All you need are a blank wall and a light that comes from a single bulb across the room. Your hands are the actors in a shadow show and, by experimenting, you can find how to move your fingers to form the shape of a swan, a rabbit or other animal. Looking at the shadow on the wall, try to adjust your fingers slightly until the picture looks best. Wiggle your fingers so that the shadows move. After you've learned to make these shadow pictures, perhaps you can invent some new ones!

**Cookbook Markers.** To save time when looking up favorite recipes, how about making several bookmarks? Scraps of oilcloth, plastic, leather or colored paper will do. Cut a strip of material 1½ inches wide and 4 inches long. Trim one end to a long point. With paints, print the name of a kind of recipe on each marker: cake, cookies, bread and so forth.

**Five, Six, Pick Up Sticks.** Some colored toothpicks are all you need for an exciting game of old-fashioned jackstraws. Drop a handful in a heap on the table; then players take turns trying to remove them one at a time without moving any others with the aid of a pick held in the hand. Red picks count 10, blue picks 5 and the others 1. The player with the top score wins.

## Riddles for Young 'uns
1. When is a doctor most annoyed?
2. Why are clocks so shy?
3. Why is it wrong to whisper?
4. When your clock strikes 13, what time is it?
5. Why is a room full of married people empty?
6. What is the difference between a conductor and a teacher?
7. What is the difference between a hill and a pill?
8. Why is it funny to see a boy darning his socks?
9. Why are you like two people when you lose your temper?
10. What did the big firecracker boast to the little firecracker?

### Answers:
1. *When he loses his patients.*
2. *Because they always hold their hands before their faces.*
3. *Because it isn't aloud.*
4. *Time to get it fixed.*
5. *Because there isn't a single person in it.*
6. *A conductor minds the train and a teacher trains the mind.*
7. *One is hard to get up, while the other is hard to get down.*
8. *Because his hands are where his feet should be.*
9. *Because you are beside yourself.*
10. *"My pop is bigger than yours!"*

**Sunday Fun.** After everyone has finished the Sunday papers, this might be fun. Give everyone a sheet of newspaper and ten minutes to create a funny hat. Odd bits of ribbon, feathers, flowers and cellophane tape can provide the trimmings. The only rule is that nobody can tear a piece of newspaper. It has to be folded or gathered into some kind of hat to be worn around the house.

**Toothpick Tussle.** Take three coffee cups and a box of toothpicks, and you're all set to play this facinating floor game. The picks are first divided evenly between the two players. They sit opposite each other with the cups face down in a row between them. The first player turns his back while the other person places one of his picks under one cup, two under another cup and three under the remaining cup. Then the first player turns around and lifts up any cup he wishes. He gets to keep all the picks he finds. The other picks go back to the owner. Now the second player turns his back while the first player hides six of his picks under the cups in the manner described. Take turns until one player wins all the toothpicks.

**Let's Play Crossword Tit-Tat-Toe.** Have you ever played tit-tat-toe with letters instead of zeros and crosses? Any number of people can play. Here are the simple rules. Each player has his own sheet of paper and pencil. He draws a tit-tat-toe pattern on the sheet. The first player now calls out any letter of the alphabet, and each player prints that letter in one of the squares on his tit-tat-toe board. Then the second player calls out another letter (or the same one). Once more each player puts the letter wherever he pleases on his board. Players continue to take turns calling out letters until nine have been called and all the squares are filled.

The winner is the person who has formed the most words. The words can be read horizontally from left to right, vertically from top to bottom, and left to right along the two diagonals.

It is possible, of course, for a player to make a perfect score of eight words, but you can be sure that this kind of thing doesn't happen often!

# BRAIN
# TEASER

Here is a famous old puzzle that has baffled people for many years.

**Family Tree**
Sisters and brothers have I none,
but that man's father is my father's son.
Do you know how this is possible?
*It is the son of the man who is speaking.*

**44**

# LET THEM
# PLAY CARDS

**—when the kids can't be dealt with.** There are roughly a thousand card games to choose from and that means play suitable for every age, stage and mood. There are card games for two, three, four and six. There are better than 400 varieties of solitaire. There are hard games and easy ones; games of chance, of bluff and skill. And I've discovered that cards are a comfort for the sick child, companion for the lonely child, pacifier for the angry child and a real godsend for everyone in bad weather.

When the rains come, for instance, children can begin slapping Jack instead of each other and venting their spleen on Hearts instead of parents. The real struggle bows out to the pretend one. This pretend struggle is, of course, one of the healthiest things about card playing. A child can bluff happily without being branded insincere. He can let loose his aggressions without being considered pushy. He can fight to win like a surly tiger and no one will tell him to be kind and cooperative. If he loses, he knows the loss is little! For cards are only a game, a make-believe struggle which apes, but is not, the real struggle. Like witches or giants, cards are simply pretend.

Letting off steam in situations where little penalty is exacted is important for all of us. It helps us to find acceptable ways of working out anger and aggression without hurting others. Cards certainly rank high on the list of harmless releases.

**Cards can teach sportsmanship.** "Listen, Pete," my daughter shouted, "cut out looking in my hand."

"Listen, Joan, I wouldn't look if you held it like you should."

"Listen, Pete, you're not s'pposed to look no matter how I hold it."

He's right and she's right, for the rules and proprieties of cards are stringent. Forms are important: cut to the right, deal to the left, keep your cards to your chest and don't look even when you can see. Unconsciously, children learn to give and take, to win without crowing, lose without crying.

Interestingly enough, the most efficient method they have of enforcing

**45**

rules is the simplest. A child can slam an angry fist on the table, brand her opponent a cheater and her rival may not even arch an eyebrow. But let her say, "O.K., if you're going to play that way, I quit," and order and rules are immediately restored. Quitting is the worst of all threats, for once the game is over someone must eventually solve the age-old problem— what'll we do now?

**Cards also teach specific skills.** Shuffling, cutting, dealing, discarding are all complex motions. At first, our youngest children could do none of these things. Their hands were too tiny to hold more than four cards at one time. But before long, they had learned to fan their hands, to deal, to perform a simple kind of shuffle. The small muscles they were learning to use will serve them well in a thousand other activities.

In the simplest of games a child must learn to recognize and match similar things: two 2's or Jacks. This is actually the first step in reading readiness—know the object, pair it with a like object and mentally discard all objects that are dissimilar. Even more complicated, the small child eventually learns that each Jack comes from a different family or suit, and that in many games one family has greater value than another.

By handling the cards he learns to recognize numbers, one through ten; to put them in sequence and finally to place greater value on the larger numbers. He can't add or subtract, but familiarity and repetition teach him that 6 is 4 more than 2. In no time he advances to really complicated games like Casino where he discovers that 2 and 4 make 6, but so do 1 and 5 and 3 and 3. Memory, complete attention and a tremendous desire to be part of the gang speed a bright child on his way and, frequently, long before first grade he and arithmetic are on friendly terms.

**What cards show.** A word should be said about parents, too. An interested mother or father can learn a tremendous amount about a child by observing him with his cards. Watch quietly while your child deals, figures and plays. Does he tense up? Or does he show careless abandon? Is he overly cautious and fearful or does he shoot for the moon with no concern for the real value in his hand? At a game he may unconsciously reveal things about himself which he represses in his daily life. A boy of our acquaintance never mastered Hearts because he couldn't bluff, even in fun.

Some of the things you learn, while watching your child at cards, may help you guide him over later hurdles. Stop, look, listen and notice how he handles himself in a tight corner, how he faces up to competition, how he reacts to success. Cards often disclose far more than a winning hand.

46

## Games that keep children happy:

Old Maid can be played by any number of people. Before you begin, take the Queen of Clubs from the pack, then deal the cards around the table one at a time. The idea is to get rid of all your cards in matched pairs (two 5's, two Kings, two 10's and so on) until one player is stuck at the game's end with the Old Maid. Play begins by removing any pairs you have from your hand and laying them, face down, on the table. If you have three of a kind, only two may be discarded; if four, all four may be discarded. When each player has discarded all he can, the dealer draws one card from the player on his left, who holds his cards in a fan. If he can add the card he picks to one he already holds and form a pair, he discards the pair; otherwise he must keep the new card in his hand. Play continues so, around the table to the left, until all cards have been paired and the single Queen left makes one player Old Maid and loser.

Concentration is a real brain sharpener. Any number can play. Deal the cards face down on the table, in any number of rows, no two cards touching. The object of this game is to get as many pairs (two of a kind) as you can.

Each person draws two cards from the table one at a time. If he draws a pair he places them before him, face down, after everyone has seen them. If he draws two unmatched cards he again shows them to the other players but returns them face down on the table, either in the places from which he took them or in different spots. As the game progresses, when a player draws one card he tries to remember where a card to match it has been discarded. If he can remember he has a pair.

Go Fish is related to another old favorite, Authors, but it doesn't take a special deck of cards. Any number of people can play and the object is to get as many sets of four as possible—four Jacks, four 3's, and so on. After the deal, each player looks over his hand and lays down any sets he may have face down. Then the player on the dealer's left asks any player for a specific card, naming both number and suit. He must have at least one card of that number himself to ask for another. If he asks for and receives his 4 of Hearts he takes another turn, asking any player for another specific card. If that player does not have the card asked for, the play moves to him. The game is won by the person who has the greatest number of sets. Go Fish can be simplified for very young card sharks by playing for pairs and by having the players simply ask for a number without having to worry about naming the suit.

There are many, many more card games to amuse and divert both young and old. Menagerie, Hearts, Spade the Gardener, I Doubt It, Twenty-nine, Stop-and-go, Bridge and the varieties of Poker, Rummy and Solitaire are only a few from which to choose.—*Jean Orcate*

**47**

# QUIET GAMES FOR SMALL GROUPS

Quiet games help to fill in the empty minutes at picnics, parties, and other gatherings when a small group is standing about. Often the family will enjoy playing them in the evening.

**Ghosts.**   The object of the game of ghosts is to add a letter to the word that is being spelled but to avoid finishing a word. Anyone who finishes a word becomes a third of a ghost, and when he is three-thirds he must drop out. The first player says any letter of the alphabet. The second adds another letter that can be used in spelling some word but that will not finish a word. Thus, if the first player said B and the second—thinking of "best"—adds E, he becomes a third of a ghost because "be" is a word of itself. When a word is finished the next player starts another. At any time a player may challenge another concerning the word he is spelling. If the player who is challenged is not spelling a word that he has actually in mind, he becomes a third of a ghost. If he can cite a word, the player who challenged him becomes a third of a ghost.

**What Am I?**   A player leaves the room, and the group decides what animal he shall represent. The player is recalled and tries to discover what he represents by asking questions about himself that may be answered by "Yes" or "No." For instance, he may ask, "Do I pull wagons?" "Do I eat grass?" "Do I have long, floppy ears?" When he has identified himself, the person whose answer helped him make the discovery leaves the group next.

**How, When and Where?**   A player leaves the room while the group selects a word; for example, "trip." The player returns and asks each person the three questions, "How do you like it?" "When do you like it?" and "Where do you like it?" The answers might be, "Long, drawn out," to the first; "In the fall," to the second; "In the hills," to the third. The player whose answer reveals the chosen word is the next to leave the room.

If the members of the group are old enough to enjoy it, words having the same sound but different meanings (as "bear," "bare") may be used.

**Shopping.** A player who is the shopper walks around, stops before one of the group, and says, "I'm going to Denver. What can I buy?" He then counts to 10. Before he finishes counting, the player before whom he is standing must name three objects that begin with "D" (as "dishes," "dog," "doughnuts"). If he fails, he must take the place of the shopper. Any city may be named. The things to be bought must begin with that city's initial.

**Rhymed Answers.** Pencils and papers are given to the players. Each player writes a question of any kind at the top of his paper and folds it over, then passes the paper to his neighbor on the right. This player writes any word below the fold and passes the paper to his neighbor on the right. All the players then open the papers, and each must write a brief poem answering the question and using the word he finds on the paper he holds.

**Teakettle.** A player leaves the room. The remaining group decides on some homonym; that is, a word that sounds like some other word or words but differs in meaning, such as rain (reign, rein). When the player who was out comes in, each person in the group uses "teakettle" in a sentence in place of the selected word. One may say "I grabbed the teakettle" (rein); another "Did you go through the teakettle?" (rain); another, "His was a very short teakettle" (reign). The player whose sentence reveals any one of these words so that it is guessed must leave the room for the next game. Other examples of such words are raise, rays, raze; pole, poll; tail, tale, tael; bare, bear; rose, rows; pier, peer.

**Imaginary I Spy.** A player thinks of an object in some special location; for instance, the ball on the flagpole. The others in the group try to find it by asking questions that may be answered by "Yes" or "No."

Sometimes it is better to have two children agree on the same object and answer the questions together.

**The Moon Is Round.** The players sit in a circle. The leader stoops and with his left hand outlines a face on the ground, saying, "The moon is round; it has two eyes, a nose, and a mouth." The others must stoop and do likewise. If they do not use their left hands, they have failed to do it properly because their imitation of the leader was not exact. Clearing the throat before starting, putting one hand on the hip, standing with a knee bent, and outlining one's own face with the left hand are variations the leader may use.

**Gossip.** The players sit in a circle, and the leader whispers a brief sentence to his neighbor on the right, who passes it on to his righthand neighbor until it has gone around the circle to the leader again. The leader then says it aloud and gives the original sentence.

**Biography.** Here's a way to see yourself as others see you. Make a scrapbook for each player, using wrapping paper for the pages and colored string to hold the leaves together. On each page write one item of an individual's life which should be mentioned in an interesting biography. This may vary with different groups. It should include, however, such items as birthplace, earliest recollections, baby days, school days, first girl, real romance, wedding, occupation, hobby, favorite friends, enemies, disappointments and epitaph. Distribute the scrapbooks and assign to each player the name of one of the other players whose biography he is to prepare. Now provide a file of old magazines, several pairs of scissors and lots of pins. The participants select from the magazines pictures which illustrate each item in the biography they are assembling. The pictures are fastened on each page and the scrapbooks exhibited when all the pages are filled.

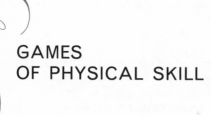

# GAMES
# OF PHYSICAL SKILL

Physical tests are given very generally and are extremely popular. Boys and girls who are unwilling to display their physical strength personally have come forward gladly to do their share for the honor of their group.

**Buzz.** Three players stand side by side with their feet well apart, the inside foot of each end player touching a foot of the player in the middle. The end players put the backs of their outside hands over their ears nearest the middle player. The middle player wears a hat, and he tries to protect it by ducking and dodging without moving his feet. He imitates the buzzing of an insect as he makes false passes at the end players, then slaps one of them on the out-turned palm with which he protects his ear. The one who is slapped immediately tries to brush off the middle player's hat. If he succeeds, he becomes the middle man. The challenger agrees that he will stand up through three slaps or that he and a teammate will take three slaps and give three slaps.

**Hand Push.** Two contestants stand facing each other with their toes touching. They have their palms also touching on a level with their chests. In this position each pushes the other's hands until one is forced to step back. The player who forces his opponent backward is the winner.

**Toe Tilt.** Two players sit on the floor or ground facing each other with their knees bent, their feet flat on the ground, and their arms clasped around their legs. Under the knees and over the arms of each is thrust a wand or broomstick. At the signal each player tries to lift with his toes the feet of his opponent. The one who succeeds, thus compelling his opponent to lose his balance and roll over on his back, wins the contest.

**Rooster Fight.** Two players stand in a circle drawn about 6 feet in diameter. Each puts his right hand behind his back, clasps his left foot with it, and then grips his right arm with his left hand behind his back. In this position they hop at each other when a signal is given, and each tries to force the other out of the circle or out of position. As soon as a player lets go of foot or arm or leaves the circle he loses the game.

Instead of holding his left foot each player may fold his arms over his chest, grasp his own elbows, and hop after his opponent. Releasing the elbows, lowering the foot, and leaving the circle are counted against the contestants.

**Hand Wrestle.** Two players face each other, grasp right hands, and place the outer edges of their right feet together. They brace themselves by putting their left feet back. At the signal each player tries to throw the other out of balance. As soon as either foot is moved, a fall is counted.

**Leg Wrestle.** Two players lie side by side on their backs with their heads in opposite directions. They hook right elbows. When the referee counts "one" they raise their right legs and touch them together. At count "two" this is repeated. At "three" they hook their right knees and each tries to turn the other over. The player who does a back somersault loses.

**Finger Bend.** Two players stand facing each other. They extend their arms over their heads and clasp each other's hands, interweaving the fingers. At the signal they back apart and bring their hands down. The stronger player will force the other to kneel. The one who has to kneel is the loser.

**Stick Pull.** Two players sit on the ground, each having the soles of his feet pressed against those of his opponent. They grasp a stick and hold it crosswise above their toes. At the signal each tries to pull the other to a standing position. The player who is pulled up or over or who releases the stick is the loser.

**Twist Stick.** Two players face each other, extend their arms overhead, and grasp a stick. At the signal they step backward and pull the stick down between them, each trying to retain his own grip and make the stick slip in his opponent's hands. The one who loses control of the stick loses the contest.—*from Handbook for Recreation, a publication of the U.S. Children's Bureau*

# MARBLE GAMES

**A-Hunting We Will Go.** Each child gets five green marbles to shoot with and a handful of marbles is placed on the floor inside a circle made with string. This is the forest and in it live orange and white-striped tigers, black bears, white rabbits, red squirrels and maybe a moose. Each animal

**52**

knocked clear out of the woods belongs to the hunter who shot the bullet. The children get so interested they don't care who bags the most game.

**Marbles.** There are many variations of the game of marbles. There is, for example, "Bounce Eye." This game requires several players, each of whom puts down a marble. The marbles are then formed into a small ring. One player begins by holding a marble in his hand close to his eye and letting it fall upon the ring; the marbles forced out of the ring by the concussion become his property, and the other players then try their skill in turn. The players are termed "bouncers."

**Picking the Plums.** A line is drawn on the ground, along which each player places a certain number of marbles. At this line the players shoot their taws in turns from a given point. The marbles knocked off the line become the property of the striker, and the game continues until no marbles remain. The marbles should be placed as close together as possible without actually touching.

**Pyramid.** Let a player draw a circle on the ground and then make a pyramid, either by placing three marbles triangularly, and one on the top of them, or else with six first, then four, and then one; the post of keeper of the pyramid ought to be taken by each boy in succession. Before a player can shoot at this pyramid, he must give a marble to the keeper; and should he strike the pyramid with his taw, all the marbles driven by the concussion beyond the circle belong to him.

**Marble Golf.** The courses themselves can be built wherever there is room to shoot marbles. The fairways, marked off by the white lines, are fifteen inches wide. Tees are small mounds of clay. All shots must be made "knuckle down." If the marble goes outside the white line on the fairway, it is brought back, and the next shot made from the point where it crossed the line.

Holes may be of any length, from about thirty to sixty feet, usually with one hazard and a trap or two to each. Tin pie plates, sunk flush with the fairways and filled with water, serve as water traps.

It is in building, and then beating, their own hazards that youngsters take special delight. One of the most popular hazards is a cast-off automobile tire, cut open across the tread, with the two openings spread apart

**53**

so that a marble shot into one opening would make the complete circuit and roll out the other onto the fairway. With insufficient force the marble will roll back and the shot will have to be made again. Shot too hard, the marble would strike the inside top of the tire and bounce back for another try. Just the right drive is needed to carry it through.

Other hazards call for lofting the marble with basketball accuracy, shooting through a revolving door, through a hole in the bottom of a barrel, and driving through iron pipes, and tantalizing mazes. The variety of hazards is almost unlimited. —*from "All Sorts of Games," a publication of the National Recreation Association*

# BEAN BAG GAMES

Playing bean bag, generally considered a kindergarten sport, interests the whole family when variety and elements of skill are introduced.

**Target Toss.** Three concentric circles should be drawn on the ground. The inner circle is 12 inches in diameter, the next circle is 3 feet in diameter and the largest is 6 feet in diameter. The player stands 20 feet away from the center of the circles; in other words, 17 feet from the rim of the outside circle. Player gets 5 throws. If bag stops within the center circle, it scores 10 points, if it stops within middle circle it scores 7 points, if it stops within the large circle, it scores 5 points. A bag landing on a line does not score. all.

**Bean Bag Box.** A box measuring 6 inches square and 4 inches deep should be fastened in one 12 inches square, same depth, which in turn is in a third box 18 inches square, same depth. This is set up on a slight incline (5 in.). The throwing line is 15 feet away. Player gets 5 throws. Bag thrown into the smallest box scores 5 points; bag thrown into middle box scores 7 points, and bag thrown into largest box scores 10 points. Bag which stops on edge of any box does not score.

**54**

**Bean Bag Board.**   This game consists in throwing the bean bag through holes in the inclined board. The board should be preferably 18 inches wide by 24 inches long. Near the lower end a 5-inch square hole should be cut. (A good-size bean bag is about 5 inches.) Higher up, another hole 8 inches square should be cut. The board is to be slanted at an angle of about 45 degrees, either by bracing it or resting it against a wall or fence. The player stands at a throwing line 12 feet from the board. Each player gets 10 throws. A bag thrown into the larger hole scores 5 points; into the smaller hole 10 points.

**Pocket Bean Bag.**   Canvas is stretched on a 4-foot square frame. The center pocket is 8 inches in diameter. Eight pockets 5 inches in diameter form a circle 20 inches from the center of the square to the center of the 5-inch circles. Entire frame may be raised 2 feet from the ground. Player stands 15 feet away and gets 10 throws. The 8-inch pocket scores 5 points and 5-inch pockets score 10 points.

# GAMES
# AT DANCES

**For teenagers or adults.**   These are fun at dances, but should be used with discretion. A dance that is going well needs fewer than the dance that is hard to get started.

In elimination dances, some method is used to gradually remove dance couples from the floor, until only one couple is left. Their element of suspense makes them fun.

Tag, or robber dances, allow a person to cut in and take a partner away from someone. They are very good for groups where there are extra boys or girls, and they add a touch of humor and excitement.

**Blind Date.**   The boys line up on one side of the room, the girls on the opposite side. Both lines turn their backs to each other. When music begins, each player backs up until he bumps into someone in the opposite line. This is his partner for the next dance. Caution: Tell the boys to back slowly. They are usually in such a hurry to get their partners first, they move back much too quickly and bang into someone. Also tell them not to look— just back straight.

**Multiplication Dance.** Definitely a good mixer to get the dance started. Select one couple to start dancing. After only a few steps, the music stops, the couple separates, the boy and girl choose new partners. The two couples dance a few steps until the music stops, separate, and all four people choose new partners; and so on until all available couples are dancing.

**Paul Jones.** Girls form a circle inside the boys' circle. Girls move clockwise, boys counterclockwise, to the music. When the music stops, the girl and boy facing each other become partners. When the music starts, they dance together until it stops again, then fall back into the circle formation. Keep the dance periods fairly short, so as to change partners frequently.

**Deer Hunting.** A pile of small paper bags is placed on a table at the front of the room. Several of the extra girls who do not have a partner start the game. At the call "All hunters stalk your deer," the girls who have a paper bag blow it up, go to a boy of their choice and pop it on his back. The girl with whom he is dancing must give him up to the hunter. She then goes to the table and gets a bag and goes stalking her deer. The bag must pop. If it merely squashes, she has made a poor shot and must blow it up again. The deer who was shot puts the bag in his pocket so the floor will not be covered with them.

**Balloon Bust.** Give each boy an inflated balloon with string attached to tie to his partner's ankle. Balloon should float out at least 2 feet from ankle (watch those nylons!). Music starts and couples try to break each other's balloons and protect their own. As balloons are "busted," couples must leave the floor. Last couple remaining on the floor with balloon intact should receive some small prize. If you think this game will be too rough on the girls' ankles, the balloons may be tied around wrists or carried in hands.

56

**Heads Together.** Each couple is given a potato (orange, etc.). They must place this between their foreheads, put their hands behind their backs and dance. As soon as the potato falls, that couple must leave the floor. If the potatoes are not falling quickly enough, a change of rhythm may help. (Rhumbas or polkas usually cause most to leave the floor. Waltzes are usually comical to watch because the dancers are trying so hard to be graceful and at the same time trying to keep from dropping the potato.)

**Tin Pan Alley.** Give each couple a card bearing the name of a popular song and give a list of the songs to the orchestra. As the songs are played, the couples leave the dance floor until only one couple remains. For a large dance the same songs may be given to several couples.—*from Handbook for Recreation, a publication of the U.S. Children's Bureau*

# GAMES ACROSS
# A JUMP ROPE

Sha-thump, sha-thump . . . you hear it as you mow your suburban lawn; as you drive along a country road. It floats through the window, open to spring, from the city street below. The slap of the rope, the thump of the feet. And with the endless chantings . . .

> "Cinderella dressed in yella'
> Went to the ball and met a fella'
> How many kisses did she re-ceive!
> 1-2-3-4-5-6-7-8-9-10!"

or one that goes, "Intery, kintery country corn—Apple seed and apple thorn . . ." or the strenuous one that must have each line enacted as the jumper goes through her paces—

> "Teddy Bear, Teddy Bear, turn around
> Teddy Bear, Teddy Bear, touch the ground

Teddy Bear, Teddy Bear, show your shoe
Teddy Bear, Teddy Bear, better skiddoo
Teddy Bear, Teddy Bear, go upstairs
Teddy Bear, Teddy Bear, say your prayers
Teddy Bear, Teddy Bear, turn out light
Teddy Bear, Teddy Bear, say goodnight
Teddy Bear, Teddy Bear, sit on a pin
How many inches did it go in!"

"Teddy Bear" is chanted from North Carolina up the east coast and out to the west. "Teddy Bear" is also very much at home in England, and has been for many years. Yet an ocean separates the children of America and the children of England. Oceans and continents separate all the children of the world but if your daughter knows the jump rope rhythm chants, she would be at home in any nation.

In France, not even knowing the language, she could leap readily into the arcing rope to

Trois petites pattes
Ma chemise brule
Trois petites pattes
La voila brulee
Ou vas-tu petit soldat
Je pars pour la guerre
Que portes-tu dans ton sac?
Des pommes de terre.

The world round, the verses seem to grow out of nowhere. Ask a child where he learned a rope rhyme and he'll say from his playmates. And where did they learn them? From their playmates. As a rule, you don't see parents jumping rope with their children, and still the verses go down from generation. Don't you remember the somewhat gruesome "Ladybug, ladybug. . ."?

"Down by the river, down by the sea
Johnny broke a milk bottle
And blamed it on me
I told Ma, Ma told Pa
Johnny got a licking
Ha, ha, ha!
1-2-3-4-5-"

and so forth until the jumper misses.—*Princine M. Calitri*

**58**

# SINGLE
# CIRCLE GAMES

*In single circle games the players form a circle, joining hands or not, in accordance with the directions. In some games a designated player stands inside or outside the circle to act as "It." If the number of players is very large, two separate circles should be formed.*

## Singing Games

The tunes for most games probably are familiar to most people and phonograph records can be obtained for them. Other well-known single circle games are Farmer in the Dell, We Go Round the Mulberry Bush, Round and Round the Village, and Did You Ever See a Lassie?.

**Oats, Peas, Beans.** For this game a player who acts as the farmer stands in the center of the circle and makes motions that everyone else imitates.

> Oats, peas, beans, and barley grow;
> Oats, peas, beans, and barley grow;
> Do you or I or anyone know
> How oats, peas, beans, and barley grow?
>
> First the farmer sows his seed,
> Then he stands and takes his ease;
> He stamps his foot and claps his hand,
> And turns around to view the land.
>
> I'm waiting for a partner,
> I'm waiting for a partner;
> Break the ring and choose one in,
> While all the others dance and sing.

Tra la la la la la la,
Tra la la la la la la,
Tra la la la la la la,
Tra la la la la la la la.

During the first verse the farmer pantomimes "you or I or anyone" by extending both hands, touching his own chest, then extending his hands again. In the second he throws out the seed with his right hand, folds his arms to stand at ease, then stamps his foot, claps his hands, shades his eyes, and turns around "to view the land." During the third he walks around the circle looking for a partner until the words "choose one in" are sung. Then he bows to the player he has selected and crosses hands with her. They skip inside the circle during the whole of the last verse.

Both become farmers for the next game, and each selects a new partner. These players also remain in the circle, so that the number of farmers doubles at each playing. The game continues until everyone is skipping.

**Looby Loo.** For this game the first verse is repeated as chorus after the second and each following verse.

Here we go, Looby Loo,
Here we go, Looby Light;
Here we go, Looby Loo,
All on a Saturday night!

I put my right hand in,
I put my right hand out;
I give my right hand a shake, shake, shake,
And turn myself about, oh.

I put my left hand in,
I put my left hand out;
I give my left hand a shake, shake, shake,
And turn myself about, oh.

I put my two hands in,
I put my two hands out;
I give my two hands a shake, shake, shake,
And turn myself about, oh.

I put my right foot in, etc.
I put my left foot in, etc.

**60**

I put my head way in, etc.
I put my whole self in, etc.

During the chorus all the players join hands and walk eight steps toward the center of the circle and eight steps back to place. During the verses they pantomime the words. On the first verse each player extends his right hand into the circle, stretches it behind his back, shakes it, and turns around in place. This action is varied as the remaining verses require.

# Running Games

**Come Along.** The players learn the names of their neighbors, then extend their left hands into the circle. "It" steps inside the circle, walks around, and takes the hand of someone. That person catches the hand of someone else, and so a line continues to grow until the whistle blows. Then everyone must hurry back to his own place and greet his neighbors by name. The last player home is "It" for the next time. If the circle is large several lines may be started from different points.

If the players seem likely to start "cracking the whip," the leader should blow the whistle at once.

**Slap Jack.** All the players except one stand in the circle, clasping hands. One player runs around the outside of the circle and tags another player as he runs. The one tagged immediately leaves his place and runs in the opposite direction. The object of each runner is to get back first to the vacant place. Whoever succeeds remains in that place, the one left out becoming runner the next time. This is sometimes varied by having the players bow, shake hands as they meet, and say, "Good morning, Good morning."

**Cat and Rat.** All the players except two join hands in the circle. One player is chosen to be the rat and stands inside the circle. Another is the cat and takes his place outside. The cat tries to catch the rat. The players favor the rat and allow him to run in and out of the circle, but they try to prevent the cat from following him by raising and lowering their arms. When the rat is caught, the cat and the rat join the circle after choosing two other players to become rat and cat. A second cat may be sent to help a cat who is slow, or the circle may slowly count 25 and then demand that the players select a new cat and rat.

**61**

**Drop the Handkerchief.** All the players except one stand in a circle. The odd player, who is "It," runs around outside the circle carrying a handkerchief, which he drops behind one of the players. As soon as this player discovers that the handkerchief has been dropped behind him he must pick it up and run around the circle in the same direction in which "It" is going, trying to catch him before he reaches the place left vacant in the circle. If he fails, so that "It" takes his place in the circle, he must be "It" for the next game.

**Numbers Change.** All the players take consecutive numbers. One player takes his place in the center of the circle. He calls two numbers, and the persons whose numbers are called must change places. While they do so the center player tries to secure one of their places. The person who is left without a place becomes the center player. This may be played indoors with the players seated or out of doors with the players standing in an extended circle.

# DOUBLE CIRCLE GAMES

*In double circle games the players form two circles, one inside the other, during at least part of the time. If the number of players is very large, they may place in two or more groups, the partners in each group taking their places in accordance with the directions for the game.*

## Singing Games

The tunes and words for these games are also familiar to most. For some of them any fast march music that can be hummed easily is suitable. Phonograph records can be obtained for a number of them so that you can learn them beforehand.

**Tucker.** If there are more boys than girls, the girls form the inner circle while the boys make a circle around them. If there are more girls, the boys form the inner circle. Fast march music is played, and immediately the girls walk in one direction while the boys go the opposite way. When the whistle blows, every boy tries to get a partner, and the ones who fail go into the center. The leader then calls various commands, such as, "Skip!" "Hop on the right foot!" "Skate!" "Slide in, slide out!" The couples obey these commands until the whistle blows again. Then the boys bow and turn away, and all the players walk in the direction in which they had walked at the beginning of the game until another signal is given by the whistle.

**Jolly Is the Miller.** The circles face in the same direction, and the couples march around the circle hand-in-hand, the girls on the inside.

> Jolly is the miller who lives by the mill
> The wheel goes round with a right good will;
> One hand in the hopper and the other in the sack,
> The right steps forward, and the left steps back.

At the last line of the song the players on the right step forward and those on the left step back to meet new partners. An extra player, the miller, who stands in the center, tries to get a partner during the change. The player who fails to get a partner becomes the next miller.

**Firefly.** The girls form the inner circle facing their partners who are in the outer circle. Any march music can be played for this game. The partners swing by their right arms for eight counts, then by their left arms for eight counts. Next they join hands and slide right during eight counts, then left eight counts. A grand right and left follows during eight counts, and the eighth player encountered is the new partner for the repetition of the game. Until the players have learned the game thoroughly the leader should call the figures.

**Yankee Doodle.** While the song is being sung or whistled the partners walk around, the girls being in the outside circle.

> Father and I went down to camp
> Along with Captain Goodwin,
> And there we saw the men and boys
> As thick as hasty pudding.

**63**

(chorus)
Yankee Doodle, keep it up,
Yankee Doodle, dandy;
Mind the music and the step,
And with the girls be handy.

During "Yankee Doodle, keep it up" the partners join hands and slide four steps in the direction they have been marching. They slide back during "Yankee Doodle, dandy." Each couple swings around with six steps during "Mind the music and the step." Then each boy moves to the girl on his left and bows during "With the girls be handy." The game is repeated with these new partners.

## Running Games

**Squirrels in Trees.** This game is played by groups of four. Three players join hands and form a small circle. This is the tree. The fourth player stands in the center as the squirrel. Two extra players are a squirrel and a hound. The hound chases the squirrel, who for safety darts into a tree. The squirrel already in the tree must get out, and he may dart into any other tree. If the hound catches any squirrel outside a tree, that squirrel must become the hound, and the hound becomes a squirrel.

**Face to Face.** The partners stand facing each other in one large circle. One odd player stands in the center and calls "Face to face," "Back to back," "Face to face," "Back to back," the players taking their positions accordingly. When he calls "All change," the players must take new partners. The center player tries to get one, too. If he succeeds, the person left without a partner must go into the center and give the commands. This game should not be used in a group of more than 50 players.

**Fire in the Mountain.** All the players except one form a double circle facing inward, each in the outer circle standing directly behind his partner. The extra player, who is "It," stands in the center. When he calls "Fire in the mountain! Run, men, run!" the players in the outside circle begin immediately to jog around while "It" and the players of the inside circle clap their hands. When "It" stops clapping, he and the inside players hold their hands over their heads as a signal that the outside players are each to try to get in front of an inside player. "It" tries to do the same, and the player left out becomes "It" for the next time.

# LINE GAMES

*In line games the players begin by taking their places in parallel lines. Usually those who have been partners or who will become partners are opposite and they face each other unless the directions specify otherwise.*

## Singing Games

**Broom Walk.** The boys form one line, the girls another, the two lines being about 10 feet apart. An odd player has a broom and sweeps back and forth between the lines. If there are four or five extra boys or girls, there can be several sweepers.

> One, two, three, four, five, six, seven!
> Where's my partner? Nine, ten, 'leven!
> To-le-do, O-hi-o,
> That is where you'll have to go!

While the first four words are sung the players in the lines walk four steps toward each other and four steps back to place. When "Toledo, Ohio," is sung, everyone dashes for a partner, the sweeper dropping his broom and trying to get one too. The person failing to get a partner must carry the broom during the repetition of the song, through which each couple skips around and goes back to place in the lines.

**Virginia Reel.** The players stand well apart in lines or sets of about six couples facing each other. The boys' line is at the left of the girls' when they turn to march. All the couples go through the figures at the same time. While the music is being played or sung the leader should call the figures, which are as follows:

Forward and bow: Each player advances three steps, bows to partner, and returns to place.

Right-hand swing: Partners advance, join right hands, face each other.

Left-hand swing: Partners join left hands and turn.

Both-hands swing: Partners join both hands and turn.

Do si do, right: Partners fold arms and walk around each other, passing on the right and walking backward to place.

Do si do, left: Partners fold arms and walk around, passing on the left and walking backward to place.

Arm right: Partners hook right arms and swing around.

Arm left: Partners hook left arms and swing around.

Head couples lead your lines away: The girl in the first couple turns to the right, the boy to the left, and the other players follow. They march down outside their respective lines, clapping hands in time to the music. When the first couple meet at the foot of the lines, they join hands and form a bridge. As the following couples meet they march under the bridge to their places, the second couple thus becoming the first.

The game is continued until each couple has acted as first couple.

## Running Games

**Crows and Cranes.**   The two lines of players stand about 3 feet apart, facing each other. A base line is marked about 30 feet behind each line of players. The base line should vary in distance from the line of players according to the space, age of players, and occasion. One team is designated "Crows," the other "Cranes." If the leader calls "Cranes," the Cranes turn and run back toward their base line, endeavoring to reach it without being caught by any of the Crows. Any players who are caught go to the side of the catcher. If the leader calls "Crows," these players run in the same manner. The team having the larger number of players at the close of a given time wins. The game may be made more interesting if the leader drawls the "r" in either Crows or Cranes, so that the players are not at first certain which word he is going to say.

**Stealing Sticks.**   The field is divided into two parts by a well defined line drawn or dug through the middle. At the center back of each side five or more sticks are placed in a pile. A prison is marked off about 4 feet square in one corner. The players are in two teams, each scattered over its own side. The object of the game is to get the opponents' sticks without being caught. As soon as a player crosses the center line he may be caught and put in prison. If he can dash to the pile of sticks and secure one, he is safe and may bring it home to his own pile. A player may be released from prison if one of his teammates can touch his hand. He may then come back to his own side without being tagged. The team that gets all the opponents' sticks and has all its members safely out of prison wins the game.

**Pom, Pom, Pull Away.** This game is suitable for any open space which is large enough to permit two lines to be drawn across with a space of 30 to 50 feet between them. All the players stand on one side behind one of these goal lines, except one player who is "It," who stands in the center between the two lines. He calls:

> "Pom, pom, pull away!
> If you don't come, I'll pull you away!"

Thereupon all the players must run across the open space to the goal line on the opposite side, the one who is "It" trying to tag as many as possible before they reach that line. Anyone tagged joins in helping to tag other players as they dash across the open space; but "It" does the calling throughout the game. When all not tagged have reached the line, "It" gives the call again, and all the uncaught players must run back to their original goal line. The players run from one goal to the other in this way until all have been caught. Then the game starts again, the first player tagged in one game becoming "It" for the next game.

**Ride Him, Cowboy.** All the players except one form in short lines (four or five persons), each player clasping the one in front of him around the waist. These lines are called bronchos. The odd player, who is called the cowboy, tries to "ride" by clasping the waist of the last player in some broncho. If he can do this in spite of the broncho's swerving about, the first player of that line must become a cowboy, because the broncho needs a better head. For six or more bronchos there should be two or three cowboys.—*from Handbook for Recreation, a publication of the U.S. Children's Bureau.*

# THE
# WONDERFUL
# WORLD OF
# MAKE-BELIEVE

*FOR A YOUNG CHILD, external and internal reality are inextricably mixed. And while children sometimes try to escape into fantasy when life becomes too difficult for them, they most often engage in fantasy play to separate more clearly the inner life of imagination from the outer life of reality—and to gain mastery over both.—Bruno Bettelheim, Ph.D.*

**69**

# DRAMATIC GAMES

## For pre-school age

Simple singing games of impersonation of adult activities like Looby Loo, Mulberry Bush, circle games of impersonation like Cat and Rat, Hen and Chickens, Flowers and Wind.

## For elementary school age

### Singing games of impersonation

Thorn Rosa—a fairy story which is acted out, not just sung with perfunctory gestures.
Roman Soldiers—in which the English and the Romans threaten each other, and then wound each other in broad pantomime.

### Pantomime games

Statues
Simple Charades
Trades—A popular playground game that combines pantomime and guessing with tag. Players divide into two groups. One group decides upon a word or words, which they act out while the other group tries to guess. A traditional dialogue takes place as each group meets at a center line. One version goes like this:

First group—Here he comes!
Second group—Where from?

First group—Tennessee
Second group—What's your number?

First group—Cucumber
Second group—What's your trade?

First group—Lemonade
Second group—Show us some

The first group gives the initials of their words, P.C. for example, and pantomime their words until somebody in the second group guesses "Picking Cherries," whereupon the second group chases the first to its safety line, those caught joining the second group. The game proceeds, each group taking turns, until one group has captured all the players, or until interest begins to lag a bit.


**For teen age**

Dumb Crambo—a good icebreaker for a group
In the Manner of the Word
Take It—A quiet game with real pantomime. One person thinks of some object—a baby, a snake, a bucket of water, a piece of ice—and with appropriate pantomime passes it to the next player, saying, "Take this and pass it on." Each in turn tries to figure out what this invisible object could be, and passes it along. When it finally gets back to the one who started it, he tells what he had in mind, and then each player explains what he thought it was. The wide range of imaginary objects is always very amusing, and the game can absorb a group for a long period of time.

Charades—simple and complex—the classic example of a dramatic game. In this game, words are pantomimed syllable by syllable. Sometimes the whole word is acted as a unit in addition to the separate syllables. Although individuals may perform in turn, players are usually divided into teams of four or more. In acting the charade, no words are spoken and no properties used. However, a player may point to or touch any part of his own body or those of his teammates. Players hold up their fingers to indicate the number of syllables and use gestures to indicate when they have decided to change to another syllable or when the guessing is very close or far afield. They may also indicate with their fingers whether the syllable they are acting is the first, second or third.

To be successful, only words which permit action and which are familiar to the group should be chosen. As the group becomes experienced, a time limit for guessing can be set, so that the game does not drag.

For a starter, the following are good words to try:

| | |
|---|---|
| Bandage | Buttercup |
| Workman | Dandelion |
| Ice Cream (I scream) | Infancy |
| Chestnut | Tulip |
| Bookworm | Seasick |
| Toothbrush | Poker (Poke her) |
| Keyhole | Rainbow |

**The Game**—A more modern version of charades. In this form, the players on each team decide on actions which the other team has to perform. These are written on slips of paper and there is one for each player. The action may be based on an advertising slogan, a book or movie title, or may require the player to demonstrate a wrestling hold, make a pie, or bathe a baby. There are endless possibilities.

After each group has chosen the required number of actions, the written slips are collected and are exchanged between teams. They are kept face down or folded until it is time for an individual to draw a slip and perform the designated action which his own teammates must identify. Players from opposing teams take turns presenting their charades. Time is kept and the team wins that takes the least time to guess the actions of all its players. The particular fun of the game is that everyone has a share in choosing charades for the opposing team, and that half of the players always know what action the others are struggling to identify.—*Adapted from Informal Dramatics, a publication of the National Recreation Association*

# PLAY-ACT
# PROBLEMS AWAY

My love affair with creative dramatics began one morning when I said to my two-year-old daughter, "Let's pretend you're in my beauty shop. You've come into my shop to have your hair curled." Until then, combing and brushing Carol's hair each morning had been met with howls and protests—"You're hurting me, Mommy! Oooww! Stop! Leave the tangles in!" But the morning I suggested the beauty shop game, Carol sat without wiggling and actually seemed to enjoy the whole hair-grooming procedure.

**Creative dramatics** is really very simple. It's transforming a real—or imagined—experience into dramatic form. The play-acting can be based either on a story a child is told or read, or on a familiar experience. It is acting out a situation in which a child participates by creating a character, and by using his own imagination to supply original dialogue.

Children create plays or dramatize situations when they play house, play school, or "play" any of the many activities in which they engage daily. In nursery schools and in elementary schools, creative dramatics is used extensively, for it is a natural form of self-expression which children love. It is an equally effective tool at home, a novel approach to problem-solving, and children enjoy the novelty of it.

**How it works.** Take our four-year-old son Robbie, a notably poor eater. He picks at his food and is very easily distracted while at the table. Ordinary admonishments and encouragements just don't work with him. Often creative dramatics is the only way we keep him from leaving the table practically foodless. A simple remark suggesting a restaurant setting—for Robbie has been deeply impressed by his restaurant visits—turns his wandering mind to the meal on the table.

Creative dramatics does not have to be used in a complicated manner. Often a sentence or two put in dramatic form can accomplish wonders. It's possible, for example, to say when a child refuses to take your hand while crossing the street, "You're the mommy (or the daddy) and I'm your child. You must help me across the street so that the cars don't hit me."

To a child who is stamping and tramping about the house, making a great deal of noise, you might say something like, "Did you know that if you were a skin diver you wouldn't be making all that noise? Skin divers move quietly, in slow-motion, like this." This is more likely to produce the desired result than saying, "For goodness sake, Tommy, can't you remember that the baby is taking his nap?"

**How it Helps.** Creative dramatics is also helpful in teaching specific lessons—particularly in preparing a young child for a situation you know may prove frightening or disagreeable to him, such as a first trip to the dentist or on a jet airliner.

The lessons don't have to be confined to experiences that are frightening

**73**

to children. Acting out beforehand what happens when you dine in a restaurant, or attend a play in a legitimate theatre, will bring benefits far beyond the polite behavior of your pride and joy. Further, if a child's first trip to the theater, or his first dinner out is an easy and comfortable experience, he will enjoy it and remember it with pleasure. You will have given him a good beginning for a lifetime of happy and appreciative experiences.—*Joann D. Rossio*

# IN NEVER NEVER LAND

Make-believe play is one of the child's major ways to discover himself and his world. A small child will try to find out what it is to be a cat, a nurse, a bus driver by acting like them. And if he says, "I see a fairy in the garden," he may only be trying to find out if there really are fairies.

"Let's pretend" can develop into full-scale dramatic play if we provide simple costumes and props. Taking different roles will give children practice in speech and action, help them prepare for real events, such as a visit to the dentist, and give them a chance to play out feelings of anger, jealousy and fear.

**Beginning years, 1-3:**  In the second year, a child imitates the sounds and movements of animals, trains, planes. A little later, he pretends to be grownup by playing at telephoning, doing the dishes, cleaning house, driving a car, tending a baby. Often, he makes believe stuffed animals are real and clings to them for companionship and security.

**Playthings:** Teddy bear, stuffed animals, toy telephone, doll carriage, small cars, wooden train, toy dishes, baby doll, blocks of different shapes.

**Early childhood, 3-6:**  The peak period of "pretend." Around three, some children have imaginary playmates ("Don't sit on that chair, Bab is

**74**

sitting there!") but will soon discard them if we treat this as a game and provide enough activities and companions. Sex differences begin, but are not consistent. Girls play mother, nurse, cook; boys play pirate, space pilot, zoo-keeper, postman. Group activities become important to boys and girls: playing family, running a store, staging an Indian attack, giving a special tea party.

**Playthings for girls:** Dolls with wardrobes, costume materials for dressing up, toy medicine cabinet, toy washing-machine, toy kitchen utensils and appliances, small carpet sweeper, doll house and furnishings, doll carriage, bassinet.

**Playthings for boys:** Plastic shaving set, doctor kit, briefcase, police outfit, cowboy outfit, Indian regalia, clown and pirate costumes, bulldozer, crane, dump truck, steam shovel, fire engine, miniature farm, fort, gas station, grain elevator.

**Playthings for boys and girls:** Nursery school blocks, cartons, and other materials for store play; toy money, hand puppets.

**Middle childhood, 6-9:** Both boys and girls act out stories they have read or heard, or make up simple plays, speaking through the mouths of puppets. Girls still play house but like to pretend they are entertaining guests or having parties as well as cooking, cleaning, and tending children. Boys play hunt-and-chase games, picturing themselves as spacemen, commandos or FBI investigators. Group games gradually become better organized, with participants assigned to special roles.

**Playthings for girls:** Costumes (princess, Cinderella, drum majorette, gypsy, ballerina, peasant), party set, hospital cart, real-life dolls, puppets, marionettes, manicure and makeup sets.

**Playthings for boys:** Tomahawk, gun, helmet, costumes and uniforms (Canadian Mountie, pioneer, sailor), stockade, tree house, sanitation truck, moving van, cement mixer, locomotive, schooner, yacht, school bus, station wagon, auto carrier, miniature cars, tank, ladder truck, freight train, police car, mobile home, wrecking truck, fire fighter, space capsule, helicopter.

**Later childhood, 9-12:** The focus is increasingly on the real world, yet the child who visits a factory, a fashion show or a newspaper office will use imagination in seeing himself in new roles. Dramatic play may take the form of charades, pantomimes, or acting in school plays.

Playthings: Marionette or puppet theatre.—*Robert M. Goldenson, Ph.D.*

# PUPPETS

The word "puppet" means "doll"—and like dolls, puppets can be made out of almost anything—rubber balls, clothespins, eggshells, corn husks, potatoes, paper bags, boxes, spoons—the possibilities are endless! They're symbols—and a symbol can be any object to which the imagination can give special meaning.

**Puppets are Valuable.** First of all, they satisfy the instinct to create—to make something. Second, in playing with the puppet, no matter how simple it is, the youngster gets a real feeling of mastery. He has complete control over its actions and its speech! Third, the youngster identifies himself with the puppet, and therefore feels free to express emotions and thoughts that he would not be able to express through his own actions and speech because of shyness or fear of ridicule or social disapproval. This third point of "identification" is particularly important, and a very special characteristic of puppetry.

To the child, the puppet is a very real person, with a life of his own, but he is also an extension of the child's personality—his "alter ego." Through the puppet, the child can fulfill his wildest dreams of being a hero, of flying through the air on a magic carpet, of conquering space, and no one will laugh at his exploits. Through the puppet, he can be a truant, a mischief-maker, a thief, a pirate, and no one will punish him. Through the puppet, he can satisfy his desire for revenge on the adults who compel him to conform to the pattern of a society he's too young to understand. They can fight, brawl, kill, cast spells, make fun of others, act silly, get in and out of trouble—and it's all in fun!

**76**

As a result, the shy youngster, or the fearful, or the anxious child is able to take part in dramatic play and story dramatization much more easily. Many youngsters who would shy away from other forms of dramatics get pleasure from puppets—and in time to take a personal part in other dramatic activities. Puppetry is an easy first step.

Anybody can make and work a puppet. And everybody loves them!

**Pre-School Age.** With small children, start off with a rubber band holding a paper doll to the forefinger. When they've enjoyed these, suggest that they look through magazines at home and find a paper doll or animal. Then show them how small bands of paper (like a cigar band) can be glued to the legs, so that the fingers fit in the bands, and the paper cut-out will stand erect. If necessary, paste the cut-out to flexible cardboard.

Let them make paper bag puppets and use these in illustrating and acting out Mother Goose and nonsense rhymes.

**Elementary-School Age.** All of the above, plus. A natural follow-up of the simple rubber band cut-outs is the real finger puppet with a dress or trousers in which the first and second fingers are placed and used as legs. A table-top or plank, sawhorse, or cardboard box can be found and the idea of staging introduced.

Keep interest high by improvising puppet characters and animals out of wooden spoons, blocks, vegetables and anything on hand. A potato makes a wonderful elephant with toothpicks for tusks!

Go on into hand puppets, representing different kinds of characters, and let the youngsters handle and use these before suggesting that they make their own.

**Junior and High-School Age.** For older groups, all of the above, plus. Age is not a major factor in puppetry. It's interest and skill that count. If puppets are familiar to them, they can make more and more elaborate ones, construct a portable stage, plan lighting and sets, and put on puppet shows for the others. From there to marionettes is a logical step.

MAKING SIMPLE PUPPETS

**Construction:** Most manuals suggest that hand puppets have papier-mache heads, or other types that require much time and skill. The directions here, for simple types of puppets, may more easily be made at home, often by the children themselves. They are not permanent, which is all to the good, since the youngsters can make them at one sitting, for impromptu dramatic activities, and can create new ones as the need arises. As they learn to improvise new puppets, and get used to them, the time will come when they'll have enough interest to ask for more permanent types. Then is when papier-mache or carved wooden heads can be made—and the idea of marionettes introduced!

**Materials needed:** Soup ladle, colander type ladle, or wooden spoon, and two handkerchiefs.

Wrap one handkerchief around the rim of the ladle so that the round section forms the puppet's face. Place the other handkerchief around your fist, holding the handle of the ladle as close to the bowl as possible. Paint or paste the features on in the proper places. Straws, grasses, etc., can be put in the colander type ladle for a mustache, etc.

## PAPER BAG PUPPETS

The size and type of bag used is No. 7, square bottom.

### For Human Characters:

1. Take the bag and open it to its greatest fullness before planning the features.
2. Indicate features very lightly in pencil, being sure not to place the eyes too high. Remember to allow for a forehead. The mouth should be placed about half-way down the bag, allowing enough space at the bottom to tie the bag onto the wrist with a piece of ribbon or crepe paper.
3. The features may be cut from colored construction paper and pasted on the bag.
4. Giving the head a nose that stands away from the bag, rather than a flat one, helps to give the head a little more roundness. A cylindrical piece of stiff paper or a triangle folded down the center usually make surprisingly good noses.
5. Be sure the features are not too small. Hair may be added with strips of paper. Various types of hairdresses may be obtained.

Eyelashes may be added by fringing a piece of paper and bending the fringes back so that they stand away from the eye. Accessories such as hats or hair ribbons may be used.

**78**

## RUBBER BALL PUPPETS

**Materials needed:**
1. A rubber ball.
   a. Size: about 2½″ in diameter.
   b. Type: may be hollow or solid.
   c. Color: depends on character.
2. A few scraps of colored construction paper.
3. Some strong glue or rubber cement.
4. A large square handkerchief or a piece of cloth the same size. (The piece of cloth usually decides the character to be made—for example: if a workman's kerchief is used, the character might be a laborer or a farmer.)

**Procedure:**
1. Cut a small hole in the rubber ball just large enough to fit the tip of the operator's index finger.
2. Cut features out of colored construction paper and glue them to the ball. A small piece of sponge or cork may be used for the nose. A three-dimensional nose looks better than a flat one.
3. Hair may be added by using colored strips of paper. Raffia, wool or rope are effective for hair. Many different types of hair-do may be obtained by cutting the paper in different ways.
4. Take the square piece of cloth, find the center, place over the operator's index finger—and put the finger into the hole in the ball. Slash in two places to allow the thumb and middle finger to come through.

## CREPE PAPER PUPPETS

**Materials needed:**
1. Crepe paper.
2. Cotton batting.
3. A small scrap of lightweight cardboard.
4. Paste.
5. A few scraps of colored construction paper.
6. A needle, thread and scissors.

**Procedure:**
1. Take a 9-inch square of crepe paper.
2. Fill with cotton batting to form the head.

**79**

3. Use cardboard cylinder for the neck. (The cylinder should be just large enough for the tip of the index finger.)

4. Cut excess paper away from the cylinder, leaving just enough to cover the neck.

5. Cut features of colored construction paper and paste them to the head. (Remember a three-dimensional nose looks better than a flat one.)

6. The costume consists of a piece of crepe paper approximately 10 inches long and 15 inches wide.

    a. Gather the width of the paper around the neck and sew it to the cardboard cylinder.

7. Slash holes for the middle finger and thumb to come through for arms.

8. If a boy's costume is desired, use a shorter piece of crepe paper to form the jacket or the blouse, which should be large enough to cover the operator's hand.

    a. Paste two gathered pieces of crepe paper to the inside of the blouse to form trousers.

9. Add finishing touches.

    a. Ears—Fold flap back and paste to the head.

    b. Hair—Paste colored strips of crepe paper or construction paper to the top of the head, or braid crepe paper and coil around the top of the head.

Short sleeves may be added. (Paste to the armhole.)

For feet, stuff a small piece of crepe paper with cotton batting. Paste up into the bottom of the trousers.


## THE PUPPET STAGE

Puppet stages can be improvised as simply as the puppets!

The most elementary stage is, of course, no stage at all—just the ground or table-top! Finger puppets walk and talk, and the imagination of the youngster gives them separate identification from the operator.

The operator's other arm, too, is a very elementary yet effective stage, easily used with hand and stick puppets. The left arm is folded, and the right hand operates the puppet between the left arm and the chest.

A narrow plank, a box, an orange crate, a shelf, a sawhorse, a table, a suitcase—all make perfectly adequate stages on which the puppets can act out any story dramatization. The operators are behind this improvised stage, and kneel or sit so that they are below the stage. (All puppets are operated from below.) To hide the operators, and yet let their voices be audible, paper or cloth is often hung from the improvised stage to the ground.

**80**

Another very simple way to give an illusion of staging is by the apron stage—which is nothing but an apron worn by the operator. When the play is ready, two youngsters hold the apron in front of the face of the operator, who uses the edge of the apron as the stage. If he has a hand puppet on each hand, a play with two characters is easy. Otherwise, he uses his left hand to handle the "props" needed by the story.

All that is needed for any puppet stage, no matter how elaborate, are four essentials:
1. a frame-like opening (the proscenium)
2. a floor ledge to indicate where the puppets walk
3. a background or scene
4. lighting

*—Adapted from "Simple Puppetry," a publication of the National Recreation Association.*

# PANTOMIME

**For Pre-School Children.** Pantomime is a method used in dramatic activities rather than an activity in itself. Young children use pantomime easily and informally.

Many nursery rhymes make wonderful pantomime games, and are better without dialogue. As simply as suggesting that Karen be Henny Penny, the children take turns being Miss Muffett and the Spider, while you or an older child recites the jingle.

Stories in which there is not a great deal of dialogue are often acted mostly in pantomime by the little children. In The Little Engine That Could any number of children can hook on to be the train, going slowly at first, then speeding up when the leader gets to the part where the Little Engine says, "I think I can, I think I can."

**For School Children and Teen-Agers.** These groups use pantomime easily in games, story dramatization, and in dramatization of songs,

**81**

ballads and poems. Impromptu pantomimes are great fun, however, and stimulate their imagination. They should be conducted very informally. At first, the parent can suggest the situation, and the youngsters can take turns individually, or as a group, in acting out, without words, such situations as:

a lady trying on a hat
a man stifling a sneeze
four or five people watching
  an exciting ball game

a boy taking castor oil
a woman seeing a mouse
stepping into a cold shower
falling asleep in a movie

These pantomimes will be so much fun that the youngsters will suggest others. This could lead to a guessing game—where the rest of the group tries to guess the situation being pantomimed by one or a group.

Games like Trades, Dumb Crambo, Who Am I, charades, and many others, all depend upon pantomime.

These teen-age groups like ideas that challenge their imagination and that they've never thought about.

Pantomiming (as a guessing game or just as an exercise) of different ways of lifting, might be an example:
a very young baby
something very hot
something very heavy
something very fragile
something very big, light, and bulky

Or they might try pantomiming hearing:
a sudden thunder crack
a faraway bell
a dinner bell

a whisper
dance music
a symphony

Or they might try to pantomime seeing:
an old friend approach
an auto crash
a house on fire
a Christmas tree on Christmas morning

Or smelling:
a burning dinner
a skunk
smoke from an unknown source
a Thanksgiving dinner aroma

**82**

Or tasting:
food to see that it's seasoned properly
hot soup
an ice cream cone on a hot day.
bitter medicine
grapes full of seeds

Or feeling:
fresh paint
warmth from a stove or fireplace
sandpaper
waves on a beach.

The group could try expressing all these first by facial expression, then by body movement, and finally as they might be expressed by different people—a small boy, an old lady, a teen-ager. From there, putting some of them together to make a plot is an easy step, and leads naturally into improvisations, stunts, and skits.

# IMPROVISATION

Improvisation adds words to pantomime. All the situations listed for pantomimes can be dramatized by facial expressions and bodily movement, and emphasized by speech. For example, after the group has tried to pantomime a person smelling smoke from some unknown source, it is very natural to go on into a simple living room scene, the husband reading his paper, the wife knitting or reading. One of them smells smoke—and the ensuing hunt for its source combines pantomime and dialogue.

Another form that youngsters enjoy doesn't require real words. In this type, a situation is selected, and the youngsters act it out, using the letters of the alphabet, or numbers up to ten instead of words. It can be very dramatic—and very funny!—and it relieves the youngsters of the necessity of finding the right words, so that their pantomime is not slowed down.

**83**

Try these:
Two truck-drivers in an argument
A mother scolding a child for breaking a dish
A policeman and a lost child
Two gossips over the back fence

Like pantomime, improvisation is a method or technique, rather than an activity, and requires no written scripts or memory work.

The main object is having fun, but by-products of proper enunciation, use of words, pronunciation, etc., are often achieved. Speech games and tongue-twisters add novelty and amusement. The youngsters learn, by experiment and practice, the importance of the right word to convey the exact meaning. They learn to listen to words and voices, not just take them for granted.

# SKITS
# AND STUNTS

Skits and stunts may be improvised or they may be learned from a script. They differ from many of the spontaneous, almost impromptu types of dramatic activities by requiring an audience. The audience may be small or large—a playground group, or the whole community—but the whole point of a skit or stunt is lost unless it's performed before a group. They work out well with pre-teens, teen-agers and adults.

A skit or stunt may require one person—or dozens. It is short, and it requires very little in the way of rehearsals, stage setting or costuming.

Sometimes a skit or stunt is really a very short playlet, original with the group or learned from a script. It usually has what the writing trade calls a "snapper" at the end—a surprise twist that gives it unexpected humor.

"Melodrammers," mock fashion shows, take-offs, exaggerated pantomimes like Wild Nell of the Prairie, all fall into this class. An orchestra made up of every known variety of improvised musical instruments, none of which can make a noise—boxes, sticks, cardboard tubes, etc., with kazoos or tissue-covered combs for carrying the tune—and a conductor who leads the orchestra through a wild pantomime of a number in the manner of Spike Jones; a singer or group of singers who go through all the gestures of singing and don't make a sound—the music coming from a record of a popular singer; a doctor performing a major operation and taking out alarm clocks, saws, chains, etc.—all are forms of skits and stunts.

**Where to Get an Idea:** They often originate in the impromptu, everyday, spontaneous dramatic activities. Some person or group gets such a good idea, or works out such an amusing situation that it just must be shown off! It is polished up until it moves swiftly—easily—and then is performed before a group, or used as part of a bigger program, such as an amateur night, a variety show, or the like.

Sometimes they grow out of dramatic games. The Nose Bag Game, for example, is an excellent way to start a teen-age group off on making up its own skits and stunts. The leader produces a paper bag—or several—in which he has placed a variety of articles around which a group must prepare and produce a skit. Each group takes one of the bags, retires for fifteen minutes, decides upon its skit, the characters, and the lines, and arranges any improvised costuming necessary. At the end of that time, each group comes back and puts on its skit for the benefit of the other groups. Out of these, the best can be polished up and used in a variety program later on.

Make sure that in producing any of these skits and stunts, no one person is singled out for lampooning, or being made to appear silly or ridiculous. The skits or stunts should always be in good taste, and given in good humor.—*Adapted from "Informal Dramatics," a publication of the National Recreation Association.*

# CREATIVE

## FUN

*IN THE CREATIVE PERSON, happiness comes from achievement and accomplishment—from the production of something beautiful or the discovery of important truths or values. If our children can hang on to their creativity up to adulthood, they may achieve this satisfaction and open up new and more beautiful worlds for us all.—Evelyn Seeley Stewart*

# HOW TO HANDLE
# A CREATIVE CHILD

*Having a creative, original child in the family is an experience that makes for both fun and problems. Of course, all children have some creative intelligence, but there is certainly a wide range of natural endowment.*

*Highly creative children may appear in any family, but their abilities can be either fostered or discouraged at school, by the family and community. Parents who recognize and value this quality can see to it that it is encouraged.*

**How to recognize unusual originality.** An attempt to draw a clear picture of such a child would obviously be absurd: the point is that each is not a type, but himself alone. Nevertheless, a number of traits do seem characteristic of most highly creative children.

Creative youngsters, for one thing, are pretty sure to be "a handful"— energetic, curious and adventuresome. They get in everything, are full of ideas which they are eager to try out experimentally.

Some of their enterprises may be risky, and some are messy and disturbing to family routine. When you find your kitchen with water on the floor, the counters buried in litter, your cooking pans and bowls full of strange gook, while your child looks up with shining eyes and explains, "But, Mother, it's an experiment!" go easy if you can. For he may have to experiment. He may be one who learns best in his own way, by direct experience, not by being told.

And if your youngster is sloppy about his projects it may be because his ideas come faster than he can use them. He hasn't the time or patience to work one out in detail before he is claimed by another, or by a modification of the original.

It is the same when he plays games. He no sooner understands the game than he wants to change the rules or invent a different game. On the other hand, he may be very particular and precise in his experiments, but sloppy and disorganized about things that don't seem so important. Neatness and social conformity probably seem boring. His development may be uneven, ahead of his age in some ways, behind in others. As he learns to accept necessary standards, things will even out.

Still, novelty and excitement probably always will have much more charm for highly creative people than routine and familiarity.

**Strong emotions** may also make such children especially vulnerable to criticism. They very soon learn that they are different from most of us, and that realization makes it harder for them to feel sure of our understanding, respect and love. Sometimes they are even unsure of themselves.

**At home,** though, creative children are not necessarily centers of trouble. Centers of activity they will be, for they love new ideas, experiments, and even violence. Nonsense and the playful exploration of hazy ideas are a delight to their creative personalities. Humor and absurdities have great appeal and these children have energy to spare for excursions into foolishness, even while getting on with more practical matters. Such people can be very jolly to have around.

All children show some of these tendencies, with one type or another predominating at different times. The key to whether a child is exceptionally creative lies in how many of these qualities a child has—how consistently, how deeply, he feels and how off-beat and unconventional his ideas are. It is not really so important to assess the degree of creative ability a child has as it is to recognize creativity in any form and give it a chance to grow.

**Limits.** We should allow plenty of elbow room for energetic and unconventional exploration and at the same time set clear, protective limits to help the youngsters learn to control the expression of his urgent drives.

Given reasonable latitude for exploration and emotional expression, an original child will blossom forth with all sorts of unexpected ideas.

If you are not particularly creative yourself, you may find it tiring to keep up with such a child's endless flow of energy and activity. Just the same, you can't help enjoying some of his astonishing ideas and being amused at some of his projects, and your own steadiness has a fine contribution to make—even a kite needs a tail to fly well, you know.

Your sense of humor, too, can make things easier. Relax and enjoy it. Encourage the whole family to kick ideas around playfully, even irresponsibly sometimes. Why, you may discover that you, yourself, are a lot more creative than you had dreamed!—*Rhoda W. Bacmeister*

**89**

# THEY SHALL
# HAVE MUSIC
# WHEREVER THEY GO

*The first musical instruments of men were their clapping hands and stamping feet. And when they clapped or stamped, it was always with rhythm . . . a regular beat. They were familiar, of course, with the pulse of their heart beat—the rhythm of the body—and the rhythm of music was also something that all people could understand. Music became important, then, to people because it was one way they could talk to and understand one another. So that long before they knew how to read or write, men had music.*

## Music for All Children

Exposure to a wide range of sounds early in life helps to awaken hearing and develop aural sensitivity: (the clack of a rattle, the bang of a pan, the chirp of a sparrow, the crash of thunder, the humming of a lullaby). This is a necessary prelude to music appreciation. Children first respond to music with their whole bodies, not just their ears, and a good half of their enjoyment consists in reacting through jumping and hopping about.

**The beginning years, 1-3:** A youngster at this age likes bold, rhythmic melodies when he is feeling energetic; soft, soothing music when he is tired. He wants to hear his favorite records over and over, especially when he is encouraged to respond by nodding, swaying, chanting.

**Playthings:** Music box, toy accordion, bells, gourd, rattle, cymbals, drum, tambourine, simple record player, singing and story records, lullabies and folk songs, records with bells, whistles and marked rhythms.

**Early childhood, 3-6:** He can now remember simple melodies, including nursery songs, folk songs, Haydn. He likes to sing but is rarely in tune.
**90**

He responds to music by pretending he is a high-stepping horse, a marching soldier, a tug boat—this helps develop coordination and confidence. Sixes may form rhythm bands.

**Playthings:** Ocarina, flute, triangle, maracas, wood blocks, tom toms, castanets, story-and-music records.

**Middle childhood, 6-9:** Sixes and sevens like to experiment with many different instruments and pick out tunes on the piano; enjoy group singing and musical games like "Farmer in the Dell." At eight and nine they can learn folk songs from different cultures and like to identify instruments through their sound. This is usually the time to start lessons on the piano, recorder or flute.

**Playthings:** Harmonica, xylophone, ukulele, kazoo, folk song and story-telling records.

**Later childhood, 9-12:** They still like to respond actively to music by clapping, stamping and shouting, but are also ready for more complicated pantomime. Few boys like social dancing, but both boys and girls enjoy folk dancing—an excellent bridge between the sexes. Those who do not take music lessons may teach themselves to strum a guitar or ukulele. Group singing around a campfire or in a recreation room helps overcome self-consciousness. At eleven or twelve they are ready for band concerts, folk music performances, and the more melodic classics.

**Playthings:** Autoharp, Sousaphone, clarinet, flute, folk records in different languages, guitar, horn, piano, electric organ, a wide variety of popular and light classical records.—*Robert M. Goldenson, Ph.D.*

# Sing Sing

Singing has always been a natural means of communication. Even in primitive times, everyone sang, and their music—folk music—covered the range of human experience. People made up songs about their work, play, love, about their children, their religion, their dreams. The singing lightened their burdens, drew them closer together, and enriched their lives.

We, too, can sing with our youngsters in our daily living. The many pleasures of professional entertainment never quite match the deep satisfaction of self-expression. And what is more joyous than a gathering of the family around the piano, singing loudly (though often off-key) all the old favorite songs or Christmas carols!

**Sing at all times.** You don't have to wait, of course, for special occasions to sing. Ironing time is good for a songfest; so is baby's feeding or bath time. You can make singing a part of almost all of your daily activities.

Sing the traditional nursery songs with the smallest children. "Hickory, Dickory Dock" may sound like nonsense to adults, but the sounds of the mouse's story have delighted generations of children. A young child also wants to hear songs about the world that he is discovering. "Twinkle, Twinkle, Little Star" and "Old MacDonald's Farm" are greatly appreciated by kindergartners.

You might begin the day with "Good Morning to You." Then, "This is the way we wash our face . . . this is the way we sweep the floor" will make an accompaniment to your tasks as your preschooler helps. Indeed, the worksong really began, as the name implies, as a natural accompaniment to labor. The evening pajama sing has become a tradition with us, too, because this gets Daddy into the fun. You can close the day with your favorite goodnight song. The spiritual "All Night, All Day" is one of the best-loved ones at our house. Our spontaneous outbursts of song may not be of great quality, but they do bring us great satisfaction just through the fun of "talking" to each other in a musical way about whatever comes to mind.

Adults sometimes question the suitability of certain songs for children. Why, for instance, should this appeal to the preschooler?

> "Go tell Aunt Rhody,
> The old grey goose is dead.

> "The one that she'd been saving
> to make a feather bed.

> "The goslings are mourning
> because their Mother's dead."

Isn't this song too gloomy for youngsters? Actually, it appeals to them. We rediscovered the song recently and it hit home with the children immediately. I received it, too, like an old friend, for I remembered my grandmother singing it in her own version.

Songs such as this one, of death, or those about anger and hostility, are popular with children because they recognize their own feelings in the song,

**92**

and so are helped to accept the troublesome aspect of themselves and of life in general.

The truth of this became apparent one day as our five-year-old, Curt, wandered into the house, improvising on "Aunt Rhody."

> "Go tell Mama
> A baby robin's dead
>
> "She fell from the apple tree
> With a broken head."

And four-year-old Nancy matter-of-factly chimed in with, "But life goes on and on, doesn't it?"

To improvise, as Curt did, is characteristic of those who sing folk songs. In fact, the art of folk singing is in what you bring to the song. A folk song belongs to whoever sings it; it's never truly finished, but is always open to change and addition.

Folk singing helps develop imagination and vocabulary, and so makes an excellent basis for creative play. I remember Curt, at two, bringing me one of his artistic creations—bits of black crayon, stuck into a dish of clay. "Baked in a pie," he announced, and suddenly, I understood—Four and Twenty Blackbirds, of course. Similarly, the children have acted out the Danish song of Little Ole with his sleepy-time umbrella, who visits good children with beautiful dreams (as told in Hans Christian Andersen's story).

**Songs From All Lands.** Since folk music comes from all countries, we can use it to satisfy and stimulate children's eagerness to lap up foreign sounds and phrases, and thus help "tune in our youngsters" to our multilingual world.

A Polish Christmas carol has been Nancy's favorite since she was three. Curt chooses the South African "Marching to Pretoria," and two-year-old David likes the French Canadian "On, Roll On, My Ball, Roll On." Imagine them, too, singing French and Hawaiian versions of "Brother John." Children are fresh and unprejudiced; their ears are sure, their tongues flexible and willing, and they have an amazing ability to memorize and repeat sounds that would seem to be meaningless.

Familiarity with a stranger's music is a real help in developing understanding of the stranger. For if a song about his own life helps a child to accept himself, so, too, songs from many cultures help a child to accept many people and discover in them a common humanity.

Our own American inheritance comes thrillingly alive through song.

"Sweet Betsy from Pike" was a part of the Gold Rush, and the Confederate soldiers who sang of the delicious "Goober Peas" were really eating peanuts. The popular riddle song, "I Gave My Love a Cherry" goes back to fifteenth century England.

These songs, as well as many other delightful ones, may be found in paper-bound books that are published by various organizations and are available for about thirty-five cents. So why not get some and use them? Tuck one into the picnic basket; keep one in the family car. I even carry one with me in my purse.

Be prepared to swap songs the way people swap stories. When taking trips to other parts of the country or to a foreign country, find out what the native songs are.

**The Joy of Singing.** Make singing a part of the fun at children's parties. Begin with something they know well, then lead into less familiar songs. "Coming Round the Mountain" is a good starter.

Don't pitch songs too low; children have naturally high voices. And let them take turns choosing songs.

You don't have to worry about singing "good" music or developing the children's taste. After all, how many times have you changed your mind about what you enjoyed? Tastes mature naturally, gradually. Further, different occasions demand different types of songs. Generally, people (and this includes children) respond to what is good.

If you have known the joy of family singing, or if you have ever sung around a firelit circle, you know that music is a language that speaks to one's inner being.

You can help your children to retain this magic in their lives just by singing, and in so doing, you will discover a source of pleasure and growth for yourself, as well.—*Jo Ann Neville Nelson*

# 88 Keys to Musical Fun

Whether children study piano—or any other instrument—they are bound to derive pleasure as well as knowledge.

More American youngsters, in fact, are learning to play musical instruments today than ever before. Of the more than thirty-three million amateur musicians in the United States, some ten million of them are children, playing instruments and getting instruction in schools and from private teachers.

There are, then, many questions parents may ask about music study.

**What is the best age for a child to begin serious music study?**
The answer—don't start him too soon. The business of learning to play a musical instrument is one of acquiring a skill. It takes concentration to do this. It requires a lot of muscular control. It takes its own kind of reading readiness, in fact.

A child of six or seven, whose interest is high and whose finger dexterity is coming along, can usually master these things. A younger child usually can't. Stop-gap measures are in order with rhythm band classes in school, toy instruments or a phonograph and children's records in the home. These will also help create musical interest.

**What instrument is best to start with, and how can you find a good teacher?**   The instrument is usually no problem. Most youngsters know what they want to play and will accept no substitutes. It may be a piano, flute, clarinet or French horn. Whatever it is, barring a physical disability which makes that particular instrument a bad choice, it's probably best to let a child begin with the instrument he wants rather than try to talk him into studying another. Beginning any instrument is tough and the youngster needs the encouragement of working on one he likes.

Finding a teacher is more complicated. You'll want a good one. You'll want one you can afford.

Where do you look for a good teacher, however? As in most studies, getting off on the right foot is all important in music. A good teacher begins solidly with the correct basic approach to his instrument. He may seem arbitrary at times (good piano teachers do emphasize proper hand position, posture, scales and finger exercises, for example), but that's necessary for the grace and ease of performance without which no instrumentalist can progress.

The best teacher in town is the person to go to first but he's frequently the busiest and most expensive. His assistant or someone else recommended by the "master" may be more available and cheaper. A good teacher's assistant will have been chosen carefully from a number of top-notch candidates and is probably well schooled in the master teacher's techniques of playing and teaching.

**Where can you get the name of the best teacher in your town?**
The music teacher at your child's school can certainly be helpful. If there's a college or university nearby, the head of its music department may be able to give you a name. Local musicians—members of organizations like the National Federation of Music Clubs and the Music Teachers National Association—will know who's who in music locally or will be able to find

out for you. Friends who have children studying the instrument your child has picked will have some pretty firm ideas of their own. Checking around like this will result in a small list of "best" teachers—there's bound to be a difference of opinion on who's best and why—and you'll need to follow up your inquiries with a few visits.

On your interviews, be sure to take your child along; this is important. Many teachers are equally qualified. But there's the human factor, too. Something valuable seems to happen when a good teacher and a child who likes and trusts him get together.

**What about buying an instrument?**  Having found your child's teacher, you can ask his help, or the help of a reputable musical instrument dealer, in finding something just as important—a good instrument for the youngster to get started on. Musical instruments are an investment, and it's poor economy to settle on just any instrument because the price is low. Before buying one you may prefer to rent an instrument for a trial period from your child's school or a local music store.

Your child's music teacher will be your best guide in this. He knows how important a good instrument is to your child's early progress and he knows a good instrument when he tries it. He also will know when the price is right.

**Now what about practicing?**  Practicing is the big job in music study, and if your child is going to progress he is going to have to work at it. This means a half hour a day, maybe even an hour; your child's music teacher will have definite ideas about this. It will mean a period when not only your child knows it's time to practice, but the family does, too, and is quiet.

Most children practice best and with the fewest squabbles in the morning before school. Practice then conflicts with fewer other activities and the child comes fresher to it.

On the other hand, there are some youngsters, especially those in their teens, who simply can't get up in the morning. For this, a frank sit-down discussion of when to hold the practicing hour is in order. Young people have extraordinary good sense in working this problem out for themselves. And having done so, they're usually challenged to stick to the solution. Usually, but not always. Some children coast along beautifully for months with only the occasional reminder about practicing and then, suddenly, just run out of steam. They seem to lose all interest in music study. Practicing becomes a chore.

96

The best thing to do in this situation is to sit tight for a while, waiting to see if the problem persists. If it does, an appointment with the child's teacher is called for.

## Why do youngsters lose interest in their music studies?

In some cases, the child has reached the limits of his ability at the time and a vacation from music study is in order. More likely, though, he has reached one of those plateaus in learning which all students reach from time to time, and a temporary relaxation of the practice schedule or a reduction of scales and finger exercises may be advisable.

A change of instrument may be a good idea, too. And that can be a shocker. I'm not sure why, but some stern stuff in most parents makes us tend to believe that when a child begins to study on one instrument he really ought to stick with it, no matter what. As a matter of fact, the opposite is often true.

This does not mean that your child should change instruments whenever the whim strikes him. Certainly no change should be made without a thorough going-over by all concerned—student, teacher and parents. But students who want to change instruments often have good reasons for doing so. And to override these reasons out of hand can spoil all music for the youngsters.

## What about popular music?

Does it really spoil the young student's technique and damage his taste, as some people have maintained? No, so long as there's variety in a youngster's musical diet.

Jazz, show tunes, folk tunes, rock'n'roll are all important parts of every American child's musical heritage which no youngster should be deprived of out of snobbery or misunderstanding. Rather, a readjustment of your own standards is the wisest thing—and a gentle, inquiring interest.

What will this readjustment of standards bring you? For one thing, you'll find that popular music has been an enthusiasm of serious musicians for centuries. Mozart and Beethoven wrote light and lovely German dances. Brahms composed Hungarian dances, using popular folk melodies. The greatest collection of Rumanian folk music available was composed by the modern composer, Bela Bartok.

These musicians knew that popular music can be good and bad—just as classical music can. And, musical consideration aside, there are social reasons why some familiarity with popular music is a plus to youngsters. A good jazz player is much in demand at parties and informal dances. He can also turn his talent to cash, performing at hotels and resorts during

**97**

school and college vacations. What is important to remember is that to play's the thing, after all, and it ought to be fun. —*Henry Levine as told to Harold Littledale*

# B Sharp at Musical Games

**Musical Alphabet.** Each person in turn names a song title alphabetically, such as "Always," "Bye Bye Blues," "Canadian Capers," "Dear Hearts and Gentle People," "Every Little Movement," "Friendship," "Goody Goody," and so on. The person staying in the game the longest is the winner.

**Musical Guesswork.** Collect a number of small articles that can suggest a song title. Hold each one up before the group. If the group is small, give a point to the first person to guess each title. For a larger group, divide it into teams, and the first person giving the answer in each team wins the point for his team. Here are a few possibilities. Add others.

| | |
|---|---|
| Banana | Yes We Have No Bananas |
| Token | The Trolley Song |
| Apple | Don't Sit Under the Apple Tree |
| Bell | The Bells of St. Mary's or Jingle Bells |
| Toy Canoe | Paddling Madeline Home |
| Baseball | Take Me Out to the Ball Game |
| Toy Dog | How Much Is That Doggie in the Window |

(This contest can be enlarged and lengthened by adding other articles, and by letting each winner sing, hum or whistle the correct tune.)

**Musical Mixup.** Select names of about 20 musical instruments, such as accordion, trumpet, saxophone, and so on. Mix up the spelling, like this: radniocac, ptruemt, ohneopxas. Give out paper and pencils for contestants to unscramble the instruments. Allow about 5 or 6 minutes.

**Song Guess.** Invite each person to come dressed to represent a song. Everyone tries to guess the title each represents. Or provide crepe paper or newspaper, and pins, and let each team dress one of its members to represent a song title. Best costume wins.

**98**

# The Rousing, Rollicking Rhythm Bands

Children enjoy making and playing simple musical instruments, and these are a help in encouraging singing as well as rhythms. Tambourines may be made by attaching bottle tops in pairs around the rim of a tin or paper plate. Cymbals can be made by nailing two tin can lids to the ends of a 2-inch dowel, making the holes loose enough so that the tins will hit each other when one of them is struck with a short length of broom handle. A tin can or wooden keg can be made into a drum by covering with a piece of cloth or leather, drawn tightly across the open end. The tops from tin cans can be hung on a stick, and used as jangles. Bottles and glasses filled in varying degrees with water may actually be tuned and will give out specific tones.

Adults, particularly teenagers and women's groups, can get a great deal of fun out of a kitchen band, and will enjoy finding and playing a wide variety of "instruments" found in any kitchen. A fork suspended by a string tried to a stick, and hit by another fork gives a sound like a triangle. A crock struck by a wooden ruler, and a basin struck by a wooden spoon will sound like a xylophone. Saucers tapped on the edge with a wooden pencil have a bell-like tone. A bunch of keys sound like sleighbells. A metal tray struck by a stick with a padded head will sound like a kettle drum. An oatmeal box with a few beans inside will produce a fine rattle. Washboards, tin cups, bottles, boxes, nails, pans of various sizes, all can be used to produce a "fun" orchestra. Working out their "parts" and putting on a concert makes a good program. —*from Handbook for Recreation, published by the U.S. Children's Bureau*

# The Sound of Music at Home

A good home music reproduction system, whether stereo or monophonic, is a practical investment for the whole family—and not necessarily a costly one. The very best time to make it is when your children are young and are just beginning their musical education. Science tells us that human hearing is at its peak among youngsters in the 10-to-19 age bracket—particularly in the ability to perceive high-frequency sounds and high overtones.

In practical home music terms, this usually means that grownups are less able to distinguish an "ideal" balance of low-frequency and high-frequency sounds. Parents are, therefore, more likely to accept an electronically reproduced sound which is unacceptable to youngsters and teen-agers.

And never before has there been so much good music available to the

**99**

public from so many sources—music from long-playing records; from high-fidelity FM radio; and from tape recordings, another science gaining in popularity.

Stereophonic sound, too, has enhanced single channel hi-fi music with realism and depth.

**What to look for.** Before you take the plunge and buy a new home music system for your family, here are a few pointers to bear in mind.

Deal with a reputable store. This applies to both packaged and component systems. Even though one dealer may offer a slightly lower price, another may give enough additional services to save you money—and headaches. The cut-rate purchase from a store which doesn't stand behind its merchandise often turns out to be anything but a bargain.

**Here's a checklist** of what good stores in the home music field usually provide in the way of additional services: (1) Trained salesmen who can answer your questions intelligently (2) Facilities for listening to a variety of music systems (3) Free delivery and, in some cases, installation of heavy or bulky equipment (4) Repair facilities.

Don't be confused by technical audio jargon. When you purchase a music system, you're buying "sound"—not decibels, output wattage or microvolts. Your own ears can often tell you more than a set of figures—and don't forget to bring your older children along for such an equipment audition. (Remember! They're the family members who are lucky enough to have the "golden ears.")

Listen critically to several systems in the store, and compare them. Bring a couple of your favorite records along—preferably good records with which you're familiar—and use the same record in testing each system.

**Arrange** for a return privilege. When it comes to music systems, nothing beats a home trial. If you can't arrange this, make sure you have the right to return or exchange a system which is defective or doesn't sound right in your home.

**Remember** that the acoustics and furnishings of your home will actually become part of your music system. Walls, rugs, draperies—even furniture—affect sound characteristics, and larger rooms require more power output than smaller rooms.—*Charles Sinclair and David Lachenbruch*

**100**

# SHALL
# WE DANCE?

*Here we dance looby loo,*
*Here we dance looby light,*
*Here we dance looby loo,*
*All on a Saturday night.*

*Everyone loves to dance—and not only on a Saturday night.*
*Increasingly, there are folk dances, square dances, barn dances,*
*proms, hops, cotillions and balls. There's a greater interest, too, in*
*the study of dance—in ballet, tap, and interpretive dancing. What-*
*ever your style is—from a buck-and-wing to a Highland fling, just*
*kick up your heels and dance, dance, dance all night!*

## Keep Them on Their Toes

Children love to dance. They enjoy physical activity and, when there is
a design to it, it gives them extra pleasure. That is why dancing lessons are
never a waste of money, to my way of thinking—although I'll admit that
I'm prejudiced. Dancing is my life.

I know that dancing is worthwhile for all children. The ones with natural
rhythm respond delightedly to that extra bit of accomplishment in knowing
how to point the foot, raise the arm or pirouette gracefully. These children
instinctively develop a love of music and an eye for color, design and form
in dance performances.

Then there are children who are not rhythmically well coordinated—
probably by nature, just as they may have blue eyes or black hair. Given
time to think, such a child knows right from left, can duplicate movements,
but he cannot do them deftly enough to keep time to music. This doesn't
mean he shouldn't have dancing instruction.

A good teacher will help such a youngster to coordinate better, and as
long as the other children don't mock his inability to keep step, he needs

**101**

to be part of the class. If he begins to notice he's out of step and to feel uncertain, he must be given the idea that this is not too important. He'll get better as time goes on. He's enjoying the music. Meanwhile, he's just hearing his own private rhythm.

In addition to developing poise and taste in music and form, dancing lessons, like any other exercise, build strong muscles and athletic skills.

There are a great many types of dancing and all can be enjoyable and helpful to children—and adults. In addition to the traditional ballet, such as Swan Lake, other forms are: modern ballet; interpretative or rhythmic dancing; tap dancing; acrobatic and adagio dancing; ballroom dancing (which most little boys detest), and various folk and peasant dances.

**First lessons.**   Children as young as four or five enjoy and benefit from going to dancing class, although they are too young for formal training. For them, dancing is mainly getting the feel of coordinated rhythmic movement.

Six-year-olds enjoy hopping, skipping, holding hands and forming a circle. Some children are leaders and need no urging to express themselves. Others are born followers. Whichever they are, in dance class they gain skills and learn cooperation.

Seven-year-olds can usually learn mildly complicated figures. I've given youngsters of this age a pre-ballet course of standing at the bar, with the very simplest exercises to develop legs, feet and ankles, have shown the children how to stand properly on the half-point and how to move their arms in a disciplined way.

Eight-year-olds are ready for formal training—most professional schools will not accept younger children—in one of the various dance forms.

**Choosing a dance.**   Suppose your boy or girl is eager to go to dancing school, how do you decide on the type of dance to be studied? First, ask the prospective student to make a choice. Your youngster will learn more if the group is one he wants to attend.

Boys, by the way, generally prefer an informal type of dancing which provides maximum physical activity, such as tap, acrobatic, folk or square dancing. Also, these dances are not as shy-making as ballroom dancing, for examples, which requires putting an arm about a girl. They also have the big advantage of providing easy introduction to ballroom steps. Polka, cha-cha, waltz, even rhumba movements can be classed as folk steps; and just watch what happens when you give a boy the chance to lead a conga line!

**102**

If your child has no preference, you can observe what sort of natural bent he or she displays. A strong sense of rhythm is good for tap dancing, for example. Or perhaps your youngster responds to formal ballet movements, or shows the imagination which is so needed for modern free movement dancing.

Something about a child's inclinations may also be learned by taking him to ballet and other dance performances and observing his reactions. He may be more interested than you think in ballet, for example.

**Finding a class.** Next comes the choice of teacher and school—an important decision, even though your child may have no professional aspirations. You will be limited, of course, by what is available near you. The school principal or a friend may be able to recommend a local teacher who is quite good.

You should expect to be able to attend a class before making a decision, to watch the instructor and see how he or she handles the children and how they respond. Notice whether the studio is clean, well equipped, heated, lighted and ventilated.

Most important is a well-qualified teacher—one whose own training has been with a recognized teacher or school. Under a good instructor, your child should progress slowly and methodically. Even talented youngsters should not be pushed ahead too quickly.

**What you can do at home.** A child's interest in dancing, as in any other activity, can be nourished by what you do at home. Why not add some ballet music to your record collection—perhaps Tchaikovsky, Stravinsky or Offenbach? The stories of the ballets are collected in many basic books.

**Your interest** in what your child is learning is important. But real dance practice should not be done at home. Fifteen minutes after dinner is enough —for dancing is strenuous and children need their energy for other things, too. Also, without supervision, the small child easily makes mistakes and may actually strain a muscle. Not before age eleven or twelve does a child become accurate enough to be able to practice alone. Real ballet slippers and work "sur les points" should not come until then.

I could talk forever about dancing, but even if your enthusiasm is more restrained than mine, remember that all children love rhythmic movement.

—*Melissa Hayden*

**103**

# THE EVERLASTING PLEASURES OF READING AND WRITING

*In spite of competing interests, there is still no greater thrill for children than conquering the printed page, and no more satisfying source of enjoyment, information and relaxation. The problem is to keep pace with our children's growing interests and abilities, and to choose carefully from the almost infinite wealth of reading material that is offered today. If you begin early to acquaint your children with books and magazines, the library and the book clubs, and if you maintain a reading atmosphere in your home, reading will be a never-ending source of pleasure for your whole family.*

## A Book for Everyone

**Beginning years, 1-3:** The first books, bound in cloth or heavy cardboard, should all have bold, brightly colored pictures. The two-year-old likes simple rhymes and imitations of familiar sounds (chug-chug)—and he will want to hear the same story over and over, and may like to play the game of telling you "what comes next."

**Types of reading material:** Picture books about farm animals, boats and cars; nursery rhymes; read-to-me stories about small children.

**Early childhood, 3-6:** Threes want to learn more about places they have heard about or visited: the zoo, firehouse, railroad yard. Fours enjoy the "real" and "true" books about trains, steamshovels, airplanes; but are equally intrigued by nonsense rhymes and stories of animals that reflect human problems, including their own. Bathtime and bedtime are favorite reading periods for fives but it is best to avoid frightening stories.

**Types of reading material:** Simple poetry, nonsense rhymes, animal tales, pure fantasy, folk tales, stories about animated things (planes, trains), information stories about farm animals, plants, pets, the seashore, the woods.

**Middle childhood, 6-9:**   Sixes still like to hear or read about talking animals, but are ready for stories about children—including their fears as well as their fun. Action tales about magicians and supermen are enjoyed by sevens, who are beginning to read by themselves—but they should be balanced by stories about the real world of farm animals and family life for girls; and cowboys, airplanes and exploration for boys—with narrow escapes and happy endings. This is the time to get them a library card, to read with them, and to start building their own library, and to take out magazine subscriptions in their name. Eight to nine is the age for stories of all kinds: legends, folk tales, animals antics, nonsense stories about heroes and heroines as well as interesting legends about every day people in our own and other countries.

**Types of reading material:** Fables, legends, stories about real heroes and heroines; boys' stories about cowboys and Indians, exploration, sports; girls' stories about family life, girls' adventures, circus life. Information material on pets, wild animals, airplanes, trains; first dictionary, poetry, rhymes, riddles, beginning science (weather, the sea, plants, space travel, etc.), first craft books (sewing, leathercraft, etc.).

**Later childhood, 9-12:**   The door to the world of books should now be opened wide and the reading diet should be rich and varied. Boys enjoy adventure stories (pirates, sailing, discovery), westerns, mysteries with plenty of action and suspense, sports stories, science discovery with emphasis on the lives of scientists, mechanics magazines. Girls prefer legends and fantasy of the Arabian Nights variety, biographies of great heroines, stories about animal life (especially horses), series stories, books on sewing, ballet and handicrafts, girls' magazines.

**Types of reading material—For boys:** Pirate stories, sea stories, accounts of exploration and discovery pioneer tales, mysteries, suspense without murder, sports and teamwork stories, animal stories; books about real heroes, inventions and inventors, elementary science; hobby books and magazines. **For girls:** Fantasy and legends, biographies of great heroines, boy-girl mysteries, pioneer family stories, sport stories, arts, and crafts pamphlets and books, stories of women at work (nurses, teachers, actresses). —*Robert M. Goldenson, Ph.D.*

**105**

## "Reading" Picture Books

"Please, lady," a little boy asked the librarian, "do you have a book without much readin' in it? I can't read readin', but I can read pictures!"

Although children may not know much about the techniques of art, they respond to illustrations of simple beauty treated imaginatively. They like pictures that express a book's mood and will wear out with looking and loving whatever is beautiful and genuine.

The last thirty years have brought an artistic revolution in the field of books for children. Many serious, well-trained artists now devote their time to illustrations for children, with the result that there is an amazing variety of beautifully-drawn, well-written books available for each child's pleasure.

And remember that books specifically teaching art appreciation are not as important in forming taste as regular exposure to good art work in story books.

It is not only illustrations that produce pleasure, of course. Responding to tactile sensations, children run their fingers approvingly over smooth paper. They appreciate clean print, distinctive design on title page and chapter headings, and good bindings.

Children love good picture books with: good design, expressive drawings, appropriate colors and pictures that speak with freshness and candor.

It is not art for art sake that children crave, but art for children's sake.

—*Charlotte Blount*

## What Children Look for in Books

**A room without books is a body without a soul.**—*Cicero*

**Children everywhere** seek the same things in books. They want books that nurture sensibility (not sentimentality) to the great human emotions. They want books that make them laugh and cry and shiver and wonder in concert with others. (This is why girls love sad books so much.)

Children also want books of knowledge, honestly presented. They do not want chemistry disguised as magic. Nor will they trust a book that pretends to have all the final answers, or suggests that facts can substitute for thought.

Children want stories that demonstrate that truth is better than cheating in human lives, that kindliness works, that selfless devotion exists, that fun is not necessarily sinful, that integrity of purpose and character are worth the self-discipline required.

Children also yearn for the balm of humor, and the majority of good children's books are basically books of humor. Perhaps we tend to underestimate humor. It is not just a release from tension, though that is important. It is not a luxury. It is a much-needed lubricant in the gears of daily life and reinforces one's sense of values.

There is one more quality that children will find in great books. This I can only call magic—that which transports a child to new worlds of fancy and excitement. The little girl who said of "Alice in Wonderland," "This is the sort of thing that glees my heart," felt this magic.

**The classics.**   It is only natural, as we look back on our own childhood, to pick out the books we loved most and to want to share them with our children. Who would not like to have his child also experience the thrill of Robinson Crusoe discovering the footprint on the beach? Or the suspense of Peter Rabbit hiding in the watering can from Mr. McGregor? Or the fun when Robin Hood outwits the Sheriff of Nottingham for the umpteenth time? Or the devotion of Christopher Robin to Pooh, the "bear of Very Little Brain"? These are high moments of pleasure for a child.

No movie version or abridgement can ever equal the enjoyment he finds in the original book. Have you read Peter Pan recently? Peter Pan is not great because of its wild plot, but because of its insight and vivid characterizations, and the effortless grace of Barrie's writing.

To read "The Wind in the Willows" after having read the condensations, is like enjoying a delicious, unhurried meal after months of gulping vitamin pills. Kenneth Grahame, who was steeped in the language of Shakespeare and Milton, wrote as if he took it for granted that the reader had all the time in the world.

Actually classics were not written for children at all. But because they were written by people who had never lost their own childhood, these books are ageless in their appeal. They are the books that continue to influence a child long after he has finished them.—*Charlotte Blount*

# Let's Write a Letter

Dear Readers,

Like thousands of other young mothers today, I want my mother to share in my children's growing up. The fun of knowing and loving their grandchildren is sort of a special dividend to our parents for having raised us successfully.

Regular letter writing is a pleasant way of being with the folks in spirit. Just a simple report of the events of the week is all it takes. I used to forget to tell some of the most interesting things until I adopted my friend Susie's method. The minute something happens which she wants to tell the grand-parents, Susie jots down a brief note. Thus the date of baby's first smile or his first step are not overlooked.

Postcards. Jean, my neighbor, doesn't have time to write long letters. I was there the morning she discovered her baby's first tiny tooth pushing through his gum. After her first exclamation of delight she said, "I must do this right now."

Jean sat down at her desk and wrote a single sentence on two postal cards. "Little mister has sprouted a tooth."

"I keep his grandparents up to date on his development this way," she explained. "It's so much easier for me than long letters, and it means so much to them."

When children are old enough to use crayons, they can draw pictures for grandmother. As they grow older they can make Christmas cards, valentines and birthday cards.

I'm looking forward to the time when they can write letters themselves. I remember as one of the richest experiences of my childhood the cor-respondence I kept up with my grandmother. Writing letters was fun. But getting a letter of my very own in answer was truly a thrill.

Sincerely,
*Annalee Ward*

# THE LIVELY ARTS
# OF ARTS
# AND CRAFTS

*Arts and crafts give children first-hand acquaintance with widely different materials and processes. They contribute to personality growth by providing opportunities to play out feelings, to discover and develop skills, and to experience the thrill of achievement. There is such a wide variety of activities that almost every child can find one or more that interest him—if we give him a chance to try them.*

**108**

# Art for the Ages

**The beginning years, 1-3:** The awakening of sensation is a necessary prelude to arts and crafts activity. Therefore, in the first year of life a child needs things to squeeze, pound, knead and smear, as well as things of different size, shape, color and pattern. Between two and three he will make mud pies, dough balls or snowballs, and will cover yards of paper with crayon strokes, water paint or finger paint. He will be more interested in feel than in the pattern or design, so don't ask him what he's making.

**Playthings:** Peg board, large nuts and screws, play dough, plasticene, large crayons, drawing board, finger paint, bright poster paint, large brushes, easel, smock, flannel board, large wooden beads.

**Early childhood, 3-6:** He now likes to make his own designs with colored paper, blocks, tiles, finger paint. He can also make cakes, crude animals and people out of clay, and may reveal his feelings in talking about them. At about five he begins to paint pictures, but they will mean more to him than to you. Now he wants to save and display his artwork. He may have enough dexterity for crude crafts: bead stringing, sewing, weaving, knitting, making book covers.

**Playthings:** Blunt scissors, cut-out books, colored paper, colored pencils, crayon sets, modelling clay, water paint, coloring books, heddle loom, loop loom, knitting spool, cardboard for book covers and boxes, raffia basket set, first sewing set, mosaic blocks, tile set.

**Middle childhood, 6-9:** Painting, drawing and clay work become more realistically detailed. A child will sometimes work on one project for several days. He likes to make useful objects: clay ash trays, coasters from coiled paper. With help, he can make decorative animals and dolls out of pipe cleaners, spools, corn husks, milk cartons, even potatoes. He enjoys making collages out of bits of string, wire, cotton, feathers, shells, tinfoil, wrapping paper, buttons, etc. Save everything!

**Playthings:** Pastel chalk, crayons, papier-mache, paper punch, staples, wire cutters, glue, paste, Scotch tape, spatter-painting set, block-printing set, casein paint, copper enameling kit, plaster of Paris, paper sculpture (Origami) set, costume-making materials, scenery materials, drawing enlarger, water color set, stencil set, doll kit.

**Later childhood, 9-12:** The peak period for crafts. Around nine, children need a chance to try many different crafts, and by twelve they will usually concentrate on one or two. They can now make more complex and artistic objects out of clay (lamp bases, figurines, glazed jewelry), papier-mache (masks, trays, puppets), wood (boxes, shelves), metal (bookends, bracelets, lanterns), plastic (place mats, boxes, table decorations), cardboard (waste baskets, doll houses, stage scenery), leather (belts, purses, bookmarks), raffia (baskets, mats), cloth (aprons, costumes, potholders). Other art forms at this stage are: mobiles, caricatures, Christmas cards, dioramas with human and animal figures.

**Playthings:** Potter's wheel, clay modelling tools, glaze equipment, small kiln, wood-carving tools, kite material, mosaic tile kit, shellcraft kit, wood-burning set, marblecraft set, perfume kit, embroidery set, metal-casting set, crochet material, sewing kit and patterns, leatherwork set, bookbinding set, harness loom, diorama set, jewelry-making kit, house designing kit, airplane design kit, plastic model maker, table mat kit, fashion designer, oil painting set, small sewing machine.

*—Robert M. Goldenson, Ph.D.*

# Finger Painting

A child needs a place where he can muddle without constant reminders about splashing the walls and spilling on the floor. At school, long low sinks, oilcloth or linoleum-covered tables and linoleum floors solve the problem. At home, a square of linoleum that can be stored in the back of a closet makes an ever-ready work surface; the sink, bathtub and washable kitchen counters are good, too. Newspapers save the floor; and walls may be protected, if necessary, with papers or inexpensive plastic.

Preschool children enjoy helping to prepare materials and to clean up after using them.

Standard equipment for cleaning up should include large foam rubber or cellulose sponges (children can handle them more easily than cloths) and a brush and dustpan small enough for young hands to manipulate. In summer, the backyard is an ideal place for muddling. What could be more practical than a splash in the hose after a session of finger painting!

**How to Make Finger Paint:**
Soften in small bit of cold water:
½ cup Argo starch

Add this to:
1 quart boiling water

Make thick starch, stirring constantly till mixture bubbles up. Remove from fire. Let cool somewhat. Add:
½ cup mild soapflakes (Lux or Ivory)
¼ cup inexpensive talcum powder (for pleasant odor and to help preserve paint)

Stir until well mixed. When cool, pour into:
Screw-top jars (Skippy Peanut Butter jars are ideal)

Color each jarful with:
Poster paint or
Vegetable coloring (gives less vivid coloring than poster paint and not usually quite so satisfying to children)

## How to Store:
This paint keeps well in the covered jars.

## Additional Equipment:
Smooth, washable work surface.
A plastic smock is easy to make and easy to clean. Some sort of coverall, old shirt or apron is essential for the painter. Roll sleeves up.
Glazed paper in large sheets. Buy either commercial finger paint paper or try glazed shelf paper.
Pan of water for rinsing off hands.
Foam rubber or cellulose sponges for wetting paper and cleaning up.

## How to Use:
Finger painting can be done on any smooth washable surface: large trays, sink, oilcloth or linoleum. Some children enjoy painting without paper, just dabbling on the work surface. But most four and fives like to keep paintings and so need paper.
If paper is used, wet it on both sides with sponge.
Smooth out on work surface, glazed side up. Work out air bubbles.
Put spoonful of paint in middle of paper. (Twos and threes need aid, usually, but older children can help themselves and should have free access to colors.)
Let child muddle freely, adding colors as desired.

**111**

Paintings may be dried on newspapers but should be moved and unstuck before completely dry.

Pictures to be kept may be pressed from the back with a warm iron and mounted attractively.

Older youngsters and adults might use their paintings to cover notebooks, wastebaskets, bookends and so forth, finishing with a coat of shellac or clear varnish.

Beautiful placemats may be made with shiny white cardboard shellacked.

For preschool children—and others, too—the aim in finger painting is not so much to "make a pretty picture" as to gain relaxing satisfaction from the pleasant feel of the paint, experimentation with motion, and the surprise of mingling colors.

## Chalk Painting

### Equipment:
1 package colored chalk.
Heavy paper (bags from the market may be cut open and used)

### How to Use:
Wet paper with sponge.
Work with chalk laid on its side.
The aim is not to draw a picture but to obtain satisfying color effects.
This is not a substitute for finger paint but another interesting medium.

## Modeling Dough

(four-year-olds up)

### How to Make:
Mix together:
1 cup salt
$\frac{1}{2}$ cup cornstarch
$\frac{5}{8}$ cup water

Cook over low flame, stirring constantly until mixture thickens into a doughy mass. Remove from heat immediately. Cool until able to handle.

Knead in:
Vegetable coloring

**112**

**How to Store:**
Shape into a ball, wrap in wax paper, and store in a covered jar in refrigerator.

**How to Use:**
Dough may be modeled freely into beads, small dishes and so on. It is especially good for making Christmas tree ornaments. For these, roll dough out between two layers of wax paper with rolling pin, then cut into fancy shapes with cookie cutters. Make small holes through which to run cord or yarn for hanging. While still damp the shapes may be sprinkled with artificial snow. Let dry several days, turning so that pieces dry evenly.

# Paste

**How to Make:**
Mix together:

$\frac{1}{2}$ cup flour
Cold water—enough to make creamy mixture.

Boil over slow fire for 5 minutes, stirring constantly. Cool. Add cold water to thin if necessary. Add:

Few drops oil of peppermint or
Oil of wintergreen (to give pleasant odor and prevent spoiling)

**How to Store:**   Keep in covered jar, refrigerated if possible.

# Papier Mache

(pulp type for solid figures)
(For older children and adults)

**How to Make:**
Tear into small pieces:

Several sheets of newspaper

Put paper into container that will not rust and soak 24 hours in:

Hot water

**113**

Shred paper until it is a pulpy mass. Squeeze out excess water. Add one of the following until mass is consistency to model:

Flour paste or
Dry wallpaper paste powder (without DDT) or
Laundry starch (either dry or cooked—this will not sour as readily as flour paste)

**How to Store:** Keep in cool place, but it will not keep well for more than a few days.

**How to Use:** This may be used to model animals and people or other articles but it is particularly good for making puppet heads. Weight a tall bottle with stones or sand and use the neck as a base for modeling head. Do not attempt to make detailed features, but make a sturdy ball for the skull and work some down around neck of bottle for neck of puppet. Let stand several days till thoroughly dry inside and out. Paint with poster paints. Finish with shellac or clear light varnish. Complete hand puppet by making "dress" to fit over hand. Use yarn or crepe paper for hair. Favorite characters for children are clowns, cowboys, kings, queens, princes and princesses, witches, and animals.

# Clay

*Googly, gooshy*
*Pittery pat,*
*Ooky wooky woo,*
*Squoojy, squooshy*
*Pattery spat,*
*Purply, greenery blue!*

*Splishery, splashery*
*Tippery tap,*
*Unky, wunky wud,*
*Squishery, squashery*
*Slithery slap,*
*Browny, blacky mud!*

*—D.K.G.*

**Commercial clay (non-hardening)** is good for making bases for papier mache projects or models for plaster casts, but for small children it hasn't the consistency for sensory satisfaction that the wet clay has. However, it is simple to store and convenient for home use.

**114**

**Commercial clay (hardening)** is the most satisfactory for nursery school use, since children like the feel and can have it as soft or stiff as they like. It is easy to store; and, kept moist, it can be used again and again. Dry pieces may be fired or painted with poster paints. For older children who want to save what they make there are special clays that can be fired in a kitchen oven, but most clays require kiln firing at very high temperature if pieces are to be water-proof and permanent. For preschool children, however, firing is not necessary except to preserve really outstanding pieces.

## How to Store:

Form clay into round chunks the size of baseballs. Punch a few holes in each.

Put balls into:
Heavy crock

Pour over balls:
Small amount of water

Cover crock with:
Crockery lid or
Layers of damp cloth

Inspect frequently to make sure clay is in workable condition. Add water when necessary. Teach children to put clay away in ball-form with holes punched to absorb moisture.

(A heavy crock which must be moved is easy to handle if set on a small platform with rollers.)

## How to Use:

Children wear smocks or old clothes (although clay washes out of fabrics easily). Work on washable surface. (A table cover of oilcloth that ties firmly to the table legs or a piece of linoleum that covers the table top is handy since it can be removed quickly, leaving table free and clean for next activity. Scraps of clay can be brushed back into crock and table cover sponged.)

Children model or muddle with a minimum of adult suggestion. They should be allowed to experiment and try out their own ideas, or just enjoy the feel of thumping and squeezing. Some two and three-year-olds like their clay quite wet. Often fours and fives do, too; but they find stiffer clay better for the more representative things they like to make. For small children hands are sufficient tools, although sometimes wooden throat sticks are handy for cutting. Match sticks make good legs for clay animals.

**115**

A jar of "slip" (clay thinned with water to the consistency of heavy cream) is a good accessory when children make objects to save. Spread on joints, the slip keeps articles from falling apart as they dry.—*from "Formulas for Fun," produced by the Nursery Training School Alumnae Association*

# TV OR NOT TV

*. . . is no longer the question. Television, it seems, is here to stay. Let's make the most of it! How? By using the many advantages of TV to the best advantage of our children.*

**First, promote good reading through television.** In the early days of television, we frequently heard the comment, "Now they'll never read another book." Much to the surprise of parents, educators and librarians, this just didn't happen. Certainly reading has been reduced in quantity, but, surprisingly, it has increased in quality. And there, I believe, lies one cue to our approach as parents.

We can improve reading by keeping track of the stories dramatized on the air—and then suggest reading other books by the same author, if not the same book. "Huckleberry Finn," on TV, leads naturally to "The Adventures of Tom Sawyer," and then to "The Prince and the Pauper," and "A Connecticut Yankee in King Arthur's Court."

To stimulate the transition from screen to book, put up a special Television Bookshelf. The name itself will remind you and your child to be on the lookout for books—and don't limit them to storybooks or even the classics. Science demonstrations, any one of the weather shows, circus, zoo and pet shows, as well as child-and-animal series can excite an interest in books.

The one thing television does better than any other medium is to open new horizons. Today, enlightenment and enrichment are not limited to programs labeled "educational." In fact, the time devoted to "high level" programs has increased in recent years. Through these programs, the child can get a provocative introduction to folk music and folkways, unusual occupations, various arts and crafts, faraway lands, as well as the inside of factories, laboratories and museums.

**Plan a television corner with your children in mind.** In the average home today, children spend more time before the television screen than in any other single pursuit. We can, and should, cut down on the amount in most cases; but we must at the same time make the viewing productive. Here are a few concrete suggestions:

Place a low table near the set, with a dictionary and an atlas on it and, nearby, an encyclopedia. If your set is in a recreation room, a wall map of the world is a good addition to the atlas. Suggest looking up questions of fact.

For younger children, have a drawer or shelf at hand, containing a drawing board or clipboard, crayons, large pads, blunt scissors and other materials needed for participation in activity programs. Also, keep a chest or box in your child's room to be used for all kinds of odds and ends that will help him carry out his newly acquired ideas—bits of cloth, tape, string, wire, pipe cleaners, and so on.

**Start projects through programs.** One of the constant cries against television is, "But it makes spectators of our children!" Actually children don't have to watch without reacting.

For instance, seven-year-old Johnny was fascinated by a time-lapse film he saw on a Saturday morning program; it dealt with the growth of plants from seeds. His father, who watched it with him, suggested a simple experiment. Together, they placed beans in a saucer of water, and within a few days healthy sprouts began to appear. Delighted, Johnny gathered all the seeds he could find—grapefruit, orange, birdseed—and tried them all. The interest grew like the plants themselves, until today, at nine, the boy has a small window greenhouse in which he raises seedlings to be planted in the garden.

Any parent can find constructive projects via television. Does fifteen-year-old Jane admire a dress worn by a favorite actress? With some encouragement and assistance, she can make one for herself. Is twelve-year-old Andy intrigued by the easy way they make brownies on a commercial? Let him try it for himself—and learn that cooking can be fun for males, too.

All you have to do is watch their faces, listen to their comments, be on the alert for budding interests, use your own imagination in finding materials! Your children will do the rest.

**117**

**Take a tip from alert teachers.** More and more teachers are recognizing television as a source of inspiration and information—and are using TV programs in their classwork.

We parents can help our children integrate television with school work in many ways. By keeping a close eye on programs to come, we can find shows that suggest subjects for research and reports.

On Sundays, the family might look over the presentations for the coming week, then post a tentative list of programs that sound interesting. The mere idea of making up a schedule is a healthy reminder to explore programs and select judiciously. It also gets the child into the habit of budgeting his time wisely.

And, of course, there are many entertaining programs which the whole family will enjoy sharing together.—*Robert M. Goldenson, Ph.D.*

# EVERY
# HOME NEEDS
# A WORKSHOP

*Even young people can make beautiful as well as useful things from wood. All it takes is a hammer, saw, nails, some scrap wood, and a liberal dose of creative imagination. Simple . . . but deeply satisfying. (And isn't that how Pinocchio was born!)*

The whole family will enjoy creating useful and decorative things in a home workshop. It's exciting to make your own toys, and exciting to do-it-yourself . . . especially when Dad's around to lend a hand.

**Supplies Needed.** Here is a list of desirable items and some suggestions concerning their possible uses.

**Wood:** Scraps and odd shapes of soft wood. Get these at a lumberyard. Combine to make engines, trains, automobiles, miniature villages.

**118**

Plywood scraps—$\frac{1}{4}$-inch thickness. Sawed-out animals for barnyards, circuses and so forth.

Turned pieces of hard wood. Tops for masts and other boat parts, candle holders, heads for wooden dolls. These pieces can be cemented if there is no center hole all ready to nail through. In general, avoid hard wood.

All kinds of wooden boxes and match boxes. These are the basis for many toys.

Clothespins of different sizes. Dollhouse furniture. Holes must be drilled before nailing.

Skewers and any size dowel sticks. Axles, masts.

Spools. Wheels, table legs, smokestacks, stands for toy parts.

Throat sticks. For jumping jacks, benches, various toy parts. These must also be drilled for nailing.

**Metal:** $\frac{1}{4}$-inch-square mesh wire, and fine screening. Fences, ladders, windows for dollhouses, insect cages.

Roofing tins. Plates for dollhouse food, Christmas decorations.

Screw eyes, hooks and rings. Couplings for trains, boat rigging, many incidentals.

Wheels and metal parts from broken toys.

Milk bottle wires. Handy lengths for many uses.

**Miscellaneous:** Ice cream spoons and picnic forks. Puppet hands—concave surface aids in grasping.

Old fabric window shades. Excellent for boat sails or puppet scenery backdrops—they take paint very well.

Corks. Smokestacks, small animals, and so forth. Can be sawed easily, but are hard to cut with a knife.

Leather. Ears, reins. Very heavy leather can be used instead of metal hinges.

**Sewing Materials:** Stockings and socks. Dolls, puppets, animals.

Felt. This is excellent for children. Cotton felt is much less expensive than wool, comes in good colors, and may be bought at makers of school pennants. Quarter-yard lengths go a long way. Use for doll clothes, saddles, and so forth.

Cloth scraps, lace trimmings, feathers, and so forth.

Buttons, for eyes.

Oilcloth. Stuffed animals and dolls.

A toy sewing machine, provided it is a standard make that can be kept in repair, is an invaluable piece of equipment. Boys like to use these, when sewing by hand would be beyond their ability.

**Sticking Materials:**   Paste. There are several excellent pastes. For large amounts, buy the cold water paste used for wall paper. This is inexpensive, comes in powder form and can be stirred up as needed.

Glue. The standard adhesive for wood. Small bottles are less wasteful, as contents dry up quickly. Toothpicks for applying insure neater work.

Cement in 10-cent tubes. This is better than glue for smooth, hardwood surfaces like spools, for metal, or wherever a waterproof adhesive is needed.

**Workbenches:**   A solid workbench of the right height makes it easier for children to learn the correct use of tools. To find an individual's correct working level, measure from floor to wrist as arms hang at sides. But allow for a child's growth or for use by different ages by making the bench somewhat higher. Then provide a broad, steady platform for the younger ones to stand upon while working.

A bench may be improvised in various ways. Any sturdy table cut to the right height will do, or a discarded flat-top desk. An old single-panel door may be bought at a wrecking company and laid across two saw horses or across two boxes. Perhaps the easiest makeshift is a good-sized heavy packing box of proper height.

Ready-built workbenches are available, of course, but it is much less expensive, and often as satisfactory, to make your own.

If you have had some experience with tools, let the building of the workbench be a family project for yourself and the children. Use a secondhand packing box and lumber, or new wood. The advantage of a box is that when you have knocked it apart, the boards for your top are all sawed square and of the same length. You will also need some 2x4's for legs and braces, and four 4-inch bolts; 2x4's cost about 6 cents a linear foot new, half that secondhand. A few extra ones are always convenient to have if you can store them.

**These are the basic tools** a good home workshop needs.

Hammer. Medium weight is best for children. Be sure to get a claw which will pull nails.

Try Square. One of the most important tools—for marking wood so that it can be cut square across at right angles to the length.

Crosscut Saw. Try to find a panel saw, measuring 20 to 24 inches. Longer ones are hard for children to manage. It is used primarily for cutting across the grain of the wood.

Vise. A portable vise is desirable, but may be both expensive and hard to get. An excellent substitute is a pair of C-clamps with a 5-inch opening.

Screw Drivers. Those from the five-and-ten are good. Get two or three sizes.

Pliers. Pick a pair with points which close tight.

Coping Saw. Used for small work, such as cutting out animal figures, and curves. Get one with a deep throat to allow for turning. Keep a good supply of #10 blades on hand.

Plane. A block plane is small and easy for children to handle. Blades can be bought separately. Remember to get the best in edged tools.

The eight tools described thus far are essentials, arranged roughly in order of importance. As you work, you will need others which may be added gradually. Of the boring tools, the easiest to manage is the bradawl. A good drillstock (cheap ones do not hold the drill securely) with half a dozen assorted drills for either wood or metal will be needed eventually, also a bitstock and bits for holes over $\frac{1}{8}$ inch. A half-round file is inexpensive and useful. Sandpaper, while not classed as a tool, is a necessity. Keep a supply of #1 and #$\frac{1}{2}$ on hand.

As square sawing is one of the most difficult things for children to learn, you may wish to add a good wide miter box to your workshop. Wooden ones cost around a dollar, metal ones about three. Any device to insure square sawing is worth the money.


**Well-Selected Nails Are Important:** The proper nail often means the difference between success and failure. A good rule is to have about two-thirds the length of the nail go into the under piece of wood.

Use slender nails for thin wood. Poor grades of wood, like box wood, are apt to split. To prevent this, drill a hole with a bradawl or drill slightly smaller than the nail.

Start nails in the top piece of wood separately until they barely prick through, then place and drive into the second piece, setting all nails only just enough to hold, until you are sure that everything is square and well-fitted. Then finish driving.

Occasionally you will have to nail from inside a small box where there is no room to hammer freely. In this case, start your nail hole with an awl, and set the nail at a slant. Use a nail set to finish driving.

In cutting two pieces with identical measurements, like opposite ends of a chest or footstool, square and cut one first, then measure the other by it.

If both are measured at first, the space taken out by the saw-cut will make them uneven.

A word about useful nail sizes may be a help. Buy what you need by the pound; assortments are not satisfactory. For storage, use glass jars or cans properly labeled. Children enjoy learning and using names of nails. A pound each of blued lath, six and eight-penny common, box, and finish nails, several sizes of brads and small flat-head nails will make an excellent start. Experience will show which will be needed most often.

## Tips on Using Tools

**Square.** Show that when held properly, the tool cannot move diagonally. A self-checking device that children love is to square all the way around the board. If done correctly, the final line will exactly meet the starting point. This is also excellent for inexperienced adults, as keeping to all four lines insures an absolutely square cut, perhaps the most important factor in good construction.

**Saw.** Few children can saw square by the adult method of holding with one hand and sawing with the other. If the wood is held firmly by a clamp, vise or a strong hand, and the child stands directly in front of his cut, holding the saw with both hands and watching to prevent the blade from tipping, results will be good. Teach them to saw lightly—the teeth do the cutting, not the push of the workman. They must also learn that the saw-cut takes space—hence always saw on one side or the other of a marked line, rather than on it. They understand this better if a second line is squared parallel to the first and about a sixteenth of an inch from it. Then tell them to saw between the lines. When not in use, a saw should be leaned vertically, resting on its handle, or hung in its place over the workbench.

**Vise.** Holding work steady is the most difficult thing for a child. Save the grownup's time by teaching the youngster the use of a vise and clamps. Small bits of wood put between the work and the metal save denting.

**Screw Driver.** This works best if it just fits the length of the slot in the screw—hence the need for different sizes. Holes bored for screws should be slightly shorter and smaller than the screw itself. Greasing the screw makes it easier to turn.

**Pliers.** Get the habit of using these frequently for straightening nails, bending wire, pulling through an obstinate needle, or saving fingers.

**Bradawl.** Start boring with the blade crosswise of the wood grain, otherwise it may split.

**Sandpaper.** Plenty of sanding always pays in the looks of a finished piece of woodwork. Much of this is best done before the parts are nailed together. But be careful to keep edges and corners sharp where they are to be attached to other parts.

**Caring for Tools.** To teach your children workmanlike habits as well as skills, spend some time with them in arranging the family tools. Organizing equipment in an orderly way will save time in the end, and develop pride in sharp tools, easily accessible.

The vertical tool board, with a picture of each tool under it is not an original idea. However, when it was followed in a school tool closet which was constantly used by teachers and children over a period of seven years, only one tool was lost! There is something about an empty picture on a tool board that makes a child want to cover it with the missing tool.

A smooth door, a wooden wall, or boards nailed against plaster will give the necessary foundation. Measure the size of the space where the tools are to be placed, and cut a piece of brown paper, cardboard or beaverboard to these measurements. One side of such a carton as comes on a mattress would be excellent.

Now lay the paper out flat and arrange the tools upon it in as logical a manner as you can. Do not place them too closely, but leave space for later additions. When everything is arranged to your satisfaction, draw around each tool with a soft pencil. These lines may be gone over later with a black crayon or a wide speedball pen and black ink, to make them stand out.

A final educational touch is to print the name of each tool beside its outline. Tack the layout to the wall and drive in nails which will hold the tools in position over their pictures.

# Things to Make and Do

**Toy making** is one of the most practical, as well as one of the most delightful occupations for the home workshop. Big unit toys, such as farms,

**123**

circuses, villages, dollhouses, or fairy-tale settings and characters may be made by the whole family, or by Cub or Brownie groups, and given away to hospitals or the Red Cross. Doing this with children is far more rewarding than working behind closed doors and presenting the toy as a surprise.

**Trains and Boats:** Block trains may be made from sections of 2 x 4 with overhanging roofs for passenger cars, a diagonally cut shorter piece for a coal car, and an assembly of small pieces on a 2-inch base for the engine. Parts which cannot be nailed may be cemented. This is better than glue for small work. In all sticking together of parts, the secret of success is in holding them firm until they are dry. Cement dries very quickly, but set it in a vise or clamp if possible to avoid slipping. The train is coupled together with screw eyes and small cup hooks.

Boats are made by the same block-building method. Start with a board of 2x4, cut to a point at one end. Build up cabins, masts, and so forth. Fasten the superstructure with elastic bands and try the boat in the water for balance before any nailing is done. Be sure to use cement instead of glue, as cement is waterproof.

A large floor ship made out of a box may be for a small boy what a dollhouse is to his sister—a constant resource for play, with delightful details which may be added indefinitely. A pirate ship in our own workshop has sails that go up and down, ladders, treasure chests with much bright treasure within, an anchor, skull and crossbones at the masthead, hammocks below decks, and seven pirates!

## How to Do-It-Yourself

**Some Methods of Construction:** Wheels are difficult to make. There are many ready-to-hand wheels if one knows how to use them— spools, checkers, buttonmolds, or wheels from broken toys, all of which should have a place in the workshop collection. Sawed sections of broomsticks or wooden curtain rods may also be used, or ready-made wheels may be bought at toy supply companies or cut to order at a mill.

When using spools, it is better to saw each one in half to reduce the width. Hold it with a wood strip under the center, and use the miter box, as it is difficult to set a spool in the vise. All spools will fit on $\frac{1}{4}$-inch dowels, but if these are used, a small nail through a drilled hole will be necessary to keep the wheel from slipping off the axle. Also remember that all axles must be absolutely square to the sides of the vehicle, or it will not run straight. The dowel may be attached to the bottom of the vehicle by running it through two $\frac{1}{4}$-inch screw eyes. Or a small square stick may be nailed on for an axle, and the ends rounded like a dowel to permit the spool wheel to turn freely.

It is easiest for children to attach wheels without using axles. Use a piece of wood not less than $\frac{1}{2}$ inch thick for the base of the vehicle, build up any kind of superstructure to convert it into an engine, trolley car, truck or fire wagon, and then nail the wheels directly to the sides of the base. Checkers make excellent wheels, but holes must be drilled exactly in the center.

To do this, draw on paper around the checker, cut and fold the circle in quarters, and mark the center by the intersection. Then, starting the drill hole with a nail or awl, drill a hole a trifle larger than a blued lath nail. Use this first checker as a pattern and drill all the others through the correctly placed hole in the first one. When driving nails to hold wheels to a base, be sure they are at right angles, and do not drive them tight.

**How Dad Can Help.** Anyone who has watched a child work without adult help will see him start out with some definite end in view, such as a house or an automobile. He takes ready-cut pieces, or quickly saws, without squaring, what he thinks will be the right size, nails each piece on as soon as he has it in hand, and usually pays no attention to sizes of nails or to whether the pieces fit or are centered. The result is apt to fall apart, or be so far from his mental picture that he is discouraged. "I made a truck, but it didn't work," a child often answers when we ask what he has been making.

Dad's job is to give suggestions about construction which will not destroy the child's idea, but will bring the satisfaction that spurs one ahead. While some children won't mind some failures, they should not have too many discouragements. Any short cut used by a carpenter, such as a miter box, should be given to a beginner. Work held firmly at the right height is as important as sharp, accurate tools.

Putting pieces together properly presents difficulties for a child. Use two thicknesses of wood if possible, and nail through the thinner into the thicker board. When attaching two pieces of wood, both too thick to nail through, nail a larger thin piece to the smaller block, then nail through this thin projecting piece into the other block.

Children do not learn a process in one lesson. The simple use of the try square, to take one example, must be taught and taught again. The younger the child, the more frequent repetition he needs. Then, too, what he undertakes must be within his powers, so that he gets pleasure from the work.

But with patience, a bit of help and expressed interest, Dad can make the home workshop an exciting and meaningful place to share with his children.—*Martha P. Lincoln and Katharine Torrey*

# EVERYONE
## LOVES
## A PARTY

*YOU ARE INVITED TO A PARTY . . . . the words themselves bring a happy glow of anticipation. There's fun in the offing and merriment in the making. So no matter what the occasion (birthday, Halloween, or just-because-you-want-one), plan now to have a party. For young and old alike, party time means pleasure time.*

**127**

# BIRTHDAYS MEAN
# BIRTHDAY PARTIES

Parties can, and should, be great fun for the young guests, the birthday child, and even for his mother.

The formula? Some simple do's and don'ts.

The first requirement for an adult facing a crew of eager what-do-we-do-now youngsters is to be prepared—in fact, overprepared. The games you never get to, the things that never were made won't be wasted. They can go into a carton, until another party comes along, and then brought out again.

**Party theme.**   Having a theme for the party is a practical and attractive maneuver. The theme becomes a link to coordinate the invitations, decorations, refreshments, party activities, and so on. A list of party themes is limited only by your imagination—hobos, funny hats, the four seasons, royalty, famous figures in history, outer space with all its creatures and machines, the circus, flowers, Mother Goose characters, and on and on.

Don't get so carried away by a theme, however, that it becomes too involved for children to understand.

Party activities can often be adapted to fit a theme. For example, Pin the Tail on the Donkey easily converts to Put the Nose on the Snowman, Pin the Tail on the Bunny, Put the Bee on the Flower.

Costume parties for young children can add to the mothers' chores without really improving the festivities. But teen-agers can handle most of the details ingeniously by themselves.

We have had an occasional dress-up party, however. Young ladies love to come-as-your-mother party; mother just has to add a few safety pins to the cause. For boys, we reversed it once and specified that they could come as their normal selves. And they were delighted not to dress up.

**How many should come?**   It may be difficult, sometimes, to restrict the number of guests. Still, a successful child's party is usually a small one.

**128**

Certainly, before the age of six, the fewer the number of guests, the better.

Parents of invited guests do not belong at birthday parties. The year has many hours for chats with neighbors and friends, and a child's party is not the time or place. (This applies to overhelpful grandparents, too.)

**What to serve.** Refreshments are of utmost importance at a party, second only to prizes and presents as far as youngsters are concerned. Remember, however, to keep the food simple. Ice cream and birthday cake appeal to most children. Many mothers order birthday cakes from their local bakery or buy a cake and decorate it specially. In our house we use prepared cake mixes and instant frostings for all cakes on a musical cake plate.

Fill the cups with milk or soda before the children are seated, and have the cake plates ready. If any parents have remained, don't let them hover over their offspring. Nothing is more dreary at a party table than a mother urging her child to eat.

**Table decorations.** Children are more concerned with presents, food, games, favors and things to do. Parents often get side-tracked by cake and party decorations. Decorations definitely belong to parties, but they should be kept in proper perspective.

Paper birthday tablecloths and napkins give a party atmosphere; streamers taped to a plain cloth with a cluster of gay balloons waving overhead can be decoration enough for most children. In addition, paper hats and blowers are nice extras. Candy baskets are enjoyed by little children, but the older ones are more concerned with the contents than with the container.

What you plan to do during the party depends, of course, upon the children's age and sex, the space available and the season of the year. But plan you must! Several days before the party, prepare a game list, and beside each game list the equipment needed for it. Assemble the equipment in one spot so that you don't have to make a last minute round-up of rags for the three-legged race or potatoes for the potato race.

Be flexible. If the children are happily diverted by one activity, don't insist on rushing on to a new one. Don't, however, make the mistake of repeating a game more than twice—even if the youngsters particularly like it.

Have a balanced plan. Perhaps two quiet games, one thing to make, a couple of active games, and for older children, table games. If the guests are strangers to each other, have a couple of get-acquainted games. For a finale, try a party-stunt punch board.

**Game prizes.**  These are inevitably a factor in parties but there is no standard rule. My younger daughter has steadfastly refused to offer prizes at her parties. She doesn't like it when someone else wins something she would like, and yet she feels embarrassed to win anything at her own party. We explain our no-prize policy to our guests, and assure them that we have a grab bag of prizes waiting for all of them at the end of the party. This eliminates a great deal of unnecessary competition.

**Things to make.**  For children over four, "making something" adds to the party's fun. Here again the party theme is helpful. Hobby and do-it-yourself centers, books and magazines supply many good, inexpensive ideas to amuse youngsters. Decide which one you think your guests will enjoy, list your needs. Assemble supplies several days before the party, and keep them piled on an out-of-reach tray until needed. Don't forget to save newspapers to protect the surface on which the children will work. Label a large paper bag with each child's name ahead of time so that once an item is finished it can be popped safely into the proper bag. The same bag can also be filled with treats and prizes that the youngster wants to take home.

Here are some of the make-it-yourself activities that have proved to be fun at our house:

**Hats** always inspire marvelous surrealistic creations. Bring out your tray piled with aluminum pie plates to use as the base of each hat. Add doilies, yarn, cupcake liners, pipe cleaners, balloons, foil, filmy wrapper material, cardboard, crayons, feathers, ribbons, glitter, and any other scrap materials that come to hand. Have plenty of paper tape, glue and staplers, and set a time limit—say fifteen minutes. If one child finishes early, let him make another hat while waiting.

**Masks.**  Very little children can find endless amusement with just large sheets of paper, scissors, paste, cotton and crayons. We once cut dozens of large animal ears out of wrapping paper. These, with paper bags, yarn, crayons, paste and staplers, made animal masks that delighted the young.

**Puppets.**  Paper bags, stuffed with newspapers and tied, taped or banded around empty wax paper tubes (cut to half-lengths) make marvelous puppets. The children will have a lovely time creating characters if you provide cotton, cellophane straws, crayon, yarn, bits of fabric, buttons, paste and string. To get them started, suggest a familiar story or fairy tale. This may lead to an extemporaneous puppet show.

Before the sit-down activities have a chance to pall, roll up the news-

**130**

papers, remove the supplies, and start the guests on an active game to work off the kinks from sitting for so long.

There are alternatives to the birthday party: pony rides, outings and the movies, for example. But they are expensive and not enjoyed half as much as a good, old-fashioned party—which the youngsters look forward to year after year.—*Eloise Julius*

# PRE-TEEN PARTIES

When they were seven or eight you gave your youngsters a party that was pretty much: musical chairs-puppets-birthday cake. When they are seventeen or eighteen, they have parties that are dancing-talking-eating.

But when they are in-betweeners, they have outgrown one but are not quite ready for the other. What can parents do to help young people have good times when they are in the fifth or sixth grade?

**Games and gimmicks**. Pre-teeners tend to be a little self-conscious at first, so plan something active to get them in motion as soon as everyone has arrived. If the weather is warm, they can go outside in the backyard.

A popular yard pastime is a net game variation of volley ball played with strong, oversize balloons and with the players keeping first one and then two balloons going at a time.

Other games that are party-starters—to be played either outside or in— are Wink and Numbered Chairs, a little more sophisticated than Musical Chairs, but just as much fun. Sixth-graders also like silly stunts done to fast, peppy music: passing a pie pan like a hot potato, first hand-to-hand in front, and then behind the back in more and more complicated routines.

**Food.** After forty-five minutes or an hour of games, announce a break— for food—preferably in a different part of the house.

It's a good change of pace for young people when they move from a

**131**

backyard or a room where they've been very active to another where they can sit down to a table that's all ready for them.

The food served should be "grown-up." A sixth-grader really doesn't want birthday-cake-and-ice-cream.

Heroes or pizza is popular, followed by a good-sized loaf cake in place of the traditional layer cake. Refreshments will probably take from thirty to forty-five minutes. While conversation at the table is still lively, get ready for the next stage of activities.

**Group activities.**   Again the guests move—this time back to the first area used inside—but now the activity is more relaxed.

"If my husband is home, he usually has the movie projector set up and set to show films of a picnic or an outing that included some of the youngsters," one mother says. "Of course they love to see themselves on the screen. And there's always wonderful ad lib commentary from the audience!"

Another pastime for the last part of entertaining could be recording jokes and tongue-twisters if you have a tape recorder. This should be supervised.

Ten minutes or so before time for departure, the tapes can be rewound and movie equipment stowed away. A definite time limit is always best.

Ask your pre-teener and some of his friends to help "put the screen away" or "put the cover on the recorder." This is a diplomatic way to remind young people of time. If they are invited from 2:30 to 5, for instance, and stay and stay after that, the nice glow begins to fizzle out.

If young people are comfortable dancing and really enjoy it, no other entertainment need be offered. It is good to remember, though, that not all young teens do enjoy dancing. Many prefer group activities which are more familiar and comfortable.—*Marthe Gross*

# PARTY MIXERS

An evening can be made or marred in the first 15 minutes while the party group is assembling. If the ice is allowed to form at the beginning, valuable time and effort must be spent in thawing it. Simple preliminary games and contests that almost run themselves can be most helpful as "mixers." As soon as all the guests have arrived, the game should be concluded and the regular program started. Here are some useful mixer games and contests:

**Cooperative Spelling.** Each guest is given a large card bearing a letter of the alphabet, which is to be fastened to his arm. He is given also a small card and a pencil. The letters are to get together to spell words. Each word spelled by an assembled group is to be written down on the cards; then the group separates and the players seek new combinations. A prize may be given to the person having the longest list, or to the members of the group that formed the longest word. This game is an especially good mixer for a large group.

**Matching Numbers.** Numbered slips are given to the guests, and they are told to match these for partners. Only two or three slips are in duplicate, however, so that during the entire program people will continue to try to find partners, unaware that this is impossible.

**Name Chain.** An excellent way to learn names in a group of not more than 25 or so is for the first person to turn to the second and say his own name. The second repeats this and adds his own name. Then the third must repeat the first and second names before adding his own name. Thus the list lengthens as the game goes on.

**Grocery List.** The boys (or half the group) stand inside a circle, and the girls (or the rest of the group) stand outside, facing in. Each girl has a small pad of paper and a pencil. Each boy starts to write on the pad of the girl opposite him all the groceries and home equipment he can think of that start with the letter "A." When the whistle blows (after 30 seconds), he moves to the next girl on his right and lists for her the objects starting with "B." So the games goes on. The girls may not help their partners. The girl with the longest list wins.

After the boys have moved five times they may be told to keep the pads on which they were writing, and the girls are asked to move to the right. They are to list on the boys' pads all the farm tools beginning with "F." This they continue for five moves. There is no winner when the game is played in this way.—*Adapted from Handbook of Recreation, a publication of the Children's Bureau.*

**133**

# PARTIES
# FOR
# TEEN-AGERS

What makes a good teenage party? Basically, some freedom—but not too much; some planning—but not too much; some supervision—but not too much; lots of food.

How much freedom? Of course, the parents cannot abdicate responsibility for maintaining suitable conduct at parties. So they should be present somewhere in the house and their presence should be known; for when trouble arises it's usually because an adult was not present to step in. A young host wants his parents "on call", but not to "take over."

A youngster in junior high or high school should be encouraged to assume almost complete responsibility for the party planning, with you as chief assistant and provider. Of course, you've had more experience than he has and will be able to get things done and remember things that he might not even think of, but it's his party.

Decide together in advance what sort of party it's to be, who's to come, what the hours are and what standards of behavior are expected.

Often it is helpful for the child host to invite two or three friends to help him plan—food and entertainment, perhaps—and get ready. This also ensures extra helpers, servers and cleaner-uppers during the affair. Thought and advance planning help insure a really successful party, where no one need feel "out of it."—*Eric W. Johnson*

# A PARTY
# WITH PUNCH

Punch is a perfect drink for large groups. Once your punch bowl is filled, guests can help themselves. Your mixing chores end right at the beginning.

Except for the soda used in some punch recipes, your drink may be prepared well in advance of the party. Punch flavor is improved by chilling for several hours before serving.

In addition to providing very pleasing refreshment, your punch bowl can also serve as a striking centerpiece. It's simple. Here's how:

Prior to the party, take a large block of ice. Fill your punch bowl with hot water. Place it on the ice block. The heat will melt out a hollow mold. When the mold is deep enough, remove the hot water. Then set your punch bowl in the fresh ice hollow. It will keep your punch chilled right down to the last serving—and provide a novel conversation piece.

**Wry toasts.** At a party, French toast is not something made with eggs and bread. It's a salutation—"A votre sante!"—to his guest's health that a clever host makes when everyone is drinking the punch. Here are some other toasts from other lands that are fun to use at party time.

American—Here's Luck!
Chinese —Wen Lie!
Greek   —Yasas!
Irish   —Slainte!
Italian —Alla Salute!
Polish  —Na Zdrowie!

British  —Cheers!
German  —Prosit!
Hebrew  —L'Chaim!
Hungarian—Ege'sze'ge're!
Russian  —Za vashe zdorovye!
Spanish  —Salud!

# SPECIAL PARTIES FOR ALL AGES

## A Play School Party

**For three- to five-year olds.** Most three- and four-year-old children can hardly wait to be old enough to go to school. So why not plan your preschooler's birthday party around a play school theme? Four children this age are enough for a good party.

**135**

A morning party including lunch has several advantages. If you have older children, they're at school so you can give the party your full attention. The party-goers will have a well-balanced meal at noon instead of afternoon refreshments which often spoil supper appetites. Best of all, the party will be over in plenty of time for afternoon naps all around.

When your young guests arrive, it's a good idea to start school right away, leaving the birthday gifts to be opened later. If you take the gifts without comment and put them out of sight, there should be no objections.

Children of this age are not ready for organized games but will do things individually in a group. Here are some suggestions for activities they enjoy.

**Gum Drop Zoo:**  Show children how to make an animal-like figure using gum drops and pipe cleaners or toothpicks. Then let each child make one. When they have finished, line up all the animals to admire and discuss. Later these may be taken home to show their mothers.

**Cut and Paste:**  Give each child an old magazine, blunt scissors and construction paper so he can cut and paste pictures or bits of color as desired. Have crayons for those who prefer to draw pictures. Be sure to protect table top with newspapers.

**Hat Making:**  Help the children cut hats from two pieces of construction paper on which you have drawn animal outlines. Decorations may be cut from magazines and pasted on. Using staples or plastic coated cloth tape, join halves of hat, front and back, to fit each child's head.

**Rhythm Band:**  Suggest children put on their hats and parade around the house singing and beating time on pans with kitchen spoons. Sing any song they all know, or have phonograph music. This is a fairly safe way for them to let off steam.

**Story Time:**  Read them a story from a child's book with plenty of big pictures to calm them down before lunch.

By then it will be time to open gifts. First, your birthday child will open his gifts. When he has finished, bring out gaily wrapped packages containing identical inexpensive toys—one for each child.

**136**

**Lunch.** Now for the luncheon table. If possible, set it up in a closed-off room before the guests arrive. Tie gay balloons to the overhead light or affix to corners of table. Arrange paper birthday party plates and napkins with a popper by each plate. Cupcakes on a pretty platter may be used as a centerpiece, inserting the right number of birthday candles in them for lighting later when ice cream is served.

A soup, sandwich and milk luncheon is always good. Candy is best left off the lunch table. Instead, you might give each guest a basket of candy to take home along with his balloon after lunch—to sweeten the hard fact that the party is over.

# A Splash and Splatter Party

**For three- to six-year-olds.** A lawn party where youngsters can splash and splatter to their hearts' content is sure to please preschoolers.

A morning party works out well because everyone can go home for naps after lunch. Invite the guests to come at 10:30 in the morning and plan to serve lunch at 12. The children should wear bathing suits and bring towels.

The success of the party depends on having ample wading pool space. If your child's pool is small, perhaps you can borrow an extra plastic pool or two to space around the yard and fill with water before the guests arrive. Have the hose connected, and a collection of empty cans and bottles for filling and pouring. A sprinkler attachment will add to the fun.

A water party starts itself and goes on for a long time under its own momentum. The youngest ones will be content to splash indefinitely, but it's a good idea to have a trick or two ready for the five- and six-year-olds.

**Tag.** For them, set aside one pool as "home base" and start a game of wading-pool tag. Explain that no player can run out of the yard (or into the adults' area) to avoid being tagged. He becomes safe and untaggable by jumping into the pool. But only one player can stay in the pool at a time; as soon as another player jumps into the pool, the first must get out and start running.

**Songs.** When the children have run themselves tired, suggest that all sit down to sing "Little Ducky Duddle." This is a favorite with the kindergarten set, so the older ones will know both words and tune, and the younger ones will join in. It goes like this:

**137**

Little Ducky Duddle
Went wading in a puddle
Went wading in a puddle quite small.
He said, "It doesn't matter
How much I splash and splatter
'Cause I'm only a little ducky after all."

If they tire of singing before you are ready to serve lunch, give each child a small plastic boat to sail. Otherwise, save the boats for going-away gifts at the end of the party.

Serve the lunch picnic style in the yard with the children sitting in a circle on the grass. And with ice cream as dessert, the party can end happily.

## Happy Easter Party

**For five- to eight-year-olds.** The Saturday before Easter is a wonderful time for a children's party. All you need to keep the young guests happily absorbed for an hour or more are plenty of hard-cooked eggs and as many kinds of colorful decorating materials as you care to assemble. The more the merrier.

Five- and six-year-olds like to make designs on the pre-dyed eggs with crayons and paste on bits of colored gummed paper, stars and ready-made pinwheel discs. Older children prefer to paint their pre-dyed eggs with water colors and add glamorous touches with beads, sequins and glitter dust. Some may want to paint funny faces on the eggs, then paste on hats and collars cut from scraps of cloth or colored paper, beards and mustaches of yarn or cotton. Others may choose to use the colorful transfer designs, initials and Easter symbols now available for egg decorating. Directions for use come with the designs.

**Invitations.** Draw a simple bunny figure on white single-fold note paper. First draw a circle around a fifty-cent piece for the body. Then add a penny-size circle for the head and sketch on large rabbit ears. Glue a bit of white cotton where the tail belongs. Your child will enjoy helping you.

On the outside, below the bunny, write: "Help! Help! Peter Cottontail begs you to . . ."

On the inside of the invitation, write, "Come to a party and help color Easter eggs on Saturday, April 16th, from 11 A.M. to 2 P.M. at Margo Whelan's home. P.S. Lunch will be served."

**To break the ice (and maybe an egg or two)** when the guests first arrive, line up the children at one end of a room and give each one a hard-cooked egg and a teaspoon. The first one to roll his egg, with the teaspoon, across the room to a finish line wins a basket to put his eggs in.

**Now to the fun of decorating the eggs.** The kitchen table or breakfast bar is fine for this, or card tables set up in the family room. If no other place is available, use the floor of the living room, well protected with several thicknesses of newspaper topped with brown paper. Set out three or four hard-cooked eggs for each child along with crayons, gummed paper and several pairs of blunt scissors. To keep the party friendly, it's best to provide each child with his own inexpensive box of crayons or water colors and a brush. When eggs are all decorated, give each child an egg carton (half-dozen size) with his name on it so he can take his eggs home.

**Easter games.** Now it's time for more active fun, so ask your helper to supervise a game of Follow the Leader. Since this is an Easter party, the leader may decide to hop like a bunny, cheep like a chick, waddle like a duck or flap his wings and crow like a rooster. While this is going on, you will have time to clear away the decorating debris and serve lunch.

**Table decorations.** If possible, the party table should be all set before the guests arrive, preferably in a room shut off from their view until lunch time. Perhaps your child will want to make Easter place cards by gluing tiny funny chicks onto folded stiff paper. Streamers of pink, yellow and pale green crepe paper hung from the ceiling or overhead light carry out the Easter egg theme with these colors repeated at the table in the paper covering, plates and napkins.

Children love the traditional centerpiece of wooly lamb surrounded by green "grass" and Easter eggs but even more fun would be an arrangement of fresh garden vegetables with a toy stuffed rabbit—or a live one in a cage. If there are several children in your family, making an egg tree for the centerpiece is a delightful group activity. Kits containing all the essentials for professional egg decorating come with directions and inspiring examples of this ancient art.

**The egg hunt.** While the children are eating lunch, you will have time to prepare for the grand finale—the Easter egg hunt. For this, hide various

**139**

kinds of candy eggs throughout adjacent rooms or, if the weather is pleasant, outdoors. Then, after lunch, give each child a basket and let the hunt get under way.

The end of the hunt is the end of the party. Each child takes home the box of eggs he has decorated, his own box of crayons or paints and his basket of candy eggs.

## A Halloween Supper Party

**For six- to eight-year-olds.** Halloween, with its grinning pumpkin faces, witches and black cats, is a made-to-order occasion for a children's party. No other time of year provides the opportunity for such delightfully scary make-believe or appeals more strongly to a child's imagination.

Since no self-respecting spook would be caught abroad before sundown, a supper party that goes on until after dark is mandatory for six- to eight-year-olds. If held the Saturday before Halloween, it won't conflict with the exciting "trick or treat" rounds on the big night.

**Invitations.** Invite the young guests to come at 4:30 and plan an hour or more of games and other activities before supper. (Children this age glory in dressing up, so by making it a costume affair the fun begins even before the party starts.) The number of guests will depend to some extent on the play space available. Eight children in a living room roughly equal twelve in a playroom.

Small jack-o'-lanterns cut from orange construction paper are invitations your child can help you make. Fold the paper and cut the invitations with one side of the pattern on the fold so the double pumpkins may be opened to read the message.

**Decorations.** Halloween is made for the colorful decorations children love so well. If the party is held in a playroom, branches of autumn leaves, bunches of cornstalks and lighted pumpkin "heads" will provide the right atmosphere. Halloween cut-outs of witches on broomsticks, owls, black cats and the like may be purchased and taped to the walls of playroom or living room.

A sit-down supper is better than a buffet for children of this age. Cover the supper table with several lengths of black crepe paper and use a large pumpkin head for a centerpiece. If you cut two grinning faces on opposite

**140**

sides of this pumpkin, the candlelit grin will delight youngsters on both sides of the table. Halloween paper plates and napkins, orange colored poppers and little paper cups filled with candy corn by each place complete the table setting. Noisemakers are a must for all.

**Food.** Supper starts with hot soup served individually in small hollowed-out pumpkins which the guests may take home to make into jack-o'-lanterns. Names written in black crayon on the pumpkins serve as place cards. Choose a hearty soup from the many condensed canned varieties: bean with bacon, perhaps, or split pea with smoked pork. Or combine two soups. Minestrone mixed with beef vegetable makes as rich and filling a brew as ever steamed in a witch's cauldron.

With the soup serve crusty French or Italian bread, celery stalks filled with nippy cheese spread and milk to drink.

Orange sherbet and "sandwitch" cookies fill the bill for dessert. For the cookies bake or buy plain chocolate cookies and put together in two's with orange tinted frosting or peanut butter blended with canned orange juice concentrate.

**Party fun.** A costume party begins spontaneously with the fun of figuring out who—or what—each guest is supposed to be. A parade around the room to music gives everyone a chance to model his costume for all to admire. Best costume wins a prize.

Next come the traditional games. For the first one, let each child try his luck at biting into an apple hanging from a string without using his hands to help. Suspend the string in a doorway (a small tack at the top of the door frame will do the trick) and tie on a fresh apple for each child. After the first bite, the apple is his to eat and enjoy.

For the second game, give each child a pencil and paper and explain that they are going to draw pictures of a witch. Each child first draws a head near the top of the paper, then folds the paper over to hide what he has drawn and passes it to the person on his right. Everyone then draws a neck, folds the paper over and passes it on. And so it goes with arms and hands, body, legs, feet. The mixed-up pictures that result are truly bewitching.

Follow this game with tape-the-tail-on-the-cat, a Halloween version of pin-the-tail-on-the-donkey.

**The finale.** Bring out large brown paper bags, scissors and rolls of plastic tape in various colors for the children to use in making bag masks

**141**

or trick-or-treat bags for Halloween. For masks, holes can be cut for eyes, nose and mouth and then the faces decorated with colored plastic tape cut into various shapes.

For strong trick-or-treat bags, put one bag inside of another, fold over top edges of bags for extra strength, staple together in several places and then staple on handles of heavy twine. The children will have fun decorating these bags with colored tape. Be sure names are penciled on each creation to avoid confusion after supper when it's time to pack up and go home.

## A Valentine Party

**For six- to nine-year-olds.**  For valentine party invitations you will need red construction paper, white ink and a heart-shaped pattern cut out of cardboard. First step is to show your child how to place the pattern on folded construction paper, so the top of the heart is on the fold, and then to draw around it. Next he cuts it out, leaving part of the top fold uncut so that the double heart is hinged at the top. Finally, he letters "Please Be My . . ." on the outside and inside writes "guest at a Valentine Party," followed by the date, time, place and his name. A first-grader can do the outside lettering but you may need to do the rest of the invitation.

Children love to deliver invitations. If possible, this should be done several days before the party. Six or eight is a good number for a party at this age, and two hours are long enough for it to last. The games come first, followed by refreshments. Be sure to have everything needed for these games ready ahead of time.

**Games** at this party, too, should tie in with the theme.

Arrow in the Heart:  For this Valentine version of Pin-the-Tail-on-the-Donkey, your child can make a large red paper heart and a paper arrow six inches long for each guest. Cut identical half-hearts from two full sheets of construction paper, join halves with cellophane tape and tape to wall. Cut arrows from white construction paper and on each one print the name of the child who will use it. When playing the game, each arrow is taped where the blindfolded child places it. The owner of the arrow nearest the center wins.

Treasure Hunt:  For this game, your child makes four red paper hearts on which to write clues. Together you write three clues and tape to three

**142**

hearts. (Your child will want to join in the hunt, too, so you write the fourth clue and keep it a secret.) The day of the party you hide each heart in a different room of the house, to prevent clues from being found out of turn. At the party you will explain the treasure hunt, then let the children find each clue and bring it to you to read aloud.

Clue #1 might read: "In the bedroom near the bed, you will find a heart that's red." Clue #2: "In the closet in the hall, you'll see boots. Go search them all." Clue #3, discovered in the toe of a boot, read: "Under the living room rug now peek. Perhaps you'll find the clue you seek." Clue #4: "In the kitchen, for your pleasure, is the box that holds the treasure." The treasure box contains an assortment of toys.

**Decorations.** Long before the party, your child can start making red and white paper chains to hang over the party table. Six-inch strips of construction paper are fine for these and they can be taped to the ceiling.

Cover the table with several lengths of red crepe paper, taped together and decorated with small lace paper doilies and heart cut-outs. For each place setting, use a large paper doily for under the plate and a small one for the punch glass, a spoon and a Valentine napkin. The heart-shaped cake described below makes a charming centerpiece.

**Refreshments.** Ice cream, cake and punch are still the favorite party foods for six- to nine-year-olds. Vanilla ice cream topped with half-thawed frozen strawberries, a heart-studded cake and cranberry punch carry out the traditional red and white Valentine theme. For a bright red punch, combine two parts pineapple-pear juice drink with one part cranberry juice.

It's nice to use heart-shaped tins for the cake and, if you use a packaged cake mix, your child might make the cake himself under your supervision. He could make the frosting, too, using one of the easy frosting mixes. In any case, let him be the one to stud the cake all over with tiny red cinnamon candies.

When the ice cream is gone, the party's over. Give each child his own Valentine basket filled with candies and a little gift to take home.

# A Treasure Hunt Party

**Eight- to ten-year-old** boys and girls are the right age to enjoy such a Treasure Hunt to the dagger's hilt.

To set the stage, mail each prospective treasure hunter an intriguing map invitation. Here's how to make one: fold an 8½ x 11-inch sheet of paper in half crosswise, then fold crosswise again and so on until, after four folds, it is 2 x 2¾ inches. Holding it with the final fold at the top, write: "Can you crack a code?" Open one fold and write: "Unpuzzle a clue?" Open next fold and write: "Then a treasure hunt is the thing for you." Unfold again and write: "The map inside shows when and where. Follow the arrows to get you there." Open last fold and use the entire sheet of paper to draw a simple map with arrows along the shortest route from the guest's house to your house, both of which are labeled. Add the date and time of the party—either a Saturday lunch or after-school supper party.

**The hunt.** The entertainment will consist of finding clues and decoding secret messages planted throughout your yard and perhaps a cooperative neighbor's. Keep your own child in the dark about these so that he can join the hunt, too. And be sure to keep the guests in the house until everyone has arrived or some of your clues may be discovered before the party starts. Although the hiding places will differ from lawn to lawn, here are some suggestions for setting up a treasure hunt:

1. Beginning at the back door, walk around the yard unwinding a ball of green string (harder to see against the grass) over and around low tree branches and through bushes. (Later, the youngsters will follow the string, finding clues as they go along.)

2. Write "Break the pink balloon" in large letters on a piece of pink construction paper. Cut it into ten or more irregular pieces and fasten the pieces to the string at suitable intervals, hiding them as much as possible.

3. Tie balloons to bushes, shutters, etc., for party decorations. Use a single pink balloon and, before blowing it up, insert a clue such as this: M-P B-R-ED N–R R–E B-SH 3 F-. N OF SE C-RN-R OF H-U-E. (When the youngsters decipher this as "MAP BURIED NEAR ROSE BUSH 3 FT. NORTH OF SOUTHEAST CORNER OF HOUSE," provide them with a measuring tape and a trowel.)

4. Draw a map showing several landmarks to guide the treasure hunters and a big X marking the spot where the "treasure" is hidden. Bury the map as indicated in the missing letters clue.

5. For the treasure itself, fill a foot locker or grocery carton with food for a picnic lunch. If using a carton, wrap it in black crepe paper, paste on paper hinges and a lock cut from gold paper. Hide foot locker or box at spot marked X on the map, perhaps a corner of the garage or the bike shed.

When the youngsters find the box, suggest they carry it to picnic tables set up on the lawn, in the garage or other spot you have selected for serving the refreshments. In the box they will find these goodies:

**144**

*Pieces of Eight:* Box of round cheese crackers
*Uncut Emeralds:* Jars of tiny sweet pickles or pickle slices
*Giant Rubies:* Basket of the small cherry tomatoes
*Gold Nuggets:* Bag of peanuts

They'll also find paper plates, cups, napkins, salt and pepper shakers, plus a choice of sandwiches such as cold sliced ham and horse-radish on rye bread and chicken salad on white bread. Wrap sandwiches in festive red and blue aluminum foil with outside labels so the pirates can divvy the spoils and, incidentally, choose a preferred sandwich.

While the pirates go through their loot and set up the picnic, offer a beverage choice of milk, fruit juice or one of the fresh fruit punches made from a frozen concentrate.

For dessert, serve ice cream on a stick and individual "treasure sack" cupcakes. For the "sacks," bake cupcakes in fluted paper baking cups with a tiny metal charm tucked into the batter in each cup before baking. Frost and set each cupcake on an 8-inch square of aluminum foil. Bring corners up over cupcakes and twist together to resemble treasure sacks. (Better alert the children to the treasures in each cupcake so there's no chance of a broken tooth or a lost treasure.)

**Games.**    After eating, these games are fun.

List the Loot: Arrange 15 or more items on a tray: rings, bracelets, pins, chains, billfold, watch, coins. After the youngsters have a one-minute look, remove the tray and give them three minutes to list what they have seen. Longest list wins.

Hot or Cold: One player is chosen to wait indoors while the others hide a silver coin in the yard. The chosen youngster then comes out to find the coin, guided by shouts of "hot" when he comes close to the hiding place and "cold" as he goes away from it.

When it's time for the party to end, give each child a treasure trove of chocolate coins in a golden mesh bag.

# Cook-It-Yourself Party

**For nine- to twelve-year-olds.**    Most children love to cook. Young ones are happy just helping mother, but by the time they are nine or ten they like to fix their favorite foods all by themselves. To them, cooking is

**145**

an exciting adventure. And since cooking with pals is even more fun than cooking alone, a cook-it-yourself luncheon party is made to order for this age group.

Your child will be thrilled to invite two or three friends for a Saturday party lunch. It's important to keep the group small because no more than four youngsters can work together successfully.

**Planning the menu** comes first. Let your child choose foods he likes but be sure they are within his cooking capabilities. Then work out with him a step-by-step schedule for each part of the meal, including such cleaning-up chores as washing utensils and sweeping the floor. Paper plates and cups will keep dishwashing to a minimum as well as make the table pretty.

**When the guests arrive,** the hostess outfits them with aprons—frilly ones for the girls, gay kitchen towels for the boys to tuck into trouser tops. With aprons on and hands washed, the youngsters are ready to look at the work schedule and decide what each will do.

One youngster makes the chocolate fudge sauce, for example, following the recipe on a package of quick fudge mix. The second makes the brownies, using a packaged brownie mix. The third prepares grilled cheese and bacon, while the fourth slices tomatoes. Whoever finishes first clears his work space and crosses off his job on the work schedule. He then goes on to another job, such as setting the table.

When the last brownie has been eaten and the last pan washed and put away, it's time to play a few games.

**Games.** Distribute pencils and paper and see who can list the greatest number of foods beginning with letters in the word EAT. Set timer for ten minutes. The winner gets a package of pudding cake mix.

Suggest that each child in turn try writing "Too many cooks spoil the broth" on a piece of paper placed on a book held on top of his head. The ones who writes most legibly wins a ball point pen.

Blindfold the youngsters and see who can best identify different foods by sense of smell (no touching or tasting allowed). You might use a slice of orange, half an onion, a little mustard, a cup of cocoa and a sardine. The winner is awarded a jar of peanut butter.

As a parting gift, present each guest with a package of easy-to-prepare cookie mix.

**146**

# A Slumber Party

**For twelve- to fourteen-year-old girls.** Slumber parties are great fun for girls in their early teens. Strange as it may seem, they're also easy to give. No fancy invitations, prizes, decorations, supervised games or other entertainment are needed. At this age your daughter and her friends prefer to be on their own. All they ask of you is food (party refreshments at night and breakfast next morning), a place to sleep when they can't keep their eyes open any longer, and suspension of the usual bedtime rules.

Liberty is the secret ingredient that makes a slumber party exciting. Staying up after the rest of the family is asleep, raiding the refrigerator in the middle of the night, whispering and giggling into the wee hours can be pretty heady stuff for a thirteen-year-old.

**Togetherness.** A good night's sleep is the last thing the girls care about, so sleeping arrangements need not be elaborate. In fact, they would be disappointed if they couldn't all sleep in one room. A simple plan is to hold the party in your daughter's own bedroom, using one pair of twin beds for a party of eight. Take the mattresses off the beds and place them on the floor, then make up both mattresses and both box springs with sheets and blankets. Your daughter can do most of this advance preparation herself with only a slight assist from you.

Guests are invited for 8:30 on a Friday or Saturday evening and requested to bring pajamas, robe and slippers. If you don't have enough pillows to go around, ask each guest to bring her own pillow, too.

**Refreshments** are expected as soon as all have arrived. If this is a birthday celebration, now is the time for ice cream and candle-lighted cake. Otherwise, girls this age are thrilled by waffles a la mode with a choice of sauces and other toppings. (Frozen waffles are so easy!) The sauces may be bought ready to serve or made at home.

It's also a good idea to have on hand plenty of chilled soft drinks, the makings for instant cocoa, and snacks such as potato chips, popcorn and assorted cookies to nibble as the night progresses.

The girls will be eager to change into pajamas, try out the novel sleeping arrangements, and start exchanging school gossip and girlish confidences. Later they may enjoy watching TV or playing card games popular with the teen-age set. They'll also while away some time with word games such as ghost, coffeepot and buzz.

**147**

As midnight approaches you may have to deliver an ultimatum: "Either be more quiet or stop the party and go to sleep." They'll simmer down when faced with these alternatives because forestalling parental interference is part of the fun.

**The morning after the night before.** You will have plenty of time to serve breakfast to the rest of the family while the party girls are catching up on their sleep. When you hear them beginning to stir, surprise them—and incidentally speed the getting-up process—with a tray of juices delivered to the bedroom door. Offer a choice of fruit blends as well as the usual orange juice, and use paper cups to save dish washing. You can serve notice then that breakfast will be on the table in half an hour. Last one down is a rotten egg!

A handsome breakfast table centerpiece of fresh and dried fruits gives a party air and a topic for conversation while you and your daughter serve the main dishes. These may be served from the kitchen or, appliances permitting, prepared at the table.

Scrambled eggs, link sausages and pancakes will do wonders toward restoring youthful vitality. For a change, melt butter in the pancake syrup. Or give a choice of pancake toppings such as brown sugar mixed with cinnamon, strawberry preserves and honey butter.

Don't be surprised if the whole group goes back to the bedroom after breakfast to resume games and giggling—conclusive proof that the party is a smashing success.

## Class Party

**For twelve- to fourteen-year-olds.** A class party is an easy way for your child to try his wings in a mixed group. Since the boys and girls all know each other well, breaking the ice should be no problem.

At this age, bought party invitations are considered more sophisticated and hence far more desirable than homemade ones. Invite the guests for 7:30 P.M. and wave them right outdoors where nibble foods and iced soft drinks are waiting and the phonograph is playing dance music.

As soon as everyone has arrived, get the party going by pinning on each guest's back the name of a movie, television or sport celebrity. It's up to each one to find out who he is by asking questions that can be answered yes or no.

Before this game begins to pall, the co-hostesses should choose partners

**148**

and start a multiplication dance. This requires someone on duty at the phonograph to stop and start the "multiplications." When the music stops, the first four dancers separate and each chooses a new partner. The music starts again and they dance until it stops . . . and so on until everyone is dancing.

What do you do if there are more girls than boys? Or if a few of the boys won't dance at all? Alternate dancing with games that involve everyone.

**Refreshments.** By 9:30 you will have a bunch of hungry teen-agers on your hands so be ready with a buffet table laden with the makings for hearty hero sandwiches, hot or cold. For these, you will want the freshest Italian bread you can buy, sliced lengthwise and then into serving portions. Depending on size, each loaf will make three or four heroes.

For cold heroes, pile platters with a variety of sliced cheese and meat. Follow with plates of sliced tomatoes, dill pickles and onions. Add catsup, mustard and Worcestershire sauce. A hero worshipper knows no limits.

For hot heroes, have a chafing dish of meat balls in tomato sauce. Pass bottled soft drinks to go with the heroes or fruit punch in paper cups.

**Climax the party** by bringing out a cake—an impressive creation frosted in the school colors. If you feel extravagant, order it from a bakery. Otherwise you can have fun making it at home. If you do, here's an easy way to make a whopper—which you'll need for some thirty teen-agers. Use four packages of cake mix and bake each cake separately in a 9x13x2-inch pan. Place these cakes end to end on a five-foot long, twelve-inch wide plank that has been covered with colored foil. Frost top and sides of cake with one school color. Write class year on top with second color. Ask the class president to serve it. *(All special parties by Jean MacGregor Whelan)*

# THE ADVENTURE OF OUTDOOR LIVING

*THE OUTDOORS, THROUGHOUT THE YEAR, provides a magnificent parade of miracles for those who can open their eyes, ears, and hearts to them. Children, in particular, feel the magic of a plushy bed of moss and walk gently where the fairies play at night. They marvel at the flickering dance of sun and shadow on summer streams and the diamond necklaces that cluster there when winter comes. The white flash of a rabbit's tail as he leaps for cover, the disapproving harrumph of a bull-frog: all are signals to a child that the world is endlessly filled with precious wonders. He watches, listens, feels, thinks—and remembers.—Catherine S. Chilman, Ph.D.*

# OUTDOOR PLAY

*Outdoor play offers a whole set of values that indoor play can rarely touch: exploring the world of rocks, water and earth; taking mild risks by climbing high on a ladder or jungle gym; roaming in groups in search of adventure; playing on teams against tough opponents; balancing on a swiftly moving scooter or bike; feeling a new sense of power as muscles and skills develop in the open air. Ideally, this gives a child a chance to experiment with a broad range of activities at every age level, and to advance from one kind of play to the next as he grows and develops.*

**The beginning years, 1-3:** As they graduate from crawler to toddler, children like to push their carriage, pull wheel toys, ride on low vehicles, and pick up stones, twigs, shells. Between 2 and 3 they need steps, blocks and planks for large muscle activity; and sand, pebbles and water for small muscle play.

Playthings: Pull toys, riding toys (play tractor, etc.), stick horse, rocking horse, horse on wheels, small wagon, low slide, low swing, wading pool with floating toys, large outdoor blocks, small wheelbarrow, parallel bars, packing cases, play house, sandbox, sand pail with shovel, molds and sieves.

**Early childhood, 3-6:** Between 2 and 3, the child is a runabout; between 4 and 5, he becomes an acrobat. Boys and girls alike constantly test their agility, nerve and growing strength by balancing on boards, climbing on packing cases or jungle gyms, speeding along on scooter skates. Beach and water play are enjoyed by all.

Playthings: Larger wagon, larger wheelbarrow, velocipede, tricycle, clown punching bag, pedal fire truck, tractor bike, pedal racing car, shoo-

**152**

fly, packing case, small sled, medium high slide, adjustable swing, child-size play house, hoop, roller skates, skipping rope, climbing rope, rope ladder, see-saw, tent, scooter, fort, toy boats, double-runner ice skates, shuffle board, beach animals, beach ball.

**Middle childhood, 6-9:** Sixes like nothing better than group games with a maximum of action and talk, and a minimum of rules and team-work: tag, hide-and-seek, London bridge, cops and robbers. In the next two years, playing "catch" becomes playing ball; and by eight or nine, baseball has taken firm hold of boys, while girls bounce balls, play jump rope, hopscotch and engage in outdoor household play. Both sexes enjoy vigorous pursuits such as bike-riding, roller skating, water sports and treasure hunts.

**Playthings:** Rubber horseshoe set, croquet set, kites, Car-gobike, bicycle with training wheels, tether ball set, stilts, pogo stick, bongo board, jumping shoes, electric Stutz Bearcat, tops, marbles, roller skates, punching bag, baseball equipment, basketball and goal, sled, amphibious car, toy boats of all kinds, hydroplane, inflated raft, beach mattress, floating ring toss game, water ball, floating volley ball game, cabana, picnic table and benches, log cabin.

**Later childhood, 9-12:** Boys and girls have now passed the running and jumping stage and are ready for the more demanding skills of standard sports—not only the physical skills, but teamwork, fair play, competition and acquaintance with the finer points of the games. They need not only good equipment but good instruction, regular practice, and the opportunity to try different sports until they find their own. Yet team sports are not the only sports children enjoy. Many children derive just as much benefit and fun from hiking, camping, sailing, bike trips, folk dancing, skiing—either alone or with others.

**Playthings:** Full-size bike, archery set, hockey equipment, deck tennis, badminton set, punching bag, outdoor gym bar, soccer ball, volley ball, tennis racquet, batting practice machine, full-size basketball, football, football outfit, golf clubs, practice golf range, trampoline, fencing set, bobsled, toboggan, ice skates, skis, figure skates, sand bowling game, swim fins, underwater mask, floating basketball game, floating volley ball game, water walker, inflated boat, surf lung, sleeping bag, pup tent, camping supplies, tree house.—*Robert M. Goldenson, Ph.D.*

# MEANWHILE....
# BACK IN
# THE YARD

*A backyard playground will often prove the reason "why children stay at home." Given a few pieces of well-chosen apparatus, the backyard can be a place for fun, safety, and physical development.*

Among the most widely used backyard play equipment are a sandbox, swing, seesaw, horizontal bar, flying rings and slide. All of these, with the possible exception of the slide, may be built satisfactorily at home. Or any of them may be purchased through a local sporting goods dealer or department store.

If the apparatus is made at home, be sure to get as durable a wood as possible. It is a good idea to paint the woodwork that will go into the ground with creosote to keep out moisture. Two coats of paint in an attractive color are suggested for all woodwork above the ground. When pipe is called for, use galvanized pipe, unless the iron will be painted.

All the apparatus should be strongly made and securely installed. Joints should be well bolted, and posts should be set in concrete. Frequent inspection and the greasing of movable parts will insure greatest service.

**The Sandbox.** Sand play has endless possibilities—from the sifting and "cooking" the preschoolers do, to the elaborate tunnel and castle construction of the big ones, not excluding grownups! (Sand rules must be definite; no throwing, no dumping on a playmate's head, no carting to other parts of the yard.)

Building an adequate sandbox is so simple that no child need be denied it. A box 4' x 6' and 1' high is large enough for two, three, or even more children. A shelf built at either end of the box will serve as a seat and a "counter" for displaying sand pies. Material: two pieces 2" x 12" x 6', two pieces 2" x 12" x 4' and for shelves, two pieces 2" x 10" x 4'; one pound #16 common nails. Add a load of clean sand.

**154**

The box may be made with a hinged cover, the legs of which support it when it is open. This cover keeps the sand dry during storms and when the children are not at play in the box it makes a good worktable.

Small garden tools, pails, shovels, tin molds and a large iron spoon should be provided. A dozen blocks about 8 inches long, cut from a piece of 2 x 4, are a valuable addition, being useful for walls and roofs of buildings, fences, and so forth. Dampen the sand occasionally and keep bottles and other articles of glass out of it.

In choosing the location for the box, take advantage of any natural shade. If this is not available, a canvas canopy may be built over the box at a small additional expense. An old army pup tent will be found to be the right size for a shelter of this kind.

**The Swing.** Safety should be the first consideration in the construction of a swing. Iron pipe is preferable for the framework, but with care a safe and substantial frame may be built of wood, well braced. Ten feet is a good height for the frame, which will be more secure if set in concrete. The seat should be 20 inches from the ground.

Chain is superior to rope for hanging the swing. Hangers should be of roller or ball-bearing type to avoid wear. For small children a swing of the chair type is preferable.

Perhaps the inside of the garage may disclose old tires. A tire suspended from a tree by means of a rope or chain makes a very good improvised swing.

**The Horizontal Bar.** Probably no playground equipment contributes so materially toward the child's physical development as the horizontal bar. Hanging by the arms and "chinning" are ideal for developing good posture. The material is as follows: 2 pieces 4″ x 4″ x 12′ white pine for uprights to support the bar, 4 pieces 2″ x 4″ x 8′ white pine for braces, 1 piece 1½″ pipe 5′ long for the bar. In order to keep the bar from turning, a hole should be bored and the bar set with a bolt.

**The Flying Rings.** These not only strengthen the muscles, but they satisfy the desire of every child to do "stunts." The following are the materials and measurements suggested by the National Recreation Association for making the flying rings: 2 pieces of wood 4″ x 4″ x 14′, 4 pieces of wood 2″ x 4″ x 8′, 1 piece of wood 4″ x 4″ x 6″, 2 metal chains and rings and fastenings. Twelve inches of soft shavings, sand, or sawdust should be kept under the rings and horizontal bar.

**155**

**Handball.** The side of the garage may be used as a backstop for a hand-ball court, or a place to which to attach a basketball goal or golf-driving net. Handball is a game which father and son may play together. The court may be of any size, but in general the following proportions should be followed: the wall space used should be four-fifths as high as it is wide and the court should be two and a half times as long as the wall is high. Twenty feet long and 10 feet wide with a wall 8 feet high are good proportions. A service line divides the court midway between the wall and the back line.

The game is played on the same principle as tennis, the hand taking the place of a racquet and the ball being driven against the wall. A tennis ball or any similar rubber ball may be used.

The driving net serves as first aid to aspiring golfers, either junior or senior. A piece of canvas about 12 feet wide is hung from the edge of the garage roof to the ground. The ball should be driven from a point directly in front of the net and not more than 10 feet away. There is no rebound, as the net is loose at the bottom.

**Portable Wading Pool.** The wading pool is made of waterproof canvas 8 feet square, with brass eyelets every 12 inches. The frame is made of three-quarter inch galvanized iron pipe 6 feet square so as to allow a depth of about 10 inches when set up.

The iron pipe supports with their bases measure 12 inches from the ground. The framework of pipe is made up of sections which may be screwed into elbows, thus making it easy to put up and take down. Any local plumber or hardware store can supply you with the pipe cut to the lengths you desire. The canvas is hung on hooks made to hang on rings which slide over the pipe. The garden hose fitted with a shower nozzle and hung over the pool will afford the means for an open-air shower bath.

A great variety of portable pools can now also be purchased ready to set up and fill.

**Other Suggestions for the Backyard.** A larger yard offers many more possibilities for home play equipment. An open space could be reserved for games, varying with the season and the interests of the children. Quoits are enjoyed by grownups—particularly fathers—as well as by the youngsters. Sometimes the space might be used for croquet. Or a miniature golf course could be laid out, with tin cans sunk in the ground for holes.

For outdoor play, get some blocks which are large and hollow, in proportioned units. The largest ones require two to lift them, calling for co-operative action and developing the large body muscles. Or provide an

**156**

assortment of crates and empty boxes, for "building" is as essential to children as to the classic beaver. Orange crates make excellent material and can so easily be converted into chairs, bookcases, tables, doll beds, or whatnot. The child should be allowed to build as much as he can unaided.

Other suggestions for backyard equipment are an archery target, dollhouse, a house (or zoo!) for animal pets, workbench for the boys or an outdoor fireplace.

**A play house** is always a good bet for hours or days of fun in the back yard. Maybe you'll want to buy a play tent, or can get some packing boxes large enough for house building. Otherwise, a tarpaulin or an old blanket or bedspread draped over a clothesline, or anchored to a fence, makes a fine place for housekeeping or office or hide-out headquarters. If the older children have a very definite idea on running their establishment, the younger ones may need a separate place of their own, and usually don't mind if it's less pretentious.

With a tarpaulin floor, this outdoor tent-house will probably be initiated with a first sleep-out adventure for the older children. On first try, they may come trailing in with their flashlights and blankets around eleven or twelve o'clock, unable to sleep because of mosquitoes or "some queer little noise"— so keep a night-light on to welcome them back to bed—just in case.

# NATURE PLAY IS
# NATURAL PLAY

*Nature play gives children a sense of belonging to a real and not merely man-made world. Raising flowers or vegetables or pets makes them realize that all live things need to be tended and cared for if they are to grow and flourish. Without realizing it, they will learn basic science lessons about nutrition, soil chemistry, sunlight and the mystery of growth. Nature play can begin extremely early and, if properly encouraged, will never be outgrown.*

**157**

# Nature Study at all Ages

**The beginning years, 1-3:**  In the first year of life children love to cuddle soft, floppy stuffed animals, even though they do not know what they represent. In the second year they may be ready to play with a dog—large, gentle animals are best—but must be taught not to be too rough. (Cats are generally too unpredictable.) Between two and three, they still like to take favorite stuffed animals to bed and babble to them for companionship or security. This is the time to visit a pet shop and feed squirrels in the park—and to hear stories about pigs, bears and other animals they have seen in books or in reality.

**Playthings:**  Stuffed animals, wooden animal cut-outs, small farm animals, animals on wheels (seal, bear, etc.), barking bull dogs, floating ducks.

**Early childhood, 3-6:**  Threes like nothing better than to observe and feed small animals (guinea pigs can take more handling than chicks, mice, kittens or canaries). They also enjoy watching the growth of narcissus bulbs, radishes or lima beans, and will gradually learn about the cycle of life and the need for food and water. Fours and Fives are budding naturalists who collect caterpillars, worms and insects. They may also start a collection of rocks, wild flowers or leaves. Now is the time to take them to a zoo and to different kinds of farms, and to tell them about harvests, barns, silos, root cellars, and the care of live-stock.

**Playthings:**  Noah's Ark, cat family, poodle family, horse van, window garden, bird-feeding station, Doxie-on-Tour, animal picture book.

**Middle childhood, 6-9:**  Nature interests develop rapidly in this period, since children can now begin to understand the fertilization and pollination of plants and basic facts about the care, feeding and reproduction of animals. But they must have a chance to observe things for themselves, not simply read about them (bush beans and white mice are probably best for this purpose). Equally fascinating are the life cycle of caterpillars and butterflies; the development of a tadpole into a frog; the day-by-day observation of parent birds building a nest and tending their young; the antics of a grasshopper and katydid in a terrarium; and the behavior of snails, turtles and fish in an aquarium. This is the time, too, to suggest nature handicrafts: making bird houses, pine cone figurines, birch bark boxes, acorn beads.

Playthings: Seed set, ant farm, indoor rock garden or desert garden, mineral kit, window greenhouse, aquarium, terrarium, goldfish tank, picnic equipment, wildlife identification books.

Later childhood, 9-12: The peak period for nature study and nature lore: why lichen are found only on one side of a tree, how squirrels help to replenish our forests. All children should have an opportunity to wander in the woods; make camping trips with parents or other leaders; visit a fish hatchery, plant nursery, dairy farm and a planetarium if available. The unorganized collections of earlier years may now develop into full-blown nature hobbies if you encourage them to keep scrapbooks, build shelves and exhibit cases, and if you are on the lookout for local specialists and organizations that will help them to develop their interests.

Playthings: Tropical fish tank, fossil lab, astronomy kit, field glasses, exhibit cases, scrapbooks, camping equipment, birdwatching kit, window or lean-to greenhouse.—*Robert M. Goldenson, Ph.D.*

# Nature Projects

**Hikes and Trips.** Parents and children will enjoy hikes or trips to the parks, country or beach. At other times trips may be made about the city to industries where nature products are used—tanneries and canneries, for example. Natural history museums, zoos, jewelers' windows, florists, fruit and vegetable shops, pet stores and meat markets all provide sources for nature study, and may yield "treasures." Buildings and fences and streets are full of metals and minerals for study. The sky in the daytime is often all too full of weather, and on clear nights boasts myriads of stars.

**Gardens.** Make gardens. They may necessarily be in a dish or a box, but plant them somewhere. Make a record of what you do and what happens and when. Make simple experiments with seed germination, and with the effect of light and gravity on plants, and study soils and flower arrangement. Deal with living things all you can. Watch them closely.

**Museums.** Children may easily have their own museums by collecting specimens of all kinds. For this:

**159**

Make a collection of the kinds of sea life and shells you find at the shore. Tell what each piece is.

Collect rocks and minerals. Place the name on each piece.

Make an aquarium and fill it with things you find in a pond. Be sure to feed and care for the tadpoles, turtles or salamanders that you put in it.

What old hornets' nests or wasps' nests can you find?

Caterpillars will be spinning their cocoons. Watch one as it is spinning and keep the cocoon. Collect cocoons.

Make a chart of seeds or collect them in bottles. Can you tell how they are scattered?

Make an insect cage and collect grasshoppers and other insects. Be sure to feed them.

Make a collection of kinds of woods.

**Nature Notebooks.** The "treasures" of a nature adventure may be put in various forms in a notebook by each child, or a large book can be made by several children. Accounts of hikes, sketches, weather charts, star stories, diaries of gardens, tales of a caterpillar spinning a cocoon, and ink, spatter or blueprints of leaves or flowers may be included.

Use nature motifs on metal and wood craft and in batik and wood blocks. Dye with native dyes where you can.

**Making Spatter Prints.** Obtain an old toothbrush, a 4″ x 4″ square of screen (not rusty) and water color paint (showcard or cheap powder water paints). Lay a pressed and dainty spray of leaves, a fern or a flower on a white or colored paper. Dip the brush in the paint. Wipe off as much as you can on the inside of the paint cup. Then, holding the screen about two inches above the leaf or flower, rub the toothbrush back and forth over the screen. Minute drops will fall, leaving the leaf in silhouette when it is removed. Caution: do not use too much paint on your brush. It should not fill the holes on the screen. Pins stuck vertically through the leaf will hold parts not perfectly pressed close to the paper. Wait until the paint dries before removing the leaf, which may be used again. Mount with name of specimen, date, and where found.

**Making Ink Prints.** With the block print ink roller and printer's ink, one may fingerprint the leaves. Roll over the vein side of a leaf with prominent veins with the roller, as you would in inking a linoleum block. Place the inked leaf vein side down on a clean piece of paper. Over it place a scrap

**160**

of newspaper. Hold paper and leaf firm with one hand, and with the fingers of the other rub over all parts of the leaf evenly. Remove newspaper and leaf, and you will find the outline of the leaf and its venation.

Leaves may be pressed on a rubber stamp ink pad and then be pressed on paper, as in the ink print. In this way prints can be made en route on a hike. Sketch and color from life the trees, flowers, birds you see in the field. Do not copy from a book or pictures.

## Nature Games

Games always prove a fascinating activity, particularly on hikes.

**Curio Collector.** To be played with a group while walking through the forest. When the curio is named the group scatters to find it. The one to discover it first gives a call and the others gather round. If she is successful the next hunt starts. The following may be selected as curios to be sought: a humpbacked tree, a tree struck by lightning, a tree with last year's cat-kins, a tree with scale insects on it, a tree infected with galls, a tree with branches on one side, last year's fruit stem, a tree that has a stone in the center of the fruit, a deciduous tree that has cones, an evergreen tree that does not have cones, a red maple that has had fruit, a red maple that has not had fruit, a twig that took ten years to grow an inch, a twig that grew ten inches in a year, a twig that grew thirty-six inches or more in a year, a sumac bush five years old, a rock with a quartz vein, a tree with a rock callus where a woodpecker has been feeding, a woodpecker's home, the work of the sapsucker, a feldspar crystal, enough pine needles to fill a thimble, fruit of the ash tree, a mud dauber's nest, a leaf miner's home, nuts gnawed by a squirrel, a robin's nest, an animal's footprint.

**Holding the Front.** Hikers travel in single file. The file occasionally is halted and the first person in the file is asked to identify a tree or plant by the side of the road or some distance ahead. If she fails she is sent to the rear of the line and the second becomes the first and is asked the next question. The person able to answer the most questions and remain at the front for the greatest period of time wins the game.

**Nature Sounds.** The group is given five minutes to see who can make the longest list of things heard in the woods during that time. It may be a crow, a cow or a rooster in the distance; or a raindrop, the rustling leaves of an oak or the swish of a pine; the tapping of a woodpecker.

**Prove It.**   Players sit in a circle. The one starting the game says: "From where I am, I can see a gray birch." The next one says: "From where I am, I can see a gray birch and a black cherry." The next player repeats all that the previous players have said, in exactly the same order, and adds another tree or bird. It may be limited to what is seen on one gray birch tree. If anyone doubts the statement, she may challenge the speaker. Anyone caught in a mistake drops out of the game.

**Roadside Cribbage.**   This game makes the miles roll by unnoticed on a hike and it may be played by two or thirty-two girls.

The group decides what things are to be looked for: kinds of birds, flowers, trees, wild animals, snakes, rabbits, bird or animal tracks.

Each player then gathers twenty-one counters, pebbles, seeds or nuts. Whenever she sees any of the objects specified she yells "peg," and throws away a counter. The girl who first "pegs" all of her counters wins. The patrol leader should see that during the game no one leaves the trail or road.

This game may be played on a city walk by "pegging" specified makes of automobiles, persons in uniform, horses, dogs and cats. It may also be played at the seashore where boats, rare shells, leaping fish, crabs or sea plants may be looked for. *—from "88 Successful Play Activities," a publication of National Recreation Association*

# THE
# PLEASURE
# OF PICNICS

*When picnics are a part of family life, wonderful things happen. For a picnic is a state of mind, and if a happy, sharing way of living can start in childhood, perhaps it can carry over into later years when life is not always a picnic.—Helen Hermann*

**162**

# Picnic Planner

The hamburgers are grilled to a turn, the buns toasted to a T and the family in a gay picnic mood. But where, oh where, is the catsup? Back home on the kitchen shelf.

A familiar story? It needn't be if you use the following picnic check list when planning a picnic and just before setting out. You may not need all the items listed, and there may be others you will want to take, but this will jog your memory on the countdown.

### 3. Basic Supplies
Hamper or basket
Insulated carriers
Vacuum bottles or picnic jugs to keep cold things cold and hot things hot
Aluminum foil, wax paper, saran
Paper plates, cups, napkins
Eating utensils
Can-and-bottle opener
Table covering, if desired
Paper towels for cleaning up

### 2. Cooking Equipment
Portable grill
Lighter fluid and matches
Newspaper to help start fire
Coffeepot
Skillet and soup kettle
Old cookie sheet to hold foods set by the fire to warm
Long-handled grill for broiling
Long-handled fork, spoon, tongs
Meat turner
Cutting and paring knives
Potholder or asbestos mitts
Steel wool to scour grill, etc.

### 1. Food Accompaniments, Comforts & Conveniences
Salt and pepper
Catsup, mustard, relishes
Worcestershire sauce
Sugar and cream for coffee
Drinking water if you are not sure of a supply at the picnic site
Canned or bottled beverages

Marshmallows to toast over the embers
Blanket to sit on or for the baby's nap
Camera and film
Portable radio
Playthings for the children
Reading material for adults
First-aid kit
Sunglasses
Sweaters, in case it gets cool
Soap and washcloths
Insect repellant; suntan oil
Big pail for carrying water

## Summer Cookouts, Family Style

There's nothing new about cookouts. They've been going on for centuries. What is new is the ease with which Americans are cooking mouth-watering meals outdoors—thanks to modern equipment, inexpensive serving aids and the many new convenience foods available. Now, almost any family can have the fun and excitement of eating in the open air whenever the spirit—or the weather—moves them.

What makes a successful family cookout? One family we know says organization comes first, followed closely by cooperation and enthusiasm. Every member has a job to do according to age and skill. Mother plans and the rest of the family cheerfully follow through on their assigned tasks. Usually father takes over the cooking unit and the children fetch and carry from the kitchen to back yard or car. And all join in the inevitable cleaning up after the last delectable tidbit is gone.

**Here are a few simple rules** to follow when planning a cookout, whether it's a family outing or an informal gathering of family and friends.

**1. Keep the menu simple,** within your known capabilities and suited to the cooking facilities at hand.

Three or four dishes with the usual nibble accompaniments are enough for most cookouts, but there must be plenty of each. As for choice of food, be sure it appeals to both children and adults. Despite the rage for barbecued ribs, charcoal broiled steaks and chicken-in-a-basket, children invariably prefer grilled frankfurters and hamburgers.

**164**

That doesn't mean that family cookouts need be stereotyped; there are many different ways of preparing and serving these stand-bys. Franks can be split and stuffed with cheese, chopped onion or pickle relish. They can be topped with chili con carne, chili sauce or sauerkraut. Hamburgers are delicious when made into flat patties, broiled and then stuffed sandwich-fashion with myriad ingredients ranging literally from soup to nuts. With these grilled meats go such favorites as baked beans, roasting ears of corn, baked-in-foil potatoes, rice, potato salad, tossed greens and coleslaw.

When it comes to planning desserts for a cookout, the simpler the better. Good choices are fresh fruits with a variety of cheeses, chilled watermelon, cookies.

Of course, all foods selected should be portable and easy to serve. Many condiments now come in special containers for cookouts and there are spill-proof, unbreakable dispensers for catsup, mustard, and so forth.

**2. Know your cooking unit** and have the necessary supplementary equipment at hand.

In addition to the cooking unit, fuel and starter fluid, there should be a work table at a comfortable height with a cutting board, a sprinkler bottle for dousing unruly flames, both canvas and asbestos gloves, potholders, at least one hinged broiler, salts and peppers, and skewers for foods to be cooked en brochette. Also needed are such working tools as tongs and a basting brush, long-handled forks and spoons, sharp knives, and pliers if a spit is being used. A long-handled wire popcorn popper comes in handy for heating potato chips and similar foods. A chef's hat for father, though not essential, does give a crown of authority.

**3. Make clean-up chores easy.** Grease grills to prevent sticking. When cooking is finished, and while the grill is still hot, brush or steel wool off all food particles so the grill will be ready for the next cookout. Replace cooking utensils with heavy aluminum foil wherever practical. Use expendable paper cups, plates, serving platters, napkins and tablecloths. Have a suitable container handy to collect the garbage and let each one do his own K.P.

## 3 FAVORITE FAMILY COOKOUT MENUS

### For A Back Yard Grill
Tote'm Burgers on Toasted Buns
Grilled Mushrooms and Tomato Halves

**165**

Macaroni Salad           Potato Chips
Individual Frozen Fruit Pies
Milk or Buttermilk           Iced Tea

**For A Patio Hibachi**
Shrimp Kebabs with Lemon BBQ Sauce
Hot 'n' Crisp Frozen French Fries
Salad Bowl           Buttered Rolls
Gingerbread, Whipped Cream Topping
Fruit Punch or Soft Drinks           Iced Coffee

**For A Fancy Barbecue**
Barbecued Chicken or Turkey
Cranberry Sauce           Assorted Relishes
Roasting Ears of Corn           Garlic Bread
"Silver-plated" Sweet Potatoes Hawaiian
Ice Cream Sandwiches (in dry ice)
Milk           Coffee

—*Blanche M. Stover*

# A Family Beach Bake

Want to beat the heat and crowds next summer? Then, for your next picnic, head your boat for a little known, but lovely, beach where you can cook out Indian-style. All you really need is a sandy beach and food.

When the boat reaches shore, unload the food and cooking paraphernalia—a bag of charcoal, two pieces of three by five-foot wire mesh, a pair of tongs and a cooking fork. (This leaves the boat free for fishing, water skiing or just cruising.) Next step is to choose a cookout spot—if on a salt water beach, well above the high tide mark. Then the youngsters start their search for driftwood and kindling for the bake pit.

While the older children are out a-gathering, Dad digs a trench in the sand—four feet long, two feet wide and one foot deep. Then his helper lines it with paper and kindling. Over this go one sheet of wire mesh, two large pieces of driftwood to hold it in place and charcoal. This is covered with a second sheet of mesh, held in place with sticks driven into the sand, to make the cooking area.

After the fire has been kindled and the coals have burned down to white heat, the foods to be baked are arranged on top of the wire mesh. The potatoes go on first, followed by chidkens, corn, crabs and lobsters. If the fire is too hot in the center, foods can be moved to the outer edges.

Low tables, easily transported by boat, make eating on the beach a comfortable adventure. (Some families use a folding bed board set on rocks for a table.) Chilled soft drinks and fruit juices quench thirst.

A beach bake is a family adventure all can enjoy. While the coals are burning down, the beach holds a thousand secrets of interest to children. There are shells to collect, crabs to unearth and clams to dig along the seashore. There are stones to upturn, frogs to catch and flowers to discover around inlets and coves of lakes and rivers.

All too soon it's time to board the boat for home, but not without burning all waste and burying the fire with sand, so the welcome mat is always out for boaters.—*Blanche M. Stover*

# A Co-op Cookout Can Be a Real Blockbuster

The big event of the summer for the youngsters on our street is our annual Block Party. On that glorious day all parents join in giving a big, bang-up cookout for the younger set. Every child cherishes throughout the year memories of the popcorn and pink lemonade, the races and prizes, the carnival stunts, peanut hunt and marshmallow roast. They remember the fun of eating supper at picnic tables set up in the street while their daddies cook hot dogs on charcoal grills and their mothers serve mounds of baked beans and potato salad.

And each year they look forward to the entertainment they put on themselves, perhaps a musical program featuring everything from a competent twelve-year-old flutist to a three-year-old would-be Krupa solemnly beating a dish pan. Or it may be a skit they have written and rehearsed in secret, played in outlandish costumes they have made themselves. Finally, there's the fun of sitting on the grass singing together "Knick-knack Paddywhack" and "John Brown's Baby" until another block party becomes a happy memory.

If you and your neighbors have never given a party like this, why not do it this summer? There's nothing like working and playing together to deepen the feeling of neighborliness and friendship, and there's no better way to give your children a happy, fun-packed day for so little money.

Spark the affair about three weeks in advance by asking all interested parents to a planning session at your house. There are a number of decisions to make, committees to be set up and plans to discuss.

**Where will you have the party?** If you live on a quiet suburban street you may get permission from village officials to close your block to

**167**

traffic during the party. Otherwise, the family with the biggest yard might offer their place for the festivities. Or you might arrange to hold the party on the picnic ground of a nearby park, or the playing field of a public school.

**When will you have the party?** It's a good idea to choose a Saturday, so that, in case of rain, the party can be postponed to the next day. Which Saturday will depend, of course, on when most of your neighbors will be able to participate.

**What kind of party do you want?** This depends on the ages of the youngsters and on how ambitious you are. The children on our block range in age from three to fourteen, with most of them under seven. If you have fewer young children and more teen-agers, a softball game would be more appropriate than potato races and peanut hunts. We like to have supper together but your group may prefer to concentrate on an afternoon of fun with ice cream and soda pop for refreshments.

**How much do you want to spend?** Our party, including supper, costs $1 per person. (Dividing the cost per family leaves small families paying more than their share.) In order to serve supper on this small outlay we ask each family to donate some of the food: a salad, a casserole or some cupcakes. Your group may prefer to pay more and have all the food purchased.

**Who will take charge of what?** We divide the responsibility by choosing a general chairman, a finance chairman, a fun chairman, a food chairman and a clean-up chairman as well as two contest officials. These worthies are not supposed to do all the work. In fact, the success of the party depends upon giving every parent a chance to contribute some time and effort. Here's what the general chairman and his committee do, for example.

1. Get permission to close the street to traffic or make arrangements to hold the party elsewhere.

2. Borrow grills, picnic tables and chairs or benches; arrange to get them to the party site.

3. Buy charcoal for the portable grills and solicit fathers to man them.

4. Arrange for music. If you are lucky enough to have a hi-fi buff on

**168**

the block, he can hook up a loud-speaker to a phonograph in the house nearest the party tables. If the party is held elsewhere, a portable phonograph will do well.

5. Plan for lighting and decorating the party area with balloons, crepe paper and bunting. Strings of Christmas lights are colorful and add to the party feeling.

## Fun and Games

1. Plan the entertainment and games. Very young children like a story-teller, a wading pool or simple games such as a peanut hunt. Older children prefer relay races, horseshoe pitching, bean bag throwing (paint a clown's face, mouth open, on a piece of wood or masonite and cut a hole in the mouth to catch the bean bag).

2. Get prizes for races and other competitive events. Some of these may be bought and some donated by families who have surplus games or toys. Small, individually-wrapped candies or sticks of gum are a good choice. Remember that children love to get prizes whether they win or not—so have a large supply on hand. We make medals from gold or silver construction paper to pin on the chest of a winner; add gold stars for further special achievement.

3. Have group singing.

4. Lay out the course and plan races. Our gang enjoys tricycle and bicycle races, roller skate crazy races (backward, knock-kneed, pigeon-toed) and wheelbarrow races.

5. Figure out how to allow for differences in age and speed of the youngsters. We do this in several ways. We have junior and senior races, the first for children under seven and the second for those seven or older. Sometimes we work out handicaps for the older or bigger children, starting at various distances behind the official starting line.

### Block Party Cookout Supper
Frankfurters and Rolls
Mustard, Piccalilli, Catsup
Lima Bean Casserole
Hot Sauerkraut
Potato Salad          Macaroni Salad
Tossed Green Salad
Coleslaw          Dill Pickles
Chocolate and Coconut Cupcakes
Pink Lemonade     Milk     Hot Coffee
—*Jean MacGregor Whelan*

# Picnic Games

**Relay Races.** The following relay races are suitable for teams of 5 to 15 persons. Usually the players stand in single file, the first in each team toeing the starting line. There may be several parallel lines of equal numbers of players, each first player toeing the line.

**Peanut Pass.** The teams stand in two lines (or in sets of two lines) facing each other. Chairs are placed at both ends of the lines, with 12 peanuts on the chair at the head of each line. Each player weaves his fingers into the fingers of his neighbors. They must not unclasp hands throughout the game. At a signal the leader picks up the peanuts, one at a time, and passes them down the lines as rapidly as possible, the last player putting them on the chair beside him. If a peanut is dropped it must be picked up without any unclasping of hands. The team which passes all its peanuts down and back wins the relay.

The game may be played with clothespins, small stones, or sticks.

**Necktie Relay.** The players stand in single file with the same number of players in each line. The first player in each of the lines is given a necktie or a large cotton handkerchief. When the whistle is blown, he turns and ties the necktie or handkerchief around the neck of the player behind. As soon as the bow is tied, the second player unties it, turns, and ties it on the third player. The line that first passes the necktie or handkerchief down to the last player in this manner wins the game. A coat may be put on, buttoned, unbuttoned, and passed on in the same way.

**Bundle Relay.** The first player in each line is given a ball or cord or tape. When the signal is given, he passes it to his neighbor but holds the end. The ball is passed from player to player, unrolling as it goes. When it arrives at the lower end it is passed up the line behind the backs of the players until it reaches the first player again. The team that first wraps itself into a bundle is the winner. The sequel to the race consists in untying the bundle by passing the ball back and winding it as it goes.

**Over and Under.** The first player in each team is given a bean bag, ball, potato, or other object. When the whistle blows he passes this object over

**170**

his head to the second player, who passes it between his knees to the third, who hands it over his head to the fourth. Thus the object goes alternately overhead and between knees to the last player, who runs to the head of the line and starts it back over his head. The game proceeds until a line has regained its original order, with the first player at the head again. The line finishing first wins the race.

**Fetch and Carry.**   The first and second players in each team join hands. When the whistle blows they run to the goal line. The first remains there while the second hurries back and joins hands with the third player. These two run to the goal line, and the second player remains while the third returns for the fourth. The team that first transfers all its members to the goal line wins the race.

**Around and Down.**   The players form in two or more teams, and each team sits down in a compact group, the players having their backs together and their legs extended. When the whistle blows, each first player rises, runs around his own team, and sits down. As soon as he is seated the second player must be up and running, and so on. The race is won by the team all of whose members have run around and sat down first.

**Follow Through.**   The players in each line stand with legs apart. At the signal the last player begins to crawl through the "tunnel" to the head of the line. As soon as he has started the next player follows. The first line whose members have all crawled through wins the race.

**Go and Go Back.**   This relay race is especially good for picnic programs because it is fun to watch. Each team need have only two or three members. The players stand at the base line. When the whistle is blown each first player runs toward the goal line until it is blown again. Then he must turn, if he has not reached the goal, and run back toward the base line. Each time the whistle sounds the runners change their direction. The race may finish at the goal line or at the base line. If it ends at the goal, the player must dash back to touch off the next player in his line.

**Alphabet Scramble.**   The players stand in relay formation. A complete set of alphabet cards is laid on a chair about 10 feet away from each

**171**

team. A baseline is drawn about the same distance back of the row of chairs. When the leader announces a word the first few players in each team—as many as there are letters in the word—hurry forward to the chairs, select the needed letters, carry them on to the baseline, and stand there holding them up, arranging themselves in the proper order as rapidly as possible. The team finishing its word first is the winner. Then these players go back promptly to their own lines, taking their places at the rear so that the next players may take the next word announced.—*from The Handbook for Recreation, a publication of the U.S. Children's Bureau*

# Group Picnics

**Large Groups.**   The chief aim of a picnic is to get people together informally and to give them a good time. Remember to plan an abundance of music and games, because both these activities encourage friendliness and are fun.

Prepare equipment for simple games and contests for the early arrivals while the other people are assembling. Quoit games, croquet-ball bowling, and other games of this sort are useful. Guessing contests are popular, such as guessing the number of seeds in a watermelon on display, the weight of a cake or a home-made loaf of bread, or the number of stitches in a seam. If baseball bats and balls are supplied, a game probably will go on during most of the day, in addition to any special game that may be arranged for the afternoon; if the space for baseball is limited, an indoor ball (14-inch) or a playground ball (12-inch) may be used instead of a regulation baseball. The smaller children may be taken at once to the sandbox, swings, and other apparatus specially arranged for them.

**Small Groups.**   In contrast to big community picnics, a small club group often gets together for an outdoor dinner, or the family packs a basket and goes somewhere for the afternoon or the day. Certain contests are especially good for such trips. For instance, on the drive or hike to the picnic spot, divide the group into two teams and assign to one team the right-hand side of the road, to the other the left. The teams count cows, winning 1 point for every cow seen and 5 points for an entirely white one. Whenever a member of one team sees on his opponents' side of the road a graveyard or any other rather special thing that may be agreed upon, he may cancel all the opponents' points and start them over. A total of 100 or 150 points may be agreed on as a game. When a side has won, the con-

**172**

test may be repeated. In hiking through the woods this game may be made more difficult by giving points for various trees or flowers and subtracting 5 or 10 for a fungus, bird, or other specified plant or animal. Collecting and identifying a leaf of every kind of tree that is passed or searching for the largest and smallest leaves or for certain kinds of leaves along the way may also be made into a form of play.—*from The Handbook for Recreation, a publication of the U.S. Children's Bureau*

# SETTING YOUR CAMPSIGHTS

*To a youngster, camping means many things. It is the awareness of growing self-reliance that comes from living away from home. It is a sense of wonder felt in studying nature at firsthand. It is suspense as the ball spins over the basket as teammates root for you. It is cooking over an open fire; later, sleeping out under the stars.*

*Above all, camping is adventure, friendship and fun!*

## Camps for Children

The fire falls low and as the ashes whiten beneath the embers, the day closes quietly. The campers sleep with the tang of woodsmoke in the air— tired, but filled with memories and dreams of outdoor adventure. This is camping at its best!

Every year, several million boys and girls throughout the country respond to the lure of outdoor life. Some will be returning to a favorite spot while others will be exposed to camp life for the first time. Just as the first school experience can have long-lasting effects, so too can the initial impression of living outdoors and away from home.

There are several important factors parents should consider, in selecting a camp, to smooth their child's way into a most exciting and maturing experience.

**173**

**Does he want to go to camp?**   Even if you feel certain that camping would be good for your child, he may not agree with you. Perhaps he doesn't know enough about what camping is. It will be helpful to get hold of a number of camp brochures and discuss them fully with him. Some camps have pictures or movies of previous camp years. Perhaps you and your youngster can see them together.

It may be that he is not yet ready for camp life. One way to judge is to determine if your youngster is secure at home, enjoys doing things independently and welcomes new experiences. If so, he is very likely to enjoy camping enormously. Many camp authorities suggest, therefore, that camping is best suited for children from the ages of seven to twelve, although some camps are specifically geared to care for much younger or much older children.

If a young child still tends to cling, it might be advisable to introduce him gradually to being separated from you. For instance, short periods of time at a day camp will assure him that being away from home can be fun and that there is nothing to fear from being separated from his parents. The chances are that this experience will help prepare him for overnight camping the following year.

Overnight camping is often a child's first step away from the familiar small circle of school and home. It is a fine opportunity, therefore, for your child to grow in mind and body and to develop pride in his ever-increasing self-reliance. Camping can sometimes be even more successful than school at teaching this self-reliance, because children live camp life so intensely.

**What is a good camp?**   Exactly what does camp life mean? How important are the facilities, the staff? To answer these questions, study several camp brochures describing a variety of programs and facilities. Read the application blank carefully. Do not assume certain things are available because they are mentioned in the booklet, and do not assume that certain activities are important for your child just because so many camps offer them. Talk to parents whose youngsters have gone to the camps previously and, if possible, talk to several camp directors and counselors.

When you know what the different kinds of camps have to offer, you can select the one that will be most satisfactory for your youngster.

**A flexible program.**   Children in the seven to twelve age group are intricately involved in the discovery of self, eager to perfect the ability they have and excited when they discover previously latent talents. A responsible camp recognizes this and offers a wide variety of activities, permitting

**174**

youngsters to explore them all, at their own pace, with sufficient time to test their prowess and interest. Like Peter Pan's Never-Never Land, camp should be a magic place "where dreams are born and time is never planned." Ask yourself, then, if the camp you're considering combines a planned but flexible program with free time for youngsters to find and develop new interests and skills.

Some good camps meet this need for flexibility by offering a fully-scheduled program, with leeway for campers to choose activities.

Remember, however, that in choosing a camp, it is of primary importance to find one which will meet the particular needs of your child. If your youngster is timid and needs the security of familiar and specific limits, he may thrive in a camp that has many protective rules and a tightly-scheduled program. Most children, on the other hand, seem to do better at camps that offer greater challenge and freedom for experimentation and exploration.

Freedom does not imply that the days should be formless—without plan or purpose. There are regular hours, of course, for swimming, team activities, workshops; definite times for meals, rest and sleep. These give form to the campers' time and provide a framework within which they can explore and pursue new interests.

**One for all.** Eating meals together, sleeping together and playing together, the children begin to acquire a sense of man's interdependence. They learn to share, to assume responsibility for themselves and for others. The effectiveness of the democratic process becomes meaningful as they live the fundamentals of brotherhood so necessary in the world today. Determine, therefore, if the campers have the freedom of making some of the decisions which affect their life together. Interfaith and interracial camps offer the stimulation of associating with people from many different backgrounds. If this is something you value, choose a camp accordingly.

In community life, it is important that the campers share common experiences as well as pursue individual interests. Perhaps they can all be responsible for the care of farm animals (such as cows or horses). Or perhaps they can all participate in the camp play. Some camps institute community service projects in near-by towns to give the campers a more intimate, broader knowledge of the lives of other people in other kinds of communities. Does the camp you're interested in have such a program?

**Sports and sportsmanship.** Most parents want their youngsters to participate fully in a program of play and sports. Camp is an ideal place for children to develop skills and muscles.

Of course, youngsters will play with all their might to win, but they should be free from the pressures of constant competition. When team cooperation rather than competition is stressed at camp, the children learn the satisfaction of having played their best and the value of good sportsmanship.

Many camps, as a matter of fact, often shift children from team to team and from position to position, giving them more of an opportunity to discover and develop their skills. Team play thus loses its imperative, anxious quality and becomes a friendly rivalry, rather than a disturbing do-or-die battle. Some children, of course, thrive in a situation where competition spurs them on to do their best. In selecting a camp, keep in mind again your child's personality and needs.

**The camp director.**   Camps most often reflect the camp director's personal viewpoint. He should be more than an administrator; rather he should be someone who is sensitive to the needs of the children and eager to make the summer an exciting, memorable one for them. Too many directors, unfortunately, talk about camping and call it education. A good director talks camping itself—campfires, swimming, fun, friendship and a child's sense of kinship with others and with nature.

Feel free to talk to the director and question him fully about the details of camp life that matter to you. A good director wants parents to know as much as possible about the background and philosophy of his camp and to know him and his staff.

**The counselors.**   Most camp authorities agree that a child's counselors are the most significant factor affecting his feelings about camp life. Ideally, counselors are emotionally mature people who have a warm, genuine enthusiasm for children and for camping. If they are sympathetic to your youngster, can share their pleasure in the camp activities with him, and provide a proper balance of guidance and independence for him, then you can be assured that your child's summer will be a good one.

American Camping Association standards suggest: (1) a minimum of one counselor for every eight campers who are eight years and older, and one for every six children who are younger than eight years; and (2) that most of the counselors should be at least nineteen or twenty years old, college students or graduates who have studied both teaching methods and child development. Recently, there has been a trend to choose older counselors, too, who are affectionate, confident and responsible persons, and can give the campers the benefits of experienced teaching and adult companionship.

**176**

When you speak to the director, determine on what basis he hires his counselors. Does he concern himself with their past experience with young children, with the attitudes they hold toward child behavior? Does he hold frequent conferences with them to discuss each child's progress, and to help newcomers adjust to various camp situations? It is important that the director and staff work well together to understand and meet the collective needs of all campers.

**Facilities.** Although a youngster will think of camp primarily in terms of fun, friends, and activities, parents should also be concerned with the camp's physical facilities.

Are the buildings—either tents or cabins—well built and maintained? (Luxurious homes, however, have no place in camp life.)

What are the safety precautions and safety conditions of the camp? Is it free from serious physical hazards, danger of fire, etc. Is the water supply safe? Are sleeping facilities adequate and safe? Is the waterfront carefully guarded? The water front director should be a responsible person, at least twenty-one years of age. All good camps have trained lifeguards as swimming counselors, but you might make doubly sure by asking about qualifications.

Is there adequate provision for medical care? It is important to have a nurse in residence and a near-by doctor on immediate call. (In case of accident or serious illness, most camps protect parents by carrying camp insurance to cover special expenses.)

Does the camp have a well-trained dietician who sees to it that the children receive tasty and well-balanced nutritious food—and enough of it? Check whether there are regulations in the state that the camp is located requiring health examinations for all who handle food in camp.

How good are the toilet and washing facilities? (The official camping standard is a minimum of one toilet to each ten campers.) What are the provisions for disposal of sewage and garbage?

**The call of the wild.** Above all, remember that camping can unleash a child's urge to know the outdoor life. The increasingly larger camp enrollment indicate that parents are becoming more aware of the need to introduce youngsters to the intimacy of living in the heart of growing things. Children should know the sound of running streams, delight in the flash of silver birch against green leaves, and walk in wonder under the special wilderness-brightness of the stars. These can be discovered in camp, and with them, a love of the out-of-doors that can last a lifetime.

In a world that has become increasingly technological, we want more than ever for our youngsters to have an appreciation of life at first hand.

Camp is a unique opportunity to become acquainted with the serenity of wilderness ways. A good camp program should not be simply a recreational program transferred from the city streets to a country locale.

The call of reveille in the freshness of early morning has, therefore, become the new call to adventure—and the means by which children can add another dimension to their lives. —*Frances Fielding-Jones*

## Camp Isn't Just for Kids

The idea of the whole family going to camp together may sound novel but it is not a new idea. For years, the religious camp meeting, such as the Chautauqua movement, for example, has included whole families in a variety of programs.

Its increasing popularity today is due to the simple fact that families who go are pleased and they pass the word on to others. The term "family camp," however, is still unfamiliar to many people. To some it raises images of roughing it in the wilderness; trying bravely to keep up with the children; eating frankfurters and canned goods ad infinitum; moving baby from one unexplored spot to another; following a rigorous schedule all day.

But family camp need not be like that at all. It is really a week or more spent in a comfortable lodging within a setting of natural beauty which allows the family to carry on its own life and also to share in community living with other families. Every camper is free to pursue his own interests, but there are numerous opportunities for the family to participate in large group activities.

At the camp where I went, families came with children of all ages. Each family was assigned to a cabin of its own, where they slept and remained together whenever they desired. Families with very young children were housed in a central building which had heat, washing machines and refrigeration. Usually, all campers ate together family style. The hearty meals were provided by camp employees, but campers took turns helping with table setting and dish washing, two or three families serving at a time and having fun doing so.

**Programs** were planned in advance in order to get good leaders. At the time I was there, a university professor had been invited to lead the adults' discussion. While the adults were in their group, the youngsters met, grouped according to age, for some activity of their own. For instance, the six- to eight-year-olds had plenty to do imprinting leaf patterns of plaster of paris, catching butterflies with homemade nets (mosquito netting sewed on wire coat hangers,) walking in the woods, identifying birds and animals. The teen-agers, a bit tired of discussing "dating and marriage," decided to work on etiquette.

Some of the program was decided day by day, everyone doing what he wished. Frequently the adults went off with other adults (for golf or antique hunting) while the children had their own activities (swimming, movies, or just racing over the hills). Often, too, whole families enjoyed taking part in a nature walk or making something of tile or learning to play badminton. One afternoon the fathers and sons organized a softball game. (The younger ones made good rooters.) The little girls painted outdoors with two teen-ager leaders; supper was planned, campfire style, by other girls; and the mothers enjoyed an uninterrupted afternoon of bridge.

One day during the week, picnic lunches were packed for each family so that they could spend all day in the country. After their return, there was usually some pleasant activity to share—stories around a campfire, group singing under the stars, zestful square-dancing.

At the camp I visited, everyone got together every few days to settle on some of the bigger programs. One week, they decided on a "parents' pow-wow" to discuss such questions as "How to keep your family together?" and "What's your idea about discipline?" They planned old-fashioned relay racing, a Saturday night dance and a concert under the stars.

**Family camps differ.**   All bring the family together, but some do more planning for activities by age group than others. Programs are never very elaborate and the keynote is informality. How much is planned depends largely on what the camper wants and on what leadership and facilities are available. Recreation is suggested by the special quality of the camp site or the special interest of campers (I have heard of judo and mushroom-hunting as camp activities). One big factor is what families can do together. Most campers plan informal lectures or discussions covering such diverse topics as politics, improving personality and painting for a hobby. Handicrafts and hobbies of all sorts enrich the camp program; those who do not like knitting may put ships into bottles or make copper plaques for their living rooms or something else. There's variety enough to suit everyone.

Family camps are usually held for one or two weeks in the summer. The ones I know provide permanent cottages and a staff for cooking and maintenance. But camp may be set up on tent sites for more outdoor living. A modified family-plan uses children's day camp centers on free weekends: in these cases it is better if campers already know each other.

Costs vary, too. Family camps sponsored by agencies, churches or religious organizations make no profit. Often the camping quarters are owned by the agencies or are available through some endowment. The sponsoring agency may even subsidize part of the camp operation. And since parents take the place of paid leaders for children, this cuts costs, too. There is the expense of preparing the camp's meals, but this is usually reasonable.

Family camps vary according to their purpose. However, the essence of all of them is the good feeling which prevails when family members share in work and play.—*Hazel McKinley, Ph.D.*

## Camps That Challenge Teen-agers

Thousands of youngsters will enjoy being at the thousands of summer camps of all kinds throughout the country. But don't be surprised if a thirteen or fourteen-year-old expresses boredom, if not outright rebellion, at the prospect of another summer at a traditional recreational camp. Even though he may have had a great time at a camp for a number of summers, he may want to do something this year that is "older"—something mentally or physically demanding. To meet this desire, more and more camp directors are busy devising programs for teen-agers that offer recreation through challenging but realizable goals.

Your youngster, like many boys and girls of his or her age, may be happiest at an exclusively teen-age camp or at a camp with a clear-cut teen-age division and program. Of course, like a great many sixteen- or seventeen-year-olds, your child may be eager to return to camp as a counselor-in-training, finding that this new position satisfies his maturing sense of responsibility. Or he may thrive best in one of the many special-interest camps that have developed in recent years.

**Special interest camps:** A number of camps offer programs in art, music and science, "all under one roof." Other teen-ager camps specialize on only one of these fields. Of course, there are usually outdoor activities, too, for the majority of these camps have facilities for recreational as well as social and cultural activities.

Is your teen-ager a drama or dance enthusiast? There are a number of fine theater and dance camps. Is he an all-round sports bug? Or is he interested in one particular sport, such as baseball, basketball, tennis, swimming or sailing? There are specialized camps that offer intensive training in such sports. Perhaps your youngster wants to go to a camp specializing in a particular language or culture, such as French or Israeli. Does he or she

**180**

like to ride? You'll find outstanding riding camps and a few genuine ranch camps, especially out West. In addition, there are reducing camps to steel the will and wilt the weight of overweight girls, Naval training camps, and flying camps offering flight training to teen-age boys.

If it's hard physical labor and rugged, strenuous living that challenge your teen-ager, he may be enthusiastic about one of the canoe and wilderness trips that many consider the ultimate in camping experience. This kind of trip, which requires special physical fitness and training, is usually best for older boys. Although some of these trips are open to twelve-year-olds, it is doubtful whether many that age are up to this kind of strenuous living. Many of the trips are conducted in the Adirondack mountains of New York, in Maine, Canada, Minnesota, in national forests and parks.

**Work camps:**   One of the many private work camps may have just the program to fill the need your teen-ager feels for disciplined, self-fulfilling, constructive work. They provide varied activities such as construction, forestry, animal husbandry, gardening. Most of them have eight-week programs.

If you have a more mature teen-ager—eighteen or older—he or she may be eligible for one of the international voluntary work camps, especially in England and Western Germany. Costs are nominal for these camps, whose goal is to develop understanding and accord among peoples and nations, through working together.

Or perhaps you want to look into one of the summer camps sponsored by religious organizations or other service agencies—an increasingly important development in creative summer activities. In these camps provision is made for strenuous manual labor in a camp setting, where your boy or girl will become part of a group of enthusiastic teen-agers who perform physical labor (usually without remuneration) on a project that is socially useful to a community. The youngsters may erect a new building, renovate existing ones, do truck gardening, harvesting or forestry, milk cows, and so on. The program is supplemented by study, recreation and trips. In addition to the real value of the project undertaken at such camps, the work program helps a child develop a sense of responsibility and discover the meaning of cooperation. In general, the camps are open to youngsters fifteen and older. Sometimes, there is either no cost or a nominal one, such as a $1 a day. In other work camps, costs range between $12.50 by the week and $250 for the whole summer.

A variety of work camps and institutional services are conducted each summer by such organizations as the American Friends Service Committee, 20 South 12th St., Philadelphia 7, Pa.; American Jewish Society for

Service, Room 1518, 120 Broadway, New York 5, N. Y.; the Disciples of Christ, Missouri Association of Christian Churches, 227 E. Dunkin, Jefferson City, Mo.; the General Conference Mennonite Church, 722 Main St., Newton, Kansas; the Protestant Episcopal Church, 281 Park Avenue South, New York 10, N. Y.; the United Church of Christ, Pottsdown, R.D. 2, Pa.; the United Presbyterian Church in the U.S.A., Room 1105 Witherspoon Building, Walnut and Juniper Sts., Philadelphia 7, Pa. and so on. In some parts of the country, the Junior Red Cross offers opportunities for "summer service" to local junior and senior high school students.

*—Meyer Reinhold*

## Camping Out

The whole family will enjoy an occasional "roughing-it" expedition— either on a camping trip or at a campsite in one of our many public parks. (At national and state parks, it's advisable to make reservations for a campsite in advance.)

Don't make roughing-it too rough on yourself, however. There are many conveniences—for comfortable sleeping and easy food preparation, for example—which will save you trouble and precious time, better used for swimming, hiking and relaxing.

If you plan to take a short trip or move around, it's sensible to travel light, of course. But for a long stay, or if the weather is cold, or stores are inaccessible, by all means take along sufficient supplies to make your camping experience worry-free and fun.

**What to Take Along.** You'll need a shelter, of course, such as a tent, a trailer, or a car-top unit. You'll need clothing which is appropriate for the area you plan to visit and for unusual weather. After these necessities are provided for, check this list for other items which campers generally consider important in planning a trip.

| | |
|---|---|
| Bedding or sleeping bags and liners | Personal toilet articles |
| Air mattresses and repair kit | Clothesline and clip clothespins |
| Bath towels and face cloths | Nails and stout cord or soft wire |
| Metal mirror | Small shovel |
| Small washbasin | Flashlights, extra batteries, and bulbs |
| Ax or hatchet | Watch or small travel clock |
| File and whetstone | Plastic dishpan |
| Icebox | Dish towels, sponge or dishcloth |

**182**

Scouring pads, soap or detergent
Paper towels and napkins
Toilet tissue
Camp lantern; extra fuel
First-aid kit and instructions
Insect repellants

Sheath or pocket knives
Folding water bucket
Tarpaulins and waterproof
    throw cloths
Raincoats, ponchos, and
    waterproof foot gear

The following items aren't really essential, but they certainly make a camping trip more comfortable.

Cot beds and pillows
Oven to use on stove or by fire
Folding table, chairs or stools
Folding toilet seat
Paper plates and cups
Camp saw with coarse teeth
Small broom or whisk broom
Small mat or rug for tent door
Folding hangers for clothes
Lighter, can of fuel, spare flints
Vacuum jug
Funnel or fuel pump for fuels
Plastic and paper bags

Folding toaster
Oilcloth for camp table
Screening for porch or eating area
Portable radio
Fire starters for wet weather
Small hand fire extinguisher
Extra eyeglasses if required
Wooden hinged-top food boxes
Compass and maps for exploring
Pliers with wire cutter
Screwdriver for all type screws
Sewing kit, cellophane tape
Toys, books, recreation gear

Cooking and table equipment that should be included:

Large cooking pot; coffeepot
Nested pots, pans; or,
    two cooking pots and frying pan
Cooking fork, tongs, spatula
Camp stove and extra fuel
Potholders or asbestos gloves
Flatware, plate, cup, bowl for each

Serving spoons and serving fork
Carving knife or sheath knife
Paring knife
Ice pick, bottle-can opener
Aluminum foil, wax paper
Matches in waterproof container
Wire grill for open-fire cooking

# SPOTLIGHT ON SPORTS

*Hey, diddle diddle,*
*The cat and the fiddle,*
*The cow jumped over the moon.*
*The little dog laughed*
*To see such sport,*
*And the dish ran away with the spoon.*

*IN THIS ANCIENT NURSERY RHYME,* "sport" *reverts to its traditional meaning of* fun *or* play. *And good sports* are *fun; they bring to everyone enjoyment, challenge, recreation, health. Wouldn't it be great sport if your whole family were sportful good sports who engaged in good sports, taking a sporting chance on others' good sportsmanship?*

# COME ON IN — THE WATER'S FUN!

Swimming is an ideal activity for people of all ages—healthful and fun. And the sooner the safer is a good adage in learning to swim.

There's extra fun when mothers follow a show-and-tell plan for teaching the basic water skills to preschoolers. This do-it-yourself method, used at The Lincoln Park Pool in Alameda, California, has been successful in waterproofing hundred of children.

**Starting with bubbles.** Using the buddy system (that is, learning with a pal, an effective method particularly with young children) or working in small groups, each mother first tells her child to put his face in the water and blow bubbles.

This soon becomes an active, funny game, one youngster striving to blow more bubbles than the next. Often the mother, by cupping water in her hands and urging her child to blow bubbles in her hands, will give sufficient incentive and courage to a timid child.

**Face floating.** Once he's used to holding his face under water for a few seconds, the child is encouraged to float free and look for objects at the bottom of the pool. The purpose of this is to have the child perform a relaxed face float—generally known as the "deadman's float." The mother can help the first few times by supporting the child's tummy over her outstretched hands.

**Kicking.** After the float position has been learned, the next step is to develop a kick. Having the child grasp the pool edge and kick to make a big splash is one way this can be accomplished. Another is for the mother to pull the youngster by his hands and have him act as the "propeller" to the boat.

In learning the kick, it is important that the motion come from the thigh, not the knee. Frequently one of the best ways to improve a child's kick is using an inner tube. He holds onto the inflated tube with his hands for buoyancy, and uses the kick as his only means of locomotion. This gives a beginner a feeling of accomplishment, for he can propel himself adequately by good, strong kicks. Within a short time, he will master the art of correct kicking, and give up the tube.

With the straight-knee kick accomplished, the child is ready to "torpedo" —a term used at Lincoln for a kicking face float. The child is first backed up to the gutter rail with his feet flat against the side of the pool, then told to put his chin in the water and push hard with his feet as he lets go with his hands.

It may take many sessions for the child to learn to cover any distance, kicking in this position, but be patient.

Meanwhile, as the learning-to-swim process advances, parents must not lose sight of the fact that swimming ability, alone, does not make a child water-safe. It is imperative that he also learn to perform a relaxed back float and to tread water.

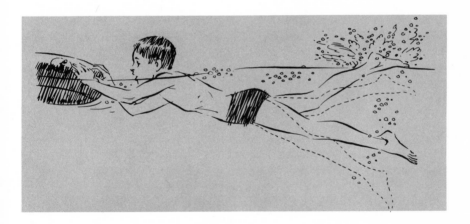

**Back floating.** Although the face float comes naturally to most children, the back float may be more difficult. Confidence is given the child by having his mother place her hands under his back—not to hold him but merely for support.

Then the youngster arches his back and pokes his tummy way up, keeping his feet together and arms outstretched. The adult's hands are gradually lowered until the swimmer is self-supporting. This takes practice and patience, but gradually the child becomes accustomed to the position. It's then, as he really relaxes, that he will float. In turn, as he floats, he will start to feel truly relaxed in the water.

**Treading water** should be learned in water over the child's depth—therefore, he must know how to stay afloat. With chin up, eyes looking up at the sky, the youngster "rides his bicycle"—moving his legs as if he were pedaling. At the same time, his hands "climb the ladder." As he becomes accomplished at treading, he can look around him, take note of his surroundings, all the while having the sure feeling that, by his own motions, he's making the water support him.

Up to this point, one of the most difficult things in working with a child is to keep him from using his arms. For beginners, only the kick should be stressed so that the proper form becomes natural and requires no extra effort on the child's part. Once the leg and thigh movement becomes second nature, an arm stroke can be developed. Perhaps the easiest and most natural arm movement for the child is an overhand, high elbow, loose arm stroke. If he reaches high with elbow up, over and out, cupping his fingers closed, he will achieve a harmonious and well-balanced stroke.

**Breathing.** Next, work on breathing can begin. It's better not to confuse a child with too many "remember this" instructions all at one time. So each major skill involved in swimming is learned separately, with proper breathing left till last. By this time, to a limited degree, the youngster can swim.

To learn coordinated breathing, the child swims with the overhand stroke, face in the water. He rolls his head to one side, so that his mouth clears the water, and breathes through his mouth; then he turns his head back, face down in the water, and exhales through both nose and mouth. It doesn't matter in which direction the face is turned upward; if it's to the left, the rhythm of breathing and swimming is as follows: as the left arm pulls back, the swimmer breathes in through the mouth, head turned to the left side. The left arm then comes forward and with the right arm back, face down in water, his breath is slowly exhaled.

This part of learning to swim takes the most concentration, requiring rhythmic coordination of arm, leg and head movements and timing of breathing. Then, when easy breathing is achieved, your youngster will have learned the basic skills needed to be at home and safe in water. Being competent at them will give him a sense of ease in the water, as well as a healthy respect for its properties. Beyond that, he'll gain the kind of pleasure and pride in accomplishment that will put him well on the way to making the water a lifetime friend.—*Patt Kirby McCauley*

# ATER SKIING

Water skiing is one of the most dashing of water sports. Any adventurous youngster who sees a graceful skier in full flight is likely to start begging for skis of his own. If he's a good swimmer who feels completely at home in the water, by all means let him have a try at it.

For skiing, a life jacket (or "ski belt") is mandatory, not optional. But except for this and 75 feet of sturdy tow rope, the best safety equipment for any water skier is a good two-person team in the boat—one person piloting, the other acting as observer and liaison to the helmsman. Smooth skiing depends on fairly accomplished boating. The pilot should be sensitive to the skier's need for a strong pull at the start, for wide, steady turns and easy stops. Be sure that skier, pilot and observer all know and agree on a few simple hand signals for such basic requests as "slow down," "stop," "turn" and "speed up."

Teach your youngster to fall compactly with his arms and legs close to his body. If he hits the water in a ball instead of with arms and legs flying, he can take spills without getting hurt. Remember that there are more than six million water skiers in the U.S. who have managed to maintain an extraordinarily good record of safety.

# URFING

Another thrilling sport is surfing. Today, from Santa Monica to Cape Hatteras to Fire Island, wherever a reef or sand bar puts a "shoulder" on the surf, teen-agers bearing surfboards are beginning to appear. Surfing is a gang sport rather than a family sport. Parents worry about it but, actually, surfing is a good deal less dangerous than it looks. True, youngsters may ride the breakers at thirty or forty miles an hour. The chief hazard, however, is not the water but a clout from a surfboard. Nevertheless, even though numbers increase the chance of a collision, no youngster should be allowed to surf alone—just as he shouldn't swim alone. When it's not a family activity, it's safest—and most fun—when it's a club activity.

# SKIN DIVING

Of all the new water sports, none has a firmer grip on its followers than skin diving. Both skin and scuba diving call for mask, fins and a "snorkel" breathing tube; scuba (the word stands for "self-contained underwater breathing apparatus") takes the above equipment, plus tanks of compressed air and the machinery to deliver it to the diver in a regulated flow.

**Is skin diving really safe?** The answer is a qualified "yes."

The basic requirement for a diver is good (not just fair) swimming skill. There are other requirements, too. Snorkeling, even just under the surface with the back of the head out of water, must be learned under controlled conditions, preferably in a pool with adequate supervision. For shallow-water diving, more practice and some conscious attention to breathing habits are necessary. For example, divers tend to fill their lungs with several deep breaths before they go under. This is fine—as long as the number of breaths is held to not more than six or seven. Because of the complicated relationship between oxygen and carbon dioxide in the human body, if you take too much air before a dive, you may black out underwater.

Another danger: the diver who has just come up has a natural urge to suck in a big, deep breath of air. The kind of snorkel that has a valve (like a table tennis ball in a cage) may not be completely open at this point, and the sharp intake of breath can seal it shut and simultaneously pull the mask tight against the face. Many children (and even unprepared adults) are likely to be panicked by the sudden cut-off of breath. A simple J-shape snorkel, rather than the valve type, is generally considered to be safer. But with this design the diver must learn to feel at home with a mouthful of water.

During the summer months, dime-store counters overflow with inexpensive fins and snorkels, but anything you buy for diving should not be chosen casually. A diving mask should fit well. Instruct your youngster to put it on and inhale through the nose. If he can feel the lens pulling toward his face and the rubber tightening against his skin, the seal is good. Lenses should be made of shatterproof glass; plastic tends to fog, distort and scratch, and is adequate only for porpoising around in a pool. Swim fins for young people should be moderate in size and stiffness; big, rigid blades call for big, strong muscles.

Snorkel, mask and fins should be the limit of diving equipment for anybody under sixteen. It's the opinion of an overwhelming number of experts that youngsters have no business strapping on compressed air tanks. Scuba diving can be very hazardous unless the diver has excellent instruction and good control of himself in an emergency. One of the common reflexes of fright, for example, is breath-holding; but holding your breath when you're diving with scuba can be deadly. And this is just one of the dangers facing inexperienced or immature divers.

This is not to say that scuba equipment isn't safe. It is—as safe as a sophisticated technology can make it. But cars are safe, too. Still, we don't put them in the hands of children too young to have mature judgment. A youngster is ready to use scuba—if he's a good swimmer and has had adequate experience with the basic skin diving equipment—at just about the time he's ready to drive. And even then he must learn the techniques of scuba under the supervision of experts, at a reputable diving-equipment shop, through a YMCA course, or at a city or county recreation center.

—*Lillian Borgeson*

# H BUOY —
# SMOOTH SAILING!

*A sailor went to sea, sea, sea,*
*To see what he could see, see, see,*
*And all that he could see, see, see*
*Was the bottom of the deep blue sea, sea, sea.*

Man is a land animal. So if your family's to be seagoing, they have to be able, first of all, to swim well.

Knowledge of swimming is far from being enough, of course, to insure safety in family boating. The real fundamentals are: a good ship with a good skipper and a good crew.

**What's a good ship?**   She's "sound and fully found"—a boat in good condition to do the job she was built for and possessing all the equipment for that job. The Coast Guard will give your boat a courtesy inspection if you want to make sure it's up to standard.

That CG inspection, by the way, naturally includes the "fully found" aspect of your boat, as well as the "sound." They'll tell you what equipment you ought to have and whether what you do have is worth keeping. Naturally, equipment varies with the size and nature of the craft, and where you're using it, but one fundamental on any boat is a life preserver (a Coast Guard-approved life preserver) for everyone aboard. And almost any small craft needs the following: waterproof flashlight (two if there are small children aboard), bailing can or pump, oars or paddles, tool kit, flares, a whistle or horn or both; and a bell of any sort is handy should you have to anchor in fog. You ought to have a Coast Guard-approved fire extinguisher attached to frame or bulkhead or seat near the steering position in a small boat. And every boat should carry spares—spare parts (shear pins, sparkplugs, etc., even a spare propeller if possible), spare line, spare sail for a windjammer and spare gas for a coffee-grinder, spare anchor in any good-sized body of water (an anchor is not a parking meter—it's a safety device) and a sea anchor for a cruising boat.

Some items not always considered necessary are especially important on a family boat: life jackets of the vest type, for instance, to be worn by all young children—good swimmers or no; on a larger boat, life lines; a place to lock matches away securely (at home they're bad enough in too-young hands; on board they're deadly). If you have a creeper or toddler aboard, you may have to tether him—not just to keep him from trying to find out what's on the other side of the gunwales, but to keep him from experimenting with how to stuff up the scuppers. A particularly important safety item for the children are shoes made with treads for wet decks.

**A good skipper.**   Nobody has to pass an examination to take the helm. So fulfilling the second requirement of boating safety—a good skipper—is up to your own conscience and common sense.

For one thing, a good skipper knows his boat and its capacity, and he never overloads. He knows what his boat can do, too, and doesn't take an open craft cruising across the Great Lakes because he knows that two hours after he's started out in calm weather the Lakes can blow up a squall with waves six feet high.

Secondly, a good skipper knows his waters. There are no signs announcing "submerged rocks" or "rip tide." He has to have charts whenever possible and know how to read them. He has to learn to recognize aids to navigation like buoys and lights. Even if he's only scooting around a small uncharted lake, he ought to find out about possible hazards from local people who know.

The skipper knows boating law—and lore—and courtesy. Many amateur small-boaters have a vague notion about something called "right of way—and that stuff," and don't realize that the Rules of the Road apply as much to them as to a freighter or a seagoing yacht! It's not very hard to know when you're on a collision course if you're driving a car. Do you know when you're on a collision course on the water—and what you have to do if the other boat is under sail? A good way to find out about the basic rules of boating is to get the official Coast Guard pamphlet on the subject.

Any power-boatman who thinks wind direction has significance only for sailing craft had better stay put in the marina. And a good boatman checks up on and heeds weather reports. A portable radio keeps you in touch at all times with local weather observations, and a skipper should at least be able to recognize small-craft warnings. Moreover, since weather is always on the move, he should himself learn something about the elementary weather signs. That mysterious word "front" you keep hearing around docks and anchorages isn't so mysterious if you've got yourself a copy of the U. S. Weather Bureau's "Weather Forecasting."

If you are a sailboat novice most of your help and information will probably come from sailing enthusiasts. Local yacht clubs or marinas usually provide some kind of programs for juniors to introduce children to sailing. Power-boatmen can turn to a local branch of the U.S. Power Squadron, represented in most boating areas. For the address of the group near you, write: U.S. Power Squadron, Box 510, Englewood, New Jersey.

**A good crew** is important, too—and your youngsters are a potential crew. Even young children can take on interesting and important jobs. Responsibilities depend, obviously, on the maturity of the children but, for example, a youngster can: learn why a boat must be kept clean and polished, its lines coiled, its equipment stowed—and therefore enjoy keeping things shipshape; learn the fundamentals of caring for an outboard; learn to keep a log on a cruise (making experience a really good teacher, for the log can note errors not to be repeated, plus appropriate praise for each crew member). He can learn to read charts and to navigate and to take the helm for a spell under supervision. When they can help care for and run the boat, the "must-do's" come easier to youngsters—like sitting quietly without rocking, dipping hands or paddling feet; like never leaping from dock to boat (or back).

However well-learned the crew becomes, they must understand that for safety one person is in charge. Unquestioned and prompt response to orders can make the difference between adventure and trouble.

And marvelously adventuresome it can be, this family boating.

*—Jean R. Komaiko and Margaret Albrecht*

# O FISH!

*Little fishes in the brook.*
*Daddy catches them with a hook.*
*Mommy fries them in the pan,*
*And Johnny eats them like a little man.*

In our complex society, fishing is important, not only as a means of recreation, but also as a superb method of establishing closer relationships between father and child by having fun together.

For the youngest beginner the best method is pole and line with plain old worms for bait. No matter what you think privately of this practice, keep it to yourself. There is plenty of time later to be initiated into the more complicated forms. Right now the primary aim should be fun with no difficult skills to acquire. Let the child help in digging the bait. This gives him as much pleasure as the actual fishing if it is done leisurely, so that there is plenty of time for questions.

Pick a place near enough home so that your child is not already tired by the time he arrives. Take along a straw hat to shade his eyes, some sandwiches or fruit just for fun, and a thermos of water so that the "I'm thirsty" business can be solved promptly. Young children are often extremely sensitive about hurting anything. Assure him that it does not hurt the worm (we don't know that it does) and that the fish is not injured if removed from the hook carefully. As a precautionary measure let him feel the sharp end of the hook with the tip of his finger, then guide his arm a time or two until he gets the hang of throwing the line into the water.

Start fishing and pray that this is the day they will bite.

Young children cannot sit still for over five minutes at a time. Nature was wise in this respect, for if they led the same sort of sedentary life that adults do, how would they ever explore and learn about the millions of things they need to know? When squirming starts, as it will in a short time if the fish aren't biting, do something to prevent boredom. Hand out a piece of chewing gum, pour a drink of water, or best of all, start a story about "When I was just your age." If there are still no bites, the perfect medium for play is right at hand—mud and water. Do insist, however, that they carry the water away from the bank to make their pies. It is a mistake to let children wade in the water where they are fishing. Too often wading would be dangerous.

Boat fishing is definitely less desirable than bank fishing because activity is too restricted. If you do go out in a boat, a life jacket of some sort is essential for the child. No child who is afraid of boat riding should ever be taken out fishing in one. Fear of one particular thing often becomes a fear and dislike of all associated things.

Always leave before your young guest is quite ready to go home, and if no fish have been caught, stop by the drug store and buy him the biggest ice cream cone in town. It may ruin his appetite for dinner, but that is of little consequence. The important thing is for the child to have a happy memory of his first fishing trip.

The age when a child can use a rod and reel depends on his muscular coordination, his previous interest in fishing and his desire to imitate his father. Some can begin at eight, others at six. Usually when Daddy starts practicing in the back yard, the child also wants to try. Use a dummy plug (no hooks), and take turns of five casts each. Perfection doesn't inspire confidence in a beginner. He feels more at ease if he sees an adult make some of the same mistakes he does. Do show him the correct form of casting, but don't insist on exact conformity to your instructions. His unorthodox approach may suit his grasp better, and in the long run be the best method for him. Again, stop before he is quite ready. After a few practice sessions in the yard, let him try casting in the water with a dummy plug until he gets the feel of it.

Your choice of the child's own rod and reel should be made only after careful consideration. Certainly he should not have a piece of worn-out, discarded equipment. All beginners should start with an anti-backlash reel. Untangling a line is discouraging for an adult, and for a child it destroys

the incentive to continue.

The age of beginning fly casting depends on the same factors as those for rod and reel, but ten is about the average age for the novice. If you feel that fly casting is an art, or if you feel that it requires an inordinate amount of skill to master, don't let the child know about your feelings. Stripped to essentials, a fly rod is nothing but a stick with a string on it, which is cast by pumping it up and down like a buggy whip. Start the beginner with a seven and one-half foot creek rod with a line only as long as the rod. For the first few practice times use a dummy lure, or cut the hooks from a brightly-colored old one. Explain the necessity for keeping the upper arm close to the side. Show that the movement is from the elbow down, and then let the child try. His adroitness and skill may surprise you. As he becomes more adept, lengthen his line very gradually, about a foot at a time. The fine points of technique should not be brought out until he has mastered these essential beginnings.

The whole process of teaching children to fish should be a gradual one. There will be spurts of interest followed by periods of complete lack of interest. With patient training, however, you will find yourself one fine day with a fishing partner who is your equal in skill, dexterity and sportsmanship. Who could ask for more?

# PEOPLE WHO PADDLE

Cruise camping or canoe camping is possible in many parts of the United States. Two paddlers in an 18-foot canoe, with up to 200 pounds of supplies, need only a foot or more of water for a successful canoe camping trip. Experienced canoeists can travel from 15 to 30 miles per day. Thousands of young people learn canoeing in camp and would enjoy continuing this exciting sport.

Competitive paddling in either individual or team events is stimulating, too. Rules and regulations of the American Canoe Association govern the events and competitions in competitive paddling. Olympic trials open to all amateurs are held every 4 years.

White water canoeing involves shooting rapids and cruising fast water streams. Courses for all competition are determined by local water conditions and full safety precautions, of course, should be observed.

# HAVING A BALL WITH BALL GAMES

Do you remember: *"One, two, three, O'Lary,*
*I spy Mistress Mary,*
*Sitting on a bumble-ary,*
*Just like a chocolate fairy;*
*One, two, three, O'Lary."*

Or perhaps: *"Gypsy, gypsy, lived in a tent;*
*Gypsy, gypsy, wouldn't pay her rent.*
*She borrowed one, she borrowed two,*
*And passed the ball to Y-O-U"!*

*These are but two of hundreds of chants we—and our children—*
*intoned as we bounced a ball. Even the very youngest children like*
*to roll a ball, then throw a ball, then bounce it, and finally play*
*games with it. Balls are inexpensive, easily available, easy to handle,*
*and popular all over the world. No wonder the refrain of our sports-*
*conscious country is so often "Take Me Out to the Ball Game"!*

# BASEBALL

**Play ball with your kids.** Fatherhood is an occupation which can
bring into play all a man's talents and abilities. Sooner or later you will
use all of them. Take, for instance, your prowess on the play fields. Every
man can help his young son—or daughter—learn some of the sports skills
which will help him with his friends today and in the years to come.

If you have average athletic ability, it will be easy. If you are a complete
duffer and poor at throwing and catching, for example, you can still help
your son when he is 6, 7 and 8—and give him the great satisfaction of feeling
that *he* is helping *you* when he reaches 10 and older. If you actually are an
athlete, however, you'll need to watch yourself; it's easy to have a youngster
feel that dad is so good—and so competitive—he doesn't have a chance.

Ball playing is generally the start. However, most 6's and 7's and many
8's will not want to stick very long to throwing a ball back and forth or
batting. Be patient. Even if you have walked six blocks to the park, lugging
your son's new bat, ball and glove, don't be surprised if he has had enough
after five minutes. Enjoy the park, and try it again in a week or two.

When the time comes for sports, he'll let you know. Suddenly he will become tireless, skills will develop fast and you will both have fun. However,
preliminary practice with you—and pointers from you—will give him a
head start. Besides, it will give you a chance, right from the beginning, to
establish the idea that the game itself is fun, not merely the winning of it.

There isn't too much you can do about playing a game of hard-ball baseball when it's just you and your son. It really takes three or four to hold batting practice, but when the time comes maybe you can bring the rest of your family into the game or include several of your son's friends.

**Catch as catch can.** In the meantime, you can practice throwing and catching—the basic ingredients of the game. The boy who is a consistent fielder is always welcome in a game, even though he may not hit very well. But if he can't be depended on in the field, he'll have to be a first-rate slugger to stay in the game.

As with other ball games, start throwing and catching a hard ball at very close range. (Using a rubber ball or soft ball is advisable with young boys or when playing on city streets, but hard-ball baseball on a playground or field should be an activity you participate in often.) A boy 6 or 7 years old should be able to catch throws at ten feet before he tries them at fifteen.

Once you get to the 15-foot range, let him practice throwing faster before working for more distance. If he can put on some steam at fifteen feet, he'll have no trouble throwing thirty. When a boy tries for distance before he has learned speed, the tendency is to lob the ball high in order to reach.

Talk it up, as you play. When he catches the ball it's a hit and you're the first baseman. Let him get rid of it fast. When he returns the ball to you straight and fast, yell, "He's out!"

Sometimes he will want to practice first base, catching the ball with one foot on base. He will want to practice pitching. He will want to be a catcher, crouching behind the plate and returning the ball with a snap. He'll want to catch flies, and you can help him to learn to catch the ball in front of his chest, not over his face. Show him how to drop to one knee the way many infielders do when fielding a grounder so that if he misses the ball his leg or body will stop it.

**Pitching.** When you are pitching the ball to your son or any other child, don't try to strike him out. With youngsters, the good pitcher is not a strike-out artist. He is the one who gives them the most hits! Stand close enough (putting your pride in your pocket) so that you can pitch straight and easy over the plate. Aim for the bat. Maybe you can hit it!

**Batting.** Teach a very little boy to hold the bat waist high, horizontal, pointing toward the catcher. Then his swing will be straight forward. If he holds the bat on his shoulder, he will tend to chop down at the ball and even when he hits it, it won't travel far. The first five hits are the most important in his life. Once he feels inside himself that he really can hit the ball, then you can help him improve his technique, holding his arms shoulder high and back.

**Flies up.**   Practice situations can themselves be games. Flies Up is simply "fungo" hitting. One person fungos the ball (tosses it up and bats it in the air) and the others try to catch it. If someone catches it on a fly, he's up. If someone catches it after it has touched the ground, the batter lays the bat in front on the plate, broadside to the field, and the fielder who caught the ball rolls it in and tries to hit the bat. If he hits it, he's up—unless the batter, crouching behind the plate, catches it on a fly.

This game is appealing to boys, but there are two factors to be aware of. A superior player will be hitting fungos almost all the time and the others will get little chance. You'll have to see that it doesn't go that way. Also, fungoing is not batting practice, though it may give the boy who can hit fungos confidence. Batting practice requires a pitcher.

**Kick Ball.** If you go to the park with your son and his friends, Kick Ball will not only be fun but will also enable the boys to learn the rules and procedures of baseball. Use a soccer ball or any similar large, tough ball. The home plate is a line three or four feet long, broadside to the pitcher. The pitcher bowls the ball; the batter kicks it. Any fair ball going outside the infield on a fly is an automatic out. Otherwise the rules are similar to baseball except that four fouls are "out."

This is fine for the little fellows who can't as yet catch or bat well enough to enjoy a real ball game but who are itching to get out and play.

**Stealing Bases.** This game rather realistically reproduces basemen's and runners' situations without a batter. Basically, it is a game for three, one runner and two basemen. When a runner is out, he takes the base of the player who makes the putout and the latter becomes the runner.

Put the bases near enough together so everyone can throw and catch comfortably, but far enough apart to insure at least occasional misses. Whenever the runner thinks he can make it safely, he tries to run from one base to another. He is out if he reaches the base while the baseman is holding the ball or if he is tagged by the player with the ball.

If the baseman on the sack toward which he is running catches the ball, the runner may try to return to his original base. Every time he gets from one base to another, he scores.

With four players, divide into two teams of two. The team that is running has one player in action, one waiting. When the first runner makes a point or is put out, the other takes his place. When a team makes three outs, sides change.

 OOTBALL

**What to tackle first.** A small child cannot possibly handle a regulation football. If you want him to play, get a smaller-sized ball.

Football is so grievously misnamed that it takes some youngsters years before they're willing to do anything but kick the ball! Let your son kick it a few times—but don't make him chase the kicks all over the field—and then get down to throwing and catching. Stand very close. At five or six feet he will be able to catch the ball most of the time, and even get off some throws that travel flat. Increase the distance only a little bit at a time.

In between, trot along side by side, throwing laterals. That will give him a feeling of going somewhere. Take turns going out for passes, with the thrower sending the ball out ahead of the runner. This is dramatic and useful—and exciting when it works.

Let him practice "hiking" (passing from between his legs) and receiving hikes. Even though only the center gets to "hike" in college football, in kids' games everyone takes his turn at it. Many boys don't discover until they are 11 or 12 that the hike is a swift throw and not a lob. Let him learn this now and he won't learn it the hard way, having the opposing linesmen swarm all over his quarterback before the ball ever gets to him.

Don't worry about tackling. His serious football games for many years will be "touch." And don't try to teach him to block. He'll learn that in playing with boys his own size. If you help him learn to handle the ball, you will be doing him a service as well as having fun together.—*Edgar Bley*

# THE SPORTS RACQUET

**Tennis, anyone?** Tennis is a game that takes time and patience to learn well. But the learning can be a pleasure for a child if he isn't made to feel that unless he performs brilliantly he will disappoint his parents. That kind of pressure, of course, will spoil a child's enjoyment of the game and hinder, not help, his progress. In encouraging children to learn tennis, start them off in an atmosphere conducive to maintaining their interest and to avoid putting pressure on them.

Eight or nine is an ideal age for youngsters to begin to learn how to play tennis. The primary stress should be on good form, concentrating on the two basic "ground strokes"—a forehand and backhand—and for those who are ready, a simple overhand serve, which is the stroke used to put the ball into play in a real game. Explain the rules for scoring and game play almost at once so that easy competitive games can begin. Particular attention can be given to proper behavior on the court.

One of the advantages of learning tennis young is its carryover value; like bicycling or swimming, tennis skills are easily renewed.

**Children differ in ability** and interest. Some children learn the forehand and backhand quickly, rally well and are ready to play the full court. Boys are likely to progress faster than girls—the more able are soon experimenting with advanced strokes (drop shots, lobs, smashes) and "rushing net" like the pros. Girls are likely to take several seasons just gaining enough strength and control to execute a beginning forehand and backhand. The overhand serve is particularly difficult for most girls, for the young child and for anyone whose coordination is not fully developed. Less athletic youngsters need encouragement and personal attention; the better students should be taught at their own pace, advancing quickly but learning to "groove" their basic strokes before attempting more complicated skills.

As the mother of one boy claimed: "This is the first sport that Tom has been able to find any satisfaction in. He's not a natural athlete, and in baseball or basketball, for instance, when he did poorly some of the other players would jeer. Naturally, he'd then become even tenser and do worse. Eventually, he quit trying. Here, he can go at his own speed and he's found another boy who is at just about the same level as he is. He knows he'll never be a great player but he's having fun and getting plenty of good exercise."

Surely such children derive as much pleasure and benefit from the game as potential champions.—*Eve F. Kraft*

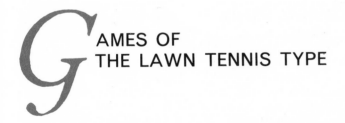

# GAMES OF THE LAWN TENNIS TYPE

A number of games of the general type of lawn tennis are not only satisfactory in themselves but also excellent preparation for playing regulation tennis. They give practice in the use of a racket and develop various skills.

Much of the equipment is less expensive than that for lawn tennis and much of it can be made at home.

**Paddle Tennis.** This game, which is played by two or four players, requires only a fourth of the space necessary for lawn tennis. For a young child, it is an excellent substitute for tennis, and it has won many older fans as well.

The court is marked like a tennis court with all the dimensions halved. A still smaller court may be used, but the proportions should be kept. The top of the net should be 2 feet 2 inches above the ground at the middle of the court.

Balls, net, paddles (instead of racquets), and posts for the game may be purchased; or lawn tennis balls and net may be used and paddles made at home.

The paddles should be made of 3-ply material 8 inches wide and 17 inches long. The handle should be built up by adding an extra piece of wood on each side. Jumping standards will serve as temporary posts to hold the net. Permanent posts should be set 3 feet deep in the ground, 1 foot outside the outer lines of the court.

The rules and scoring are the same as in lawn tennis.

**Tether Tennis.** A 13-foot pole should be set 3 feet deep in the ground, or a straight tree may be utilized and a line painted around it 6 feet above the ground. A staple or heavy screw eye is set at the top of the pole, and a heavy nylon cord or fishing-rod cord 8 feet long is tied to it. This may be a chained or double-twisted cord. A cover large enough for a tennis ball should be knotted or crocheted from nylon cord, and the bottom drawn together with a lacing, so that when the ball is worn out it can be replaced. The ball is to be fastened to the cord so that it will hang $7\frac{1}{2}$ feet from the top of the pole.

On the ground around the pole a circle is drawn 6 feet in diameter, bisected by a straight line about 20 feet long (10 feet on each side of the pole). On an imaginary line crossing this one a serving spot should be marked on each side, 6 feet away from the pole.

The game is played with lawn tennis rackets or with wooden paddles of about the same size as a tennis racket.

Two persons play this game. Each in turn starts from his serving spot, trying to strike the ball in such a way as to wind its cord around the pole above the 6-foot mark before his opponent is able to prevent this and to make it wind in the opposite direction.

**Badminton.** This is a game of Indian origin. It is played with racquets lighter than those used in lawn tennis, and instead of a ball, a shuttle is used. The shuttle is made of cork. Badminton may also be played indoors. The rules are the same as those for lawn tennis.

A court may be chalked on the lawn, forty-four feet long and twenty feet wide. Across the center is a net two feet six inches in depth, and when hung, it should be five feet from the ground to the top of the net at the center.

Either two or four may play the game, as in tennis. The object of the game is to return the shuttle before it hits the ground, playing as in tennis. Failure to do this gives the opposite side one point. A fault gives the service to opponent. Score the game as in tennis.

# BALL GAMES FOR GROUPS

**Dodge Ball.** The players are divided into two equal groups. One group stands around outside a clearly marked circle 30 feet in diameter. The other group scatters about within the circle. The players outside the circle try to hit those in the center with a basketball or volleyball, while the center players dodge to avoid the ball. They may jump, stoop, or resort to any means of dodging except leaving the ring. Players hit above the hips are not out, but any player hit below the hips must leave the circle. No outside

player may step inside the circle to throw the ball. If the ball stops in the circle a player may step in for it, if it should not roll within reach. When two center players are hit by one throw of the ball, only the first one hit leaves the circle. At the end of a minute the groups change places for the next half-inning, the center players becoming outside players and the outside ones going to the center. The score is the number of players left in the center at the end of the inning. The team with the higher score at the end of five innings wins the game.

**Kick-over ball.** The players are divided into two teams which are seated on the floor with the feet of one team almost touching those of their opponents. The players support themselves by placing their hands on the floor behind them. A basketball or other large ball is thrown down the line of feet, and each team tries to kick it over the heads of the opponents. When a team succeeds, it scores one point. The ball may not be touched with hands, but it may be blocked with the shoulders. Nothing is scored if the ball goes between the players or out at the ends; it must go over the heads. If the players on a team kick the ball over their own heads their opponents score a point.

**Volleyball.** The official volleyball court is 40 by 80 feet in size. It is divided across the middle between the end lines by a net, the top of which is 8 feet above the ground at the center. However, a much smaller court may be used. The boundaries of the court should be clearly marked with lime or other material. The ball should not weigh more than 10 ounces; a lighter ball may be used.

The game is played by two opposing teams that may vary from 6 to 12 or more persons on a side. As few as 2 persons on a team to as many as 15 can play successfully.

The players are numbered and serve the ball in rotation. The server stands on the back line and bats the ball over the net with his open hand. If his opponents fail to return it, a point is scored for the serving side. Only the serving side may score.

In trying to return the ball, three different players may touch it if necessary, but the same player may not touch it twice in one service.

If the server fails to bat the ball over the net, or the serving side fails to return it when it is batted back, the service goes to the other team. At a change in service all players change their positions on the court, rotating clockwise to bring the new server to the upper right hand corner of the court. Fifteen points constitute a game.

**Call ball.** All the players except one form a circle and take numbers. The odd player stands in the center and tosses the ball high up within the circle, at the same time calling the number of some player. The one called must quickly run to catch the ball on the fly—or on the first bounce if the players are unaccustomed to handling a ball. If he catches the ball he tosses it up and calls the number of some other player. If the ball is not caught, the center player gets it and again tosses it up.

**Stride ball.** The players stand in a circle with their feet apart, each foot touching a neighbor's foot. The ball is rolled swiftly about inside the circle, each player trying to make it pass between another player's feet. When anyone succeeds, the player who let the ball escape must drop out. The space between the feet may be protected by using the hands but not by closing the knees or stooping. The game ends when only three players are left in the circle.

**Kick up.** The players lie in a circle on the floor with their feet toward the center. A light ball (or a balloon) is tossed on their toes. It must be kept in the air by using the feet only, a point in the score being lost each time the balloon touches the floor. This game should not be played more than about three minutes at a time. It may be used as a relay race by dividing the players into teams of four or five persons and furnishing a ball to each team.

**Basketball goal.** A regulation basketball goal and backboard may be purchased, but it is quite as satisfactory to nail a barrel hoop or metal ring on the garage wall or on a homemade backboard 6 by 4 feet in size. The rim of the hoop should be set 10 feet from the ground (and 1 foot from the bottom of the backboard, if a backboard is used). Boys and girls not only will practice shooting baskets but also will develop many games around a single goal.

**Backyard golf.** Tin cans sunk in the ground so that their tops are flush with the surface make good holes for putting practice. Tin can golf is played with six of these holes. The holes need not be at any certain distance apart, the size of the yard governing the size of the course. The object of the game is to see who can complete the six holes in the least number of strokes. When a player drives his ball off the course or in any place where it is impossible to play, he may forfeit two strokes and place the ball on the ground nearest the place where it left the course. A player must not place his ball more than six feet from the hole he has just completed when going ahead.

**Miss the bell.**   A bell is suspended in a hoop about 8 inches in diameter, and a small ball is given to the players. They take turns tossing the ball, trying to send it through the hoop without causing the bell to ring. One point is scored each time the ball goes through, and three points are scored if the bell does not ring.—*from Handbook for Recreation, a publication of the U.S. Children's Bureau*

# OWLING THEM OVER

**Bowling is a striking sport.**   Bowling's got just about everything these days to make it one of America's favorite family recreations. Modern million-dollar lanes (most are completely automatic) are open twenty-four hours a day. Some are almost cities in themselves—located near shopping centers and providing their own lounges, shops, restaurants, entertainment and nurseries staffed by trained personnel, to look after the very little ones while the rest of the family plays.

Even young children play these days, for balls (supplied free by the management, though some bowlers prefer to bring their own) come in varying weights—ranging from nine to sixteen pounds.

Many bowling centers encourage children's leagues for school-age youngsters who like to play regularly.

The lanes ring with laughter as everyone gives the game all he's got. Of course, like other skills, bowling takes much practice, but the novice has as much fun as the expert—partly due to the atmosphere of relaxed goodwill and the vigorous (though not too strenuous) exercise provided.

Rules and regulations are few. The special shoes that are needed can be rented on the spot. Otherwise, play as you are, and often, with the whole family. You're all bound to enjoy the kind of high fun, low cost and convenient pleasure that has brought this ancient popular sport back to the top again.—*Lynn Marett*

# H, SAY, CAN YOU SKI?

Skiing is the fastest growing winter sport in the nation, with some four million Americans whizzing down mountainsides from Maine's Sugarloaf to Oregon's Mt. Hood, and more joining the fun each year.

Skiing is made-to-order as a family sport for the good reason that every member can join in, toddlers as enthusiastically as teen-agers (not to mention grandparents). To complement skiing, the bigger resorts offer a real smorgasbord of activities: ice skating, tobogganing, swimming in heated pools. There are sleigh rides and dog sled rides, and children can come bouncing down gentle slopes on small discs called "snow saucers," or scoot over the snow on "shoe skates"—miniature skis just slightly longer than a child's overshoe.

Well over 750 ski resorts are nestled in the country's mountains and hills, and this number is increasing by ten per cent every year.

**Slopes are steep, but not the prices.** When the idea of a ski holiday comes up, the first question is likely to be "how much?" Happily, you don't need a luxury budget, for there are many modest priced resorts.

On winter weekends from about Christmastime through early March, ski slopes are a beehive of activity, but from Monday through Friday they are as quiet as the falling snow. Many resorts offer "specials" at reduced rates to attract skiers during this midweek interlude.

Some resorts offer housekeeping rooms or cozy cabins which will sleep about ten. If you have a large family or plan to share a vacation with friends, investigate the private chalets which cluster about most big ski areas. Many owners are happy to rent their places for a week or a weekend, particularly to families. Here you can cook your own meals and have the luxury of privacy, often for less than you would pay for motel rooms. The manager of the ski area is the man most likely to know what facilities are available.

**What to wear?** In general, it's a good idea to pack along several layers of clothing for each person. As the sun gets high, outer layers are shed. Necessary equipment includes goggles or sunglasses, mittens, ear covering and head gear. Flannel pajamas can double nicely for long-johns. Don't forget sunburn cream or lotion; sun bounced off snow inflicts a wicked burn.

You can decide to buy equipment for your youngsters or rent it. Wooden skis and poles come in special junior sets. The more popular metal skis are expensive, so to cut a few financial corners, you might ask the ski shop owner about second-hand equipment, since most take trade-ins, or wait for end-of-season sales. Ski clubs often have equipment pools where children can be outfitted in other youngsters' gear.

Properly fitting boots and skis make almost magical difference in skiing. Boots should slip on over two pairs of socks, one heavy and one light, and still be narrow enough to feel the edge of the ski. Since the heel is responsible for a good part of the work of skiing, it is important that the boot lift with the heel. To judge ski length, stand a ski at your side and reach for the sky with one arm. The tip of the ski should come to the base of the thumb. Poles should be long enough to rest under the arms.

**Lessons lessen the risks.**  Lessons should be the first order of business for a family of novice skiers—whether the beginner is four or sixty-four.

Some children are born sliders to begin with (bannisters, polished floors). They look on skiing as entirely logical and wonderfully desirable. Although some instructors maintain that a child can be put on skis as soon as he can walk, one director of a ski school warns in gentle accents, "Never, never force the little ones to learn. Give them skis if you want but let them set their own pace."

Another instructor offers this guide, "When a child can throw and catch a ball or ride a bike or roller skate, he's ready to try skiing." Most instructors agree that the best learning years are from seven to nine.

In our poll of some thirty-five professional ski instructors, all agreed that classes for children in the five to seven age group should be more play than work. Children's instructors have a whole repertoire of learning games.

What about accidents? Most ski accidents can be traced to one of three causes: overconfidence, fatigue or poorly fitting boots and skis.

A motto to ski by might be, "Don't push beyond your ability." To encourage skiers to stay within their limits, ski slopes are marked off into novice, intermediate and expert slopes. Most accidents happen to beginners or intermediates whose friends lure them up slopes too advanced for their ability.

"The best candidate for an accident," a veteran skier says, "is the person who is in poor condition to begin with and who gives in to the temptation to make just one more run when he knows he's bone tired." Veteran skiers

feel parents should insist on the whole family doing some conditioning exercises before heading for the slopes. Since leg muscles get the biggest workout, exercises should stress running in place, climbing stairs and going through skiing motions. Hiking and bicycling are also good.

The growth in popularity of skiing has brought safety and comfort to the slopes. Equipment has been improved, with such features as safety bindings to reduce the chances of broken limbs. Now, when there is any undue stress the boot automatically pops off the ski and a safety strap keeps the ski from sailing down the slope.

**How to get a lift.** New, efficient lifts whisk thousands up the hills each hour. Almost every ski area has an assortment of rope tows, pomas (where a round disc at the end of a pole slips between the legs), T or J bars and chair lifts.

Best of all, mountaintops that oldtimers could only yearn for are now laced with long, wide, beautiful runs. And a pastime that was once exclusive is now fair game for any family.—*Shirley Welton*

# G O FLY A KITE

Here's a pastime as old as the hills that each generation discovers anew. In fact, kiteflying has more than tripled during the past five years, partly because the new kites have better framing and better designs. The materials used, too, whether cloth or plastic, are very much improved.

Today, sport kites—which can be made from hobby kits—are coming into their own, replacing the strictly homemade ones. Modern kite construction differs from traditional chiefly in the fact that there are more non-rigid models today—that is, kites without spars or sticks which may break if they fall to the ground or bang against a tree.

If you're not already a devotee of this satisfying sport, these simple instructions will help you get your kite happily off the ground:

• First, choose your spot. The ideal place to fly is in a field without trees or open body of water nearby. Study smoke from chimneys to get wind direction. Stay away from power lines, and from buildings, where down drafts make flying frustrating.

- Stand with your back to the wind, toss the kite into the air and let out some line. If the kite starts to sink, stop letting out line until it gains some height—or run a few steps against the wind.
- If the kite dives suddenly, let out the string rapidly so that it will float to the ground instead of crashing.
- Don't drag the kite on the ground toward you. Go to it, lift it and start the launching procedure again.
- If there is little wind and you have a partner with you, let him lead out the kite some fifty feet or more. On a signal from you, your partner launches the kite in the air, against the wind. Then jerk it up rapidly so that it will rise quickly above the small ground currents.
- When you do get the kite into the air, let your waiting partner—undoubtedly a child—have a turn holding it. The first time out, you had better get the kite into the air, so your youngster won't get discouraged if his first launching is unsuccessful.

The ordinary paper kite comes unequipped with string, but you can make a line for it out of any good grade of wrapping twine. You can wax the string to make it more durable by letting the string run lightly over a softened candle, a little at a time, until it has a greasy feel to it.

Some of the best string for light kites is No. 10 nylon silk string. Don't go in for expensive fishing line, unless you use the kite for fishing. And don't use wire of any kind unless you're a professional kiteflier.

Paper kites can be bought in any candy or novelty store or you can try making your own as you did, perhaps, when you were a child. The more durable sports kites can be found in most toy and hobby stores.

*—Will Yolen*

# BACKYARD SPORTS

**Shuffleboard** is played by two teams of two players each. Each team has three wooden disks 3 inches in diameter and 1 inch thick.

One player from each team stands back of the "10-off" space at each end. (Shuffleboard courts sometimes differ, however, for scoring.)

The first player shoves a disk toward the opposite end, trying to make it stop on a high number on his opponent's side. If the head of his shovel passes the back line of the diagram, the play does not count. A member of the other team takes the next turn, and this continues until each player has played three times. Each one tries to dislodge his opponent's disks as well as to place his own. If a disk touches any of the lines, it does not count in the scoring.

At the end of the round each player counts up the total of the numbers on which his disks rest, and the players at the opposite end begin to play.

**Horseshoe pitching.** The game of horseshoe pitching is widely known and very generally enjoyed. The stakes over which the horseshoes are to be pitched should be 8 inches above the ground. The regulation distance apart is 40 feet, but for young players this may be reduced to 30 feet or even less. Two or four players may take part. If there are four, they play in two teams, with teammates standing at opposite stakes. Each player (or each team) has two horseshoes, and they take turns pitching them.

The game consists of 50 points. If a player rings the stake with one of his horseshoes, he scores 3 points. If both of his horseshoes ring it, he scores 6 points. Points are awarded also for putting horseshoes near the stake, the nearest one scoring 1 point. If both the nearest ones belong to one player, he scores 2 points. A combination of one "ringer" and the nearest horseshoe scores 4 points. Only one player scores in a turn; if both make "ringers," each cancels the other. If the horseshoes of opponents are equidistant from the stake, no points are awarded for either of them. First play in the next turn is given to the member of the winning team at the opposite stake.

Horseshoes and stakes made especially for the game may be purchased. A copy of the official rules is usually packed with each pair of horseshoes.

**Barrel hoop quoits.** A quoit game similar to that in which horseshoes are used may be played with barrel hoops. The stakes over which the hoops are to be tossed should be about 2 feet above the ground and 15 feet apart. One point is awarded each time the hoop rings the stake.

**Croquet.** The regulation croquet court is 30 feet by 60 feet, but the game can be adapted to the available lawn. Either a grass or a dirt court may be used. The game is played by two to eight players. Croquet sets may be secured at reasonable prices in toy and sport shops; a set of rules comes with the equipment. Mallets may be improvised from old stair rails or other lumber, wickets from heavy wire; and other hard balls may be used.

**Croquet ball bowling.** Blocks of wood or tin cans may be set up for tenpins, and croquet balls may be used for bowling. A smooth floor or a smooth, level piece of ground is needed. One point is scored for every tenpin that falls, and 15 points are scored if all fall at one shot.

**Archery.** A section of wallboard can be propped up over the glass in the garage doors (scrap boards would serve as well but would be heavier to handle), making the driveway a fine, safe archery range.

Archery sets serve as birthday presents too, and neighboring children can bring their own. They first plant a homemade red flag on a stick out where the driveway enters the street, then shoot down the length of the driveway to the garage doors. On the cement strips of the driveway, paint a 30-foot line, a 50-foot line and a 65-foot line, to take care of the arguments! When shooting suction arrows, aim at the target painted right on the wallboard. When using target arrows, hang up a big burlap bag full of dried grass and affix renewable paper targets to it. When the children are older, add the game of darts here.—*Marian Churchill White*

# WINTER SPORTS

In areas where there are cold winters or within easy access of snowclad mountains, there are winter sports clubs formed around a variety of winter sports, including ice skating, ice boating, skiing, coasting, tobogganing, snowshoeing, dogsledding, horse sleighing, and bobsledding. These activities are fun for everyone in the family.

**Ice skating.** Before the ground freezes, my husband levels off the space we use for a vegetable garden the rest of the year, banking dirt all around the edge to make a six- or eight-inch wall. When the ground freezes, he gets the garden hose and begins to build up the ice.

This freezing is done only when the temperature is below 32, and in our winters, may have to be done two or three times as the ground thaws and refreezes. He works slowly, putting on water in a fine mist at first until the bottom is well coated with thin ice. Once this is on, he can apply water a little faster, but we never try to flood it all at once. In good, bitter weather we go out and spray on water for ten minutes or so, come in and thaw out for ten minutes to let it freeze well, then go out and put on another layer. The water eventually levels out into a smooth skating court, one which rests directly on the ground, and no novice can possibly fall through. The ice is probably two inches thick, on an average.

This will take terrific punishment from all the boys and girls in the neighborhood all day long, and when dark drives them home and we haul down the red-ball skating flag from the garage roof, we take a couple of minutes to run a fine spray on the scarred surface. This freezes during the night, and come morning there is a glassy rink again.

Yes, it does take some upkeep, but it more than pays for itself in peace of mind. No big boys knock a puck through a crowd of little skaters here, no one can fall in, Mother can step out if someone falls down especially hard, and warm dry shoes and hot cocoa are only ten feet away in the kitchen.

—*Marian Churchill White*

# HIKING AND WALKING

Physical fitness benefits are more likely to be accrued by hiking and walking as daily regular activities. In going on long hikes, the pace, distance, and ruggedness of terrain should be gradually increased.

Many local, State, and National parks and forests offer good trails and scenic spots for long interesting nature walks.

Hiking clubs may be established in cooperation with American Youth Hostels. This national organization will help local clubs in the establishment of inexpensive lodging places (youth hostels) for hikers traveling across country and needing overnight sleeping accommodations.

—*President's Council on Physical Fitness in Youth*

*There are many other sports activities, of course, which the family can enjoy together. Some of them are obvious—such as golf, horseback riding, hockey and squash—but what is needed for these is, primarily, transportation to get to where the facilities for participating in them are.*

*Other sports, more homebound—such as roller skating and hopscotch— are also fun and well known throughout the country. And roller-skating parties are a delightful way for the whole family to get together. Try one!*

*As a matter of fact, try one-two-three—any number of sports suggested in this section which you may not have attempted before. You're sure to discover new skills, new interests. And it would be most sporting of you to try!*

# KEEPING FIT FOR FUN

"*A COUNTRY IS AS STRONG really as its citizens and I think that mental and physical health, mental and physical vigor, go hand in hand.*

"*I hope that we will not find a day in the United States when all of us are spectators except for a few who are out on the field. I hope all Americans will be on the field, that they will concern themselves with the education of their children, with the physical development of their children, with the participation in the vigorous life, and then also, as their children get older, inculcate into them a desire to maintain that vigor through their normal life.*"—*John F. Kennedy, former President of the U.S.A.*

*Jack, be nimble; Jack, be quick;*
*Jack, jump over the candle stick.*

*Even Mother Goose was aware of the value of being nimble, alert and physically fit. From earliest times to the present, a sound mind and a sound body have both been deemed essential to overall good health and to a good life.*

# HOW DOES YOUR CHILD RATE?

Physical fitness, like over-all good health, of which it is an essential part, is not something that can be once achieved and then forgotten. In order for your body to serve you well, you've got to serve it well by getting enough exercise, in games, sports or calisthenics, or just walking and running. Sounds easy, doesn't it? Yet too many of our young people can't meet even the lowest acceptable standards of physical fitness.

How do you and your child measure up? A variety of tests to measure strength, flexibility and agility may be used. Here are three easy ones:

**Test for strength.** Find something to use for a chinning bar. This first test is the pull-up for boys, or the modified pull-up for girls. Boys grasp the bar with palms forward, and hand with arms and legs fully extended and feet free of the floor. For girls, adjust the bar to chest level. Girls extend their legs under the bar so their arms hang, fully extended, straight down from the bar.

In exercise, the boy pulls himself up until his chin is over the bar, then lowers himself slowly until the arms are fully extended again. The girl pulls herself up until her chest touches the bar, then lowers herself until the arms are again fully extended. Then up again.

Any boy should be able to do one pull-up. If he's fourteen, the minimum is two; the minimum if he's sixteen is three. The girls aged ten to seventeen should be able to do a minimum of eight modified pull-ups.

**Test for flexibility.** We'll use the sit-up, for both boys and girls. The child lies on his back, legs extended and feet about twenty-four inches apart. The hands are on the back of the neck with fingers interlocked. Hold his ankles, keeping the heels on the floor. Now he sits up, twisting the trunk and touching the right elbow to the left knee. Then he goes back down and up again, this time touching the left elbow to the right knee. Boys ten to seventeen years old should do at least fourteen of these, girls of the same age, at least ten, in rapid succession.

**Test for agility.** We'll use an exercise known as the "squat thrust," for both boys and girls. Start at the position of attention; the action is in four movements. First, bend the knees and place hands on the floor in front of the feet. Fingers are pointed forward. Arms may be between, outside of, or in front of bent knees. Now, in one movement, thrust the legs backward so the body is straight from shoulders to heels (the normal push-up position). Now, in one movement, return to the squat position, and in the final movement to the erect position.

Time this test. Boys ten to seventeen should do a minimum of four correct squat thrusts in ten seconds, girls three thrusts.

Don't be surprised if your child can't perform these simple feats. He has plenty of company.

**The effect on adults.** Some people have the misconception that exercise is not essential to good health and fitness. A few even think it endangers health. Yet medical men forcefully point out the fact that exercise is essential to good health. Not only skeletal muscles, but heart, lungs—all vital organs—benefit from vigorous activity and actually increase in efficiency.

Conversely, the less that the heart, lungs and circulatory system are called on to do, the less they can do. Against overweight and the attendant medical problems it can bring, regular exercise is one of your best protections. As for the spectre of heart disease and heart attack, for those entering the middle years, prevention is better than cure—prevention in the form of consistent exercise. If you're about forty and you've never played tennis or done much of anything else, don't start something very strenuous now, with a bang. But let your children start now (tennis, or whatever appeals to them) and they'll still be going strong when they're long, long past forty.

**Fitness at home.** The schools, of course, can do—and are doing—a great deal to help youngsters keep physically fit. And so can you. What you do at home is vital. What are your attitudes towards physical fitness, recreation and sports? The way you feel will determine your youngsters' delight in, or rejection of, physical activity.

What does your family like to do? For one family it may be hiking; for another, gardening. It may be bowling, boating, swimming or mountain climbing. The point is, do something—something the whole family enjoys doing—and do it often.—*Charles "Bud" Wilkinson*

# HOME EQUIPMENT

Play equipment which will contribute to physical fitness and which parents should be encouraged to install in their yard, basement, or rumpus rooms include—

## For Smaller Children

Jumping ropes
Horizontal ladder
Mats
Chinning bar
Jungle gym

Tether ball
Climbing ropes and rings
Balance beams
Table tennis sets
Skates and scooters

## For Youth and Adults

Chinning bars
Parallel bars
Mats
Striking bag
Rowing machine
Pully weights
Swedish stall bars
Weight training equipment—
    barbells and dumbbells
Peg board

Rings
Horizontal ladder
Climbing ropes
Jumping ropes
Table tennis sets
Tether ball, badminton, and other
    sports equipment
Metal-spring and rubber cable exercisers
Stationary bicycle

**Family Activities.** There are many activities which the family may enjoy together. Some of these can be done informally, others through organized programs. Many are even adaptable to competitive situations in which family members compete as a unit or "team."

The following activities along with innumerable others can provide vigorous and enjoyable family participation, (some of these are described more fully in the chapter dealing with sports):

Swimming
Roller skating
Bicycling
Walking and hiking
Camping
Folk, square, and other forms of dancing
Mountain climbing
Ice skating, skiing, and other winter sports
Boating, canoeing
Water skiing, skin and scuba diving, and
    other water sports
Fishing
Table tennis, badminton, tennis, golf, bowling,
    and other sports

*—President's Council on Physical Fitness in Youth*

# *T*HE THRILLS OF TUMBLING

Tumbling is natural fun. The toddler head-over-heels in the grass, the early teen leapfrogging over every hydrant in town—both are spontaneously working out basic tumbling skills. They're tumbling not because it's emotionally and physically therapeutic (although it is), but basically because they love it.

**Why give a tumble?** A well-balanced tumbling program can develop all the right muscles—the long slim ones. While most youngsters enjoy it,

there is no way to predict which ones will have native ability, for tumbling often reveals skills in highly unlikely candidates, including handicapped ones. In fact, it has been found that as children learn to handle themselves physically, they also acquire greater social skills and emotional stamina. A child also develops speed and agility, explosive leg power, hand-eye coordination and body strength which are the basis of all sports, and which are a built-in education for safety.

Tumbling is a natural activity for children because it follows their pattern of development. Body maturation begins with the big muscles; only later do the finer, small-muscle movements come into play. A child is born with the need to develop these big muscles, to go from one achievement to the next. He tests himself; if he can sit up, then maybe he can stand, then walk and, look ma, he's running, seemingly never to walk again.

Running and tumbling, jumping and diving are, therefore, basic to the business of growing up.

**Safety standbys.** Tumbling is essentially a noncompetitive sport in which the individual is pitted against himself. But tumbling is not fool-proof, though unfortunately it gives this illusion. The supple body twisting through the air at an intercollegiate meet gives no hint of the basic skills it took patient years to learn. If difficult feats are attempted before fundamentals are mastered, gymnastics may result in physical injury. Flinging one's body around in space is serious business.

The technique of spotting, therefore, is the most important safety tool in gymnastics. The instructor stands by, ready to catch the student at any point if danger develops. He can ward off an unbalanced maneuver with a flick of his hand and guide the student into faultless execution. He spots his students on all equipment, even at the mats. For the same forward roll which pulls a football player out of a fall on the field can result in a broken neck if it is improperly taught.

In a good tumbling program, students learn to spot and be spotted the first day they walk into class. Safety is not only a matter of rules. It also includes skill in teaching.

Don't put your child in a tumbling program unless you're sure it's a good one. Meet the instructor first. Watch him work a group so you get a feel for his attitude. Be certain he can maintain discipline; without it a group of tumbling youngsters can disintegrate into bedlam.

In addition, don't push your child. Most experts feel that children under eight years of age should be out skipping and jumping, rather than in a formal tumbling program. Then, when they're ready, they'll find tumbling healthful, helpful and fun.—*Shirley Sirota Rosenberg*

# WE LIKE BIKES!

Not only is biking inexpensive and great fun for the whole family; it is also very healthful. Why? Because it's mild, steady exercise, not too strenuous, yet good for the circulation and for those muscles which seem non-existent before one starts. All of us who bike look better, feel better and sleep better because of our hobby.

Of course, before you take off, there are some practical things to know.

1. Don't buy a bike unassembled unless you are handy and able to put together a partially knocked-down model.

2. Don't buy a bike with gears and hand brakes for a very young child. They are more delicate to operate than the simpler models. For older children and adults, standard touring models with no more than three gears are sufficient.

3. If you have a reliable bike shop nearby, chat with the owner for advice about the right bike for your needs, proper wheel size and so forth.

4. Whatever bike you decide on, make sure that the seat is sufficiently high for comfort. It will be a proper fit if, when you're sitting and have your foot on the pedal at low position, your leg stretches out straight.

5. Your handle bars should be adjusted so that you lean slightly forward when you ride but there is no strain placed on your arms.

Buying your bike is only part of the picture; it is vital for your safety to keep it in good mechanical condition. Experts say you should have a bicycle checked twice a year, a reasonable and worthwhile investment when you realize that this will make your travels smoother and safer. You should also have a horn or a bell as your warning sound, a light (visible for 500 feet), a carrying basket and a lock, either the chain or padlock variety. If you live in a large city where bike thievery is a problem, make sure that your bicycle serial number is registered with the police. (Some cities recognize bike licensing, which adds protection in case of thievery.)

Finally, before you set out, be sure you know the safety rules of bicycling.

Bulwarked by these few do's and don'ts, pedal in peace and discover for yourself the pleasures of sun, air and low pressure exercise.

—*Jean R. Komaiko*

# GAMES ON BIKES

**Ring Tossing.** The idea of this game is similar to that of pitching rings from a horse on a merry-go-round—only this time the bicycle (instead of the horse) is in action.

Use a board about 28 inches square. Drive 23 nails, 3 inches long, part way into it. Distribute the nails equally about 2 or more inches apart. The board is then suspended at a height of about 5 feet from some stationary object. A foul line is marked four feet from and parallel to the board.

Each contestant is given four jar rings which he holds in his throwing hand. He rides slowly toward the board and begins tossing the rings at any distance. If his bike touches the foul line, he sacrifices one throw and he must start a new run.

Several runs can be made to ring the nails for a total score. The cyclist who finishes first is the winner. Since the rider keeps only one hand on the handlebars for steering and balancing, this game should be played by better cyclists.

**Shoe Scramble.** This is the old shoe scramble game that always gives participants a lot of fun. Players are divided into two teams and placed at opposite ends of the playing field. Their shoes (not tied together) are placed in a pile in the center of the field.

At the starting signal, all the contestants ride forward to within 10-feet of the shoe pile where they dismount, find their shoes, put them on, remount their bikes and return to the starting line.

Prizes may be awarded to the team returning to their end of the playing field first, or to the individual player who returns home in the fastest time.

**Ride, Sheep, Ride.** A home base is selected. Two groups of riders are divided into the "sheep" and the "hunters."

The "sheep" and their leader ride out to hide. They decide on a set of signals which will be called by their leader. Signals might be a short, sharp blow on a bike horn, or whistle, or a word such as "Indians" which might mean "lie low." Two horn toots or the word "Cowboy" might mean "move up toward base." A long horn blow or word "Soldiers" could mean "get ready to ride for home base."

The leader of the "sheep" returns to the base when all of his players have been hidden. He then accompanies the "hunters" on their search. As the hunt continues, the leader calls his signals. When he thinks the hunters are far enough out, he yells: "Ride, Sheep, Ride."

At that call, the "sheep" emerge from hideouts and ride for home base in an attempt to get there before the "hunters". The full team who reaches home first become the "sheep" and the game continues. If cover is not plentiful, have more bases, fewer players in each group and more groups.


**Circle Tag.**   Two groups of riders line up in a single line at the opposite sides of a very large circle, with the players of each team facing in the opposite riding direction.

The circle should be large enough to permit the players to ride and maneuver their wheels with ease. The boundary of the circle should be well defined by blocks, chalk, sandbags or anything of a soft nature.

Using different color paper for each team, members are identified by a piece of crepe paper tied around their arms or diagonally across the upper part of their bodies.

At the leader's command of "Go", all the players ride as fast as possible in the opposite direction. The idea of the game is to try to tag as many members of the opposite team as possible.

As soon as a player is tagged, he is eliminated. He withdraws from the playing circle while the remaining players try to tag each other. The team with the most players untagged at the end of a given time wins.


**Umbrella Race.**   This is a funny race. Boys and girls compete on separate 100-yard courses. They hold open umbrellas overhead, steering their bikes with one hand.

A prize is given the rider who completes the course in the fastest time. Any rider who permits the umbrella to fall below his or her shoulders is immediately disqualified.


**Whip Game.**   There are many variations of the Whip Game—but here's one that is played frequently—and which you'll surely enjoy.

Each player has a whip which is made out of cord tied to a piece of wood.

A piece of paper is suspended by a string from some stationary object. The contestants ride by and with their whips try to rip off the paper.

The rider who rips the paper off closest to the string is the winner. Designate some distance from which the rider must swing his whip—not too far away or too close, but most certainly within arm's length.

# FUN
# ON
# WHEELS

*VACATION TRAVEL is an ideal family experience. It gives each member a new look—at all the others, at the world. Going places together means doing things together. It strengthens family understanding and creates memories and interest to share long after the return home.—Michael Frome*

# PLANNING
# A FAMILY TRIP

**Traveling with young children can be wonderful—if it's well planned.** On New Jersey's Garden State Parkway, there's a very exclusive restaurant which admits adults only when they are accompanied by children under five. In Washington, D.C., the National Gallery of Art now furnishes strollers without charge so that parents-with-infant-but-without-sitter can enjoy its great collection.

Family travel has soared in the past decade. California's Disneyland as well as hundreds of other playlands have mushroomed everywhere—and parents enjoy themselves at least as much as youngsters. The historical attractions emphasize family appeal, too. Colonial Williamsburg, for example, now offers a two-hour "Tricorn Hat Tour" for youngsters seven and older, during which they learn an 18th-century manual-of-arms, lock friends in the public gaol and receive a tricorn hat as a permanent souvenir. Their parents, meanwhile, are free to explore the sights of Williamsburg at their own level.

The National Park Service, host to 55 million persons annually, gears most of its facilities and programs to families with children. Trails, museums and guided walks are planned for all ages. Exhibits have eye appeal even for youngsters below reading age.

Activities for youngsters are being steadily expanded in the parks. At Yosemite National Park in California, you can now enroll your youngster of seven or older in the Junior Rangers—to participate in craft programs, conducted walks and evening campfires. At the Jackson Lake Lodge in Grand Teton National Park, Wyoming, children five and older gather every evening at 5:30 before the big picture window that frames the snow-capped Grand Tetons for a story hour with the social hostess.

All across America, from campgrounds to motels, luxury resorts and city hotels, in transportation by land, sea or air—the vacationing family is welcomed and wanted. But if you want to take full advantage of the new facilities, the better facilities, the generally improved travel conditions— start ahead of time. Reservations for most state and national parks must be made very early.

**186**

So get the family together tonight, tomorrow, next weekend—and start plotting your summer course.

**1. Decide where you want to go.**   Consider, for instance, the major travel events of the year with features for children. Basically, children are good travelers. They react with curiosity and interest to new vistas, a thoroughly healthy outlook worth encouraging. But remember their capacity to absorb is limited. Weigh your youngsters' needs and the result will be a far better vacation for all.

**2. Consult the sources that can help you.**   Travel agents have a wealth of information and their services cost little—sometimes nothing—since they receive commissions from transportation lines and hotels. If you are going by car and are an automobile club member, visit the club early for literature and maps. Oil companies also furnish extremely useful maps and booklets (your service station operator will file your request with the company's touring service).

Today, all forms of transportation offer special provisions for families traveling with children. For example, on first-class trips, hostesses aboard the major U. S. and international airlines provide everything from nursing bottles and canned baby foods to disposable diapers and bassinets (no charge). For older children, the airlines furnish books, games, magic slates, even toothbrushes and toothpaste. Many families find it practical to fly rather than spend days on the road—then rent a car at their destination. (If you're going by plane, look up the special family rates, applicable to first-class flights between noon Monday to noon Thursday, which bring costs down substantially.)

Write the chamber of commerce or official travel bureaus (simply address State Travel Bureau at the capital city) of states you may visit. Explain that you have children and request literature about state parks, accommodations, family attractions.

Several states now issue publications on the subject of vacationing with children.

New York's "Kid Stuff," for example, provides a good directory of fifty attractions, complete with a schedule of hours and admissions. The New York State Travel Bureau provides practical, useful information for a youngster and his parents about such places as its Frontier Town, where he can strut like a cowpoke; the 1,000 Animal Zoo, where he can pet and befriend the animals; the real railroad train he can drive and, for his sister, some wonderful doll collections.

**3. Study the range in accommodations**—with an eye on your budget, of course. Plan your overnight lodgings and place necessary reservations.

**Cabins and cottages** come closest to the atmosphere of home. The family doesn't have to dress for every meal. Doing your own cooking saves money—but see that it doesn't cancel out "vacation" for Mother. Cabins in national and state parks are in great demand, so act early for reservations. For cottages at mountain and seaside resorts, the Chambers of Commerce at the communities you have in mind provide lists of establishments and rates.

**The resort hotel** is for a rest. It costs more than camping or a cottage, but scarcely more than a motor tour with motel stops. The advantages: social programs, planned entertainment, athletics for both parents and children and emphasis on leisure. Many of the fine seashore and mountain hotels and resorts have counselors to lead the children in entertaining and educational activities, such as nature walks and arts and crafts on rainy days.

Many hotels, in many cities throughout the country, welcome children under fourteen without charge when they're with their parents.

**The modern motel** allows you to drive to the door of your room, unpack with dispatch and establish headquarters for the night. Even the most luxurious new motor hotels offer family quarters as well as playground, swimming pool and often baby-sitting service.

Select a motel with care. Be sure it is in pleasant surroundings and set back from the road so that you will get a good night's rest. If you want to find a moderately priced motel, you will have to stop your day's driving early, as you know, but you will do it anyway with children. The approval signs of such organizations as Quality Courts, Best Western and the American Automobile Association are worth looking for.

**4. Read about the places you are going to visit** and the country you will pass through. Even if your youngsters are too young, you ought to read in advance for your own enjoyment. The unknowing may enjoy themselves regardless, but the knowledge that comes from travel properly planned is a truly wonderful and lasting benefit. Besides adult literature,

**188**

fine children's publications prepare children for the places they are to visit and add to their appreciation.

Even if your children are infants, you needn't stay home—or leave them behind—not in this new family-minded land of travel. By summer you will need a vacation and you can afford it, for in America's broad expanse there are places to go and things to do to match every purse and taste.

This doesn't mean you must be with your children constantly during the course of your trip any more than you want to be with them constantly at home. Through wise planning, you should be able to design a vacation in which you and your children can share certain pursuits together, but be apart at times. You'll want to take books for summer reading, games, crayons, note paper, pencils and other small items that will provide pleasure for the youngsters on rainy days or during rest times. Certainly, everyone who owns a camera will want to use it all along the way.—*Michael Frome*

# GAMES FOR
# THE ROAD

**Diversions, plain and fancy, keep the young ones entertained when you travel by car.** I use many little tricks to break up a day's driving. For instance, I buy only five gallons of gas at a time. This means that we stop more often to stretch our legs and the kids get a chance to run around a bit.

I also try to maintain a flexible approach to the day's driving. I am not one of those drivers who considers the road something to be conquered rather than enjoyed. When we see a park, we pull up. My wife and I stretch out on the grass while the kids work off voltage. Similarly, we picnic a lot.

We've discovered that in standard cars it's a big mistake to put anything inside except people. The children need all the room they can get for wriggling and squirming. If our luggage overflows the trunk, we strap it to the rear bumper of the car and cover it with a tarpaulin.

Once we're sure of these basic physical comforts, we try to plan activities —fun on wheels—for the children.

**Billboard Alphabet.** One player watches the right side of the road and the other the left. When a child sees the letter A in any word in a sign on his side, he calls it out. Then he looks for a B, and so on. Allowing only one letter from any one sign, the child who first completes the alphabet wins the game.

**Odd and Even Plates.** Two players compete in this contest. While watching oncoming cars, one child counts the license plates that end in odd numbers, while his opponent scores the even ones. We set a goal of 25 or 50 points as the winning score and sometimes give 2 points for out-of-state plates.

**Guess What I Saw.** This is a simple observation game that even tots can play. One child spots something along the road and the other players try to guess what he saw.

Michael begins by telling us how many letters are in the name of the object. Then he gives a fairly vague clue, relating to size, color or some detail. The other players must guess what it is before I clock off two miles.

**Six Cities.** When we stop for gas we pick up several copies of state or regional road maps. Then my wife gives the names of six cities or towns to the children. The first child to locate and circle all six with a colored crayon is the winner.

**How Many Routes?** This one's for the smaller children. Simply give them two cities fairly far apart on the map. You can help them locate the cities. They must draw as many different map routes between the two as they can.

**Bring It Back.** In a forest area, it's our custom to take a fifteen or twenty-minute walk through woods and fields. I bring along a list of simple nature objects that we are likely to come across, then we divide into teams to see who brings back the most things on the list.

**I Hear.** This is a resting game. We all sit quietly and write down the sounds we hear within a five or ten-minute period. Sounds might include

**190**

bird calls (properly identified), breeze in the trees, water flowing, a train whistle, a squirrel scolding, and so forth.

**Petal Guess.** My wife has devised a number of simple lottery games that work nicely. She comes back from a walk with a flower, and asks each child, "How many petals does it have?" The closest guess wins the flower. Play the same game with the leaves of a fern or an ear of corn.

**Who Am I?** Even David Junior, the youngest in our family, can play "Who Am I?" We select a new identity for him. Then he has to ask questions—"Am I a person?" "Am I animal?" "Am I in a story?"

By this time he knows the answer because we always decide that he is either Winnie the Pooh or Miss Westervelt, his nursery school teacher. Yet he always gets a kick out of the game.

Whoever is "It" must ask his questions during five miles worth of travel and then has three guesses to discover the secret identity.

**Continued Story.** This is a game for children who have just started to talk—or can't stop talking. One of us starts to tell a story and suddenly breaks off in the middle. The next player must pick it up immediately and keep it going. This continues with each player as he has a turn. The last one must wind up the tale with a grand climax.

**Never Say It.** We begin this game by deciding that a certain word, such as "I" or "No," must not be spoken. Then we start a general conversation in which we each try to trick the others into saying the forbidden word. Whenever this happens, the loser gets a penalty point. We talk ten miles' worth, and after that the player with the fewest penalty points wins.

**Alphabet Story.** Each word of a made-up story must start with a successive letter of the alphabet from a to z.

Most of us are familiar with other word games—ghost, coffee-pot, twenty questions, for example—which also make good trip time-passers.

**Card Games.** We lay a suitcase on its side on the back seat and cover it with a cloth to keep the cards from skidding. The children like to play

Slap Jack, War, Go Fish, Old Maid, Concentration and others. Here are the rules for a special favorite.

Seven of a Kind. If there are three players, prepare a deck of twenty-one cards, with seven cards in each of three suits. If there are four players prepare a deck of twenty-eight cards, seven in each of four suits. For five players, make it thirty-five cards in the deck, with eight or nine in each suit. Deal seven cards to each player. The purpose of the game is to get seven cards of the same suit in your hand. Each player looks at his hand and passes an unwanted card to his left. The idea is to keep cards that give promise of building into a strong suit, and unload isolated cards. The first player to hold seven of a kind calls out, "seven of a kind!"

**What bothers children** most while car-riding is their inability to move freely. Here are some physical games to be played in a moving automobile.

**Do This and Add Something.** My wife usually starts by clapping her hands several times. Then daughter Paris claps her hands, then sneezes. Now Michael claps his hands, sneezes and scratches his head. David Junior claps his hands, sneezes, scratches his head, and stamps his feet. Each player continues to add one action to those of the player before him. The last player able to repeat everything correctly and add a new action is the winner.

**I'm Taking a Jet Plane.** This is all in pantomime, showing things the players might take with them on a jet plane. I might start by showing a suitcase. Paris could then pantomime a suitcase and an umbrella. Michael could add a fiddle, and so on.

**O'Grady Says.** This is the old "Simon Says" with a new name. Paris, being the oldest, usually takes the part of O'Grady and lets my wife referee. Paris gives commands such as "O'Grady says bounce up and down." Michael and David Junior must then obey immediately. But if she omits the phrase "O'Grady says," they must not obey. The purpose of the game is to give the kids exercise. We try to keep the game going at a good pace and usually forget to keep score.

**Six and Zero.** Ask the children to make a "six" in the air with their right hands. Then have them make a clockwise circle, or "zero," on the floor with their left feet. Next they must try to do both simultaneously.

**Make 'em Laugh.**   At some point in his life almost every child plays this game spontaneously. It's simple. One child faces another, and by using silly gestures or by laughing himself, he tries to make the other laugh. A variation is "make 'em yawn."

**Drawing Doodles.**   My wife, our vice-president in charge of doodles, draws a few on a sheet of paper. They may be straight, curved, spiraling or curlycue. Then the children must incorporate them into a picture.

**Map of Home.**   Little children might try to draw the house or apartment, back yard or front street. This game is reassuring to small children who get a little homesick on a long trip.

**Alphabet Book.**   Equip each child with a fairly large hard-cover notebook. Then let them work singly or as a team on one "Alphabet Book." Their first job is to clip (using blunt scissors) large capital letters from magazines and paste them in alphabetical order on successive pages of the notebook. Now they must cut out pictures from the magazines and paste them in under the proper letters.

This is the kind of game that children put aside for a time and return to later. And it's excellent spelling practice for all youngsters.

**Pipe Cleaner Sculpture.**   Imaginative youngsters work these fluffy, pliable cleaners into animals, birds, people, planes and mechanical objects.

**Crayon Leaf Prints.**   Place a green leaf on a flat smooth surface. Put a sheet of white paper over it. The child now rubs the paper gently and steadily with a crayon holding it lightly with one hand so the leaf will not move. As the child does this, the edges, veins and stem of the leaf will appear.

**Free Play Activities.**   Many preschool children are very talented at keeping themselves occupied once they have the toys and materials handy.

A parent can make a list of practical play things for car traveling. It always helps to add some surprise items for good measure. We have found that a cardboard box with a young child's name on it is indispensable.

**Singing.** Also try teaching songs to little children. In addition to the familiar songs, preschool children delight in making up new ones. Use familiar tunes like "Skip to My Lou" or "Mulberry Bush" and let the three or four-year-old invent songs about the trip, family, friends, nursery school, fire engines—the whole wide world.

**Story Telling.** When David Junior requests a story, he may indicate an old favorite, he may want a new one, or he may even specify a subject, saying, "Tell me about the time that big dog came into our house." If he wants an old favorite, we have his story book in the carton. If he wants a new one, we improvise on boat trips, visits to his grandparents, stories of farm life, or ad lib fables of foreign countries and faraway places.

You'll often find that all children need to enjoy themselves in a car is to be left alone. They have skills and inventiveness of their own, and if they're getting on well enough, let well enough alone.—*Dave Garroway*

# TOYS TO TAKE ALONG

A young child's span of interest is short; therefore it is necessary to take a varied collection of toys for him.

A rag doll, for example, with a wardrobe that can be buttoned on and taken off, or trains or automobiles three or four inches long that can be run along the arm of a chair or on a Pullman table, are active and dramatic outlets after a time spent in drawing pictures with crayons. The same is true of the hand puppets and the little animals which the children may make in their quieter moments out of pipe cleaners and then dramatize into a circus or a menagerie.

On a train or a boat, because of the motion, it is not advisable to allow a child to keep his attention focused too long on a small space. For this reason, older children should be provided with some amusement besides books. A map game will enable them to follow their own journey—and incidentally to learn something about geography—with wooden pegs that fit into holes beside the names of cities along the way. A compass design board makes all sorts of intricate geometric designs at a mere shift of a pencil, and a few minutes' work with a box of crayons completes the resemblance of designs to stained-glass windows.—*Charlotte Ross Mochrie*

# HUNDREDS OF
# HOBBIES

*SOMEONE ONCE DESCRIBED A HOBBY as something which is either absolutely fascinating (if it's your own) or which seems a ridiculous way to waste time (if it's someone else's)! The best hobby, then, is one which is truly, completely your own—something which brings you pleasure. So what if you're the only student of oneiromancy in your neighborhood!*

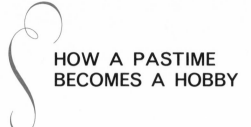

# HOW A PASTIME
# BECOMES A HOBBY

Hobbies deserve special consideration since they are frequently the most enduring, challenging and rewarding form of play. A pastime becomes a hobby when it is pursued intensively and developed systematically. An absorbing hobby will, therefore, give a child the satisfaction of becoming a specialist and something of an authority on one subject. It will also develop habits of perseverance and thoroughness, and make him a more interesting person.

You can help your children find hobbies by exploring their interests with them, to discover activities that attract them and suit their personality and abilities.

They will also need help and encouragement in developing the hobby once it is found. Be on the lookout for books and pamphlets, organizations and neighborhood specialists, as well as materials of all kinds.

Hobbies often get their start with the transient interests of early childhood, but they rarely reach full development until the preteen or teen years. The following categories comprise most types of hobbies—although no classification can be exhaustive, since the most satisfying and creative hobbies frequently rise out of one small facet of a subject.

**Collections:** Stamps, coins, rocks, flowers, leaves, shells, insects, figurines, dolls, toy soldiers, autographs, beads, puppets, tiles, bells, postcards, recipes, posters, pewter, pottery, bottles.

**Animal Hobbies:** Raising hamsters, mice, rabbits, guinea pigs, tropical fish, pigeons, canaries, lizards, etc.; grooming and showing a cat or dog; bee-keeping; birdwatching.

**Entertainment Hobbies:** Magic, sleight-of-hand, puppet shows, checkers, chess, bridge, word games, puzzles.

**Science Hobbies:** Weather study, chemical experiments, amateur radio, intercom systems, astronomy, microscopic studies, satellites and space ships, fossils, archaeology, botany, zoology, ornithology.

**Special Crafts:** Woodworking, woodcarving, jewelry-making, dressmaking, bookbinding, printing, weaving, plastic crafts, model-making.

**Special Arts:** Sketching, water color painting, oil painting, engraving, wood cuts, etching, cartoons, ceramics, sculpture, photography (portraits, landscapes, stereo, home movies, scientific photography), music (band, orchestra, folk singing, choral singing), dancing (acrobatic, ballet, folk, tap, ballroom, modern).

**Gardening:** Rock garden, water garden, window garden, greenhouse, plant breeding, hydroponics, special varieties (gladioli, African violets, cacti, etc.).—*Robert M. Goldenson, Ph.D.*

# IT'S FUN TO WORK WITH YOUR HANDS

Hobbyists, craftsmen, even doctors tell you there is nothing more relaxing than the satisfaction that comes from actually making something.

**Billfolds.** These are probably the most popular projects for leatherworkers. They make suitable gifts for all occasions and embody many essential processes in the making.

**Belts.** Making belts is always interesting because of the varied ornamentation and their usefulness. Stamped belts may be personalized with a name.

**Bags.** A large variety of bags can be made by the leather-worker. These range from ladies' zipper and carved handbags, ladies' shoulder strap bags to custom-made camera cases, and gadget bags or overnight toilet cases.

**Briefcases.** A project of a compact zippered briefcase requires ingenuity, craftsmanship, design. Briefcases lend themselves to originality.

**Leather for the Home.** Working and producing beautiful leather accessories for the home, for gifts, for personal use is a hobby the entire family, from the youngest to the oldest, can enjoy. Beautiful articles of furniture upholstered with luxurious leather can add sparkle and comfort to the home. Unusual lamps, table tops, waste baskets, only to name a few things, are being done by the leather hobbyist to add to today's pleasure of more enjoyable living.

**Mosaics in Ceramics.** One of the oldest artistic media, mosaics have become newly popular as a contemporary form of art . . . an art which is as colorfully decorative as it is long-lasting and useful.

Mosaics are pictures or patterns made by inlaying small pieces of ceramic tile, glass tile, shells, metal, stones, etc., on a flat surface. Making mosaics is an art-hobby that almost anyone can do and achieve beautiful results. For a starting project, try covering a table top, or making a decorative serving tray, dish, or planter.

Only a few materials are needed for mosaic work. Choose from several kinds of tiles. You'll need, also, a pair of tile cutters, or "nippers," file, sandpaper, cement, and grout, plus a brush for applying grout, a sponge for cleaning afterward, and, of course, the base to which you are applying the tiles. (This can be a wooden box or bowl, a table, tray, or any object which you wish to decorate.) You can buy these materials separately if you prefer, but complete kits are also available, containing tiles, cement, grout, and base object (table, tray, etc.) as well as instructions.

**Copper Tooling.** Tooling or embossing copper foil is becoming very popular as a hobby. It's easy to learn, fun to do, and tools and materials cost very little. Brass, copper, and aluminum are most commonly used for tooling; copper tools most readily and a pleasing variety of color effects can be obtained by applying heat or certain chemicals.

Some articles suitable for tooling are: Wall plaques, costume jewelry,

**200**

baggage tags, decorated facings for bookends, jewelry boxes, etc. A tooled metal design can be mounted on stiff leather with cement, or fastened to wood with escutcheon pins. Copper wall plaques are especially attractive mounted on cork.

Materials needed for tooling are: Copper foil; modeling tools; background stamp or stamps if desired; tracing paper and a sharp pencil, for tracing designs; a straight edge (a steel rule); scissors; a piece of sheet rubber; rubber cement, vaseline, and "metalfill" or other filler compound.

**Copper Enameling.** Distinctive and unusual costume jewelry can be made by copper enameling. Of course, you will improve with practice, but beginners turn out quite handsome pieces of work. The copper shapes are not expensive, and experimenting can produce beautiful articles (as well as being downright fun!).

Enameling on metals is done by heating powdered enamels on a metal surface until a certain temperature causes the powder to fuse in a glass coating over the metal base. Enameling is done on copper, gold, or silver. As copper is the easiest to handle, and the least expensive of the three, it is recommended.

Copper may be cut to shape, but many copper pieces may be bought already cut to form, and these are much easier to use. Besides the copper pieces, you'll need a kiln, enamel colors, glass threads, flux, solder for attaching backs (jeweler's findings) if you are making earrings, cuff links, etc., and the backs to be attached. You'll also need a file, tweezers, palette knife, putty knife, a small brush, asbestos, emery cloth, and gum agar. Kits may be purchased which contain the necessary articles, or you may buy each individually.

**"Slapsticks".** This craft started with the children, due to its low cost and the fact that it is easy to do. Many young children have made a number of useful articles for gifts and household use. Only a few, inexpensive materials are needed: the "slapsticks," cement or glue, and sometimes accessories according to the project being made; cork discs, wooden beads, reeds, elastic, plastic lace, and other materials.

Complete kits, containing all necessary materials, as well as ideas for a number of projects, may be obtained either for individual or group projects.

**Aluminum Designing.** Aluminum is a popular craft metal because of its attractiveness, durability, and low price. It can be purchased in sheets,

**201**

rolls (foil), or pre-cut shapes (circles, squares, bracelet blanks, etc.); and is suitable for a variety of techniques: Tooling, etching, embossing, and hammering, or beaten metalwork. (Aluminum is not suitable for enameling by using heat, because of its lower melting point.) Hammered aluminum makes handsome and sturdy trays, bowls, coasters, and similar articles; tooled pieces make attractive plaques, costume jewelry, and decorative "tops" for jewelry and trinket boxes. Etching can be done on bracelets, ash trays, coasters, and larger household articles.

**Basketry.** Basket making is an ancient craft, the principles of which have altered little since primitive times. Even a few generations ago, woven "cane-bottom" chairs were found in every home; Grandma's work basket held the mending; and various other types of baskets were used for laundry, gathering eggs or fruit, etc.

Nowadays, baskets are highly popular for table use; and also for away-from-the-table meals such as hamburgers or chicken-in-a-basket on the patio, in front of TV, etc.

Materials needed for basketry are simple and inexpensive; reed or other materials used for weaving, roundnosed pliers, diagonal cutters, small hand-knife, and an awl. (The only "tool" you need for raffia is a needle.) Round reed, flat reed, cane, raffia, and synthetic fibers are used for weaving. Wooden bases for baskets and trays, smoothly sanded and with holes bored for spokes, can be used also.—*from "Have a Hobby for Pleasure and Profit," a publication of Employee Relations, Inc.*

# THE COLLECTING CRAZE

The collecting urge begins around six and consists of any and everything that catches the child's fancy. The house will stay a little less cluttered if containers are provided for the treasures. Cigar boxes are perfect for the young collector. The outside paper may be removed with steel wool and the boxes painted, but they are loved just as much if left natural. Limit the number of boxes to the amount of space in the house because all of them will be filled. The amateur collector of any age is indiscriminate. His emphasis is on quantity, not quality. This is a normal process of growth and he should be left alone, even though his accumulations look suspiciously like trash to adults.

The collections are among the child's most cherished possessions and they should never be thrown away without his permission. As he grows and matures, he will discard. One ten-year-old had thirteen collections all active at the same time. Her wise parents interfered with none of them. Later, in a surge of room cleaning, she sniffed disdainfully at box after box, wondering aloud why in the world she had wanted that "old junk."

**Rock Collections:** Rocks make interesting and instructive collections. Even the two-year-old picks up pretty pebbles and carries them around. Smooth, rounded stones can be found along the banks of a swift stream. Visit a rock quarry and, besides watching the method of mining, notice the difference in the newly mined fragments and those that have been exposed to weathering. Examine tilts and seams in the steep banks along the highway. Were they caused by the earth's tilting or by being folded under great pressure? Leaf prints are often found in coal and fossils of shells in limestone. Nothing proves to the child so conclusively as these fossils that parts of the earth were once under water. Rocks are often grouped according to hardness. Test to see which ones will scratch others. Slate will write and was used for that purpose before pencils were thought of. Mica can be split into thinner and thinner sheets. Sandstone will crumble. Soapstone can be shaved with a knife into powder, then mixed with water to make marbles. Make lists of things man uses from the earth. Would our kind of civilization have been possible without them? If we do not conserve our natural resources, what will be the result?

**Insect Collections:** Making cages for insect collections develops ingenuity and resourcefulness. A lemon crate covered with mosquito netting or screen wire is effective for many kinds of specimens. Shoe-box containers are convenient and fun to use because they are like miniature houses. Remove the cardboard from the lid, leaving an inch of margin. Replace the cardboard with cellophane held in place on the sides with transparent tape. Punch holes for ventilation. The simplest cage for small insects is a lamp chimney placed in a flower pot filled with damp soil. A small square of netting held in place with a rubber band makes the cover. This is a superb place for lightning bugs because they can be used as a bedside lamp with no danger of escape. For a large outdoor cage, roll a yard of screen wire into a cylinder, sew or wire the long side and cover the top with netting. Sink the cage in loose dirt in a shady place. This will accommodate several specimens and, if some of them eat the others, explain the struggle for existence all living forms must make.

One seven-year-old was given an elaborate dollhouse with a whole family of dolls. The same week she had the great fortune to find not one, but two, lady bugs. She and her father made them a house from wire covered with netting, with a door that opened and closed. The dollhouse was used thereafter to house the lady bugs and other insect families.

**Leaf Collections:** All children like the bright leaves of fall, and even the youngest likes to pick up and carry the crimson ones. Do not stress names but do notice the difference in sizes, shapes and colors. Some have smooth edges, others are toothed and still others lobed. The brightest colors occur when heavy frosts are followed by sunshiny days. Pick a number of the prettiest leaves to mount. Press them in a weighted book for two or three days, then iron under waxpaper with a warm iron. Mount them on paper with gummed tape.

**Fall Flowers:** They are gaudy and gay and, unlike the spring ones, plentiful enough to pick. Goldenrod, black-eyed Susans and asters are all favorites of children. These can be pressed between blotters under weights and mounted in a scrapbook, but the colors fade to a dull brown. This is the time to collect grasses and everlasting flowers for winter bouquets. Hang them upside down in a warm place to dry. Pine cones of varying sizes can be dried and saved for Christmas decorations. Dried cattails last longer if given a thin coat of shellac. Contrast the growing places of goldenrod and cattails. Plants, like people, are selective in the places they like to live.—*Carmen Stone Allen*

**Stamp and coin collections.** Although these are somewhat more expensive hobbies to pursue, they are absorbing interests that usually last well into adulthood. They are educational, too, teaching youngsters a great deal about the history and geography of the world. And, of course, a good stamp or coin collection becomes, in time, valuable monetarily as well. There are now thousands of collectors throughout the United States, and many catalogs, magazines, and specialized newspapers dealing with current information about both stamps and coins.

**204**

# STARTING SCIENCE HOBBIES

Interest in scientific phenomena is one of the clearest indications that children do not automatically draw a line between play and learning. Exploration of the stars, minerals, insects and the processes of nature is simply a means of satisfying curiosity and getting to know their world. Scientific interest remains on a more practical than theoretical level throughout elementary school. Even so, they learn many of the laws of nature through (a) playing with machines, such as steam engines, (b) observing and collecting living things, (c) using apparatus such as magnets or lenses, and (d) constructing their own instruments, such as radios. Our job as parents is to see that they have a taste of all these types of experiences.

**The beginning years, 1-3:**  Scientific interests do not begin as science, but through direct contact with materials like mud, clay, rubber and water; and processes like fog condensing on a window pane or blowing on a pinwheel. Children must therefore have an opportunity to sharpen their senses and powers of observation by having a wide variety of objects to watch, squeeze, bang, bite, dig, pour and float.

**Playthings:**  Sand box and utensils, sponge, bubble pipe, peg board, balloons, funnel, floating toys.

**Early childhood, 3-6:**  They like to observe every-day processes: water becoming steam or turning to ice, compass turning north, a magnet picking up a nail, a cake rising in the oven. This is the time to awaken interest in the way machines operate, the way stars and insect wings move, how live things grow and reproduce. Take them to see a huge freight engine, an oil derrick, an airport, a building under construction.

**Playthings:**  Magnifying glass, compass, magnet, cooking utensils, sun dial, hour glass, aquarium, terrarium.

**Middle childhood, 6-9:** Be prepared for hundreds of questions on how things work and why, but also let them find out for themselves through using scientific instruments and through simple experiments such as changing the angle or a toy airplane wing, breaking up light with a prism, fertilizing a plant, condensing steam to make "rain."

**Playthings:** Prism, telescope, microscope, field glasses, electricity kit, crystal or transistor radio kit, magnetism set, feed and germination set, electrical steam engine, map-making set, weather station, elementary chemistry set.

**Later childhood, 9-12:** This is the time to expose your child to many different fields of science in the hope that one or more will strike fire. If he becomes intrigued, he will need help from adults—a parent, an uncle or teacher—to develop the interest further through visits to specialist, laboratories and museums as well as through special materials.

**Playthings:** Fossil laboratory set, geology set, solar cell kit, black light kit, optics set, star spotter, insect set, microscope with slides, photo-electric kit, chemistry laboratory, model planetarium, radio kit, microbiology set, astronomical telescope, intercom system, electronics lab, computer kit.

*—Robert M. Goldenson, Ph.D.*

# TAKING
# SCIENCE
# OUTDOORS

One of the aims of science teaching is understanding our environment. The summer months provide many opportunities for investigating by the child whose explorations may go no farther than the backyard.

They may be as simple and natural as making mud pies. Water added to dry, powdery dust changes the texture to a slushy, oozy mass. To demonstrate the different types of soil, make some of the pies from loam, others from sand and a third group from clay. Let them dry in the sunshine, then test to find which are easiest to crumble and which disintegrate first in water. Discuss the types of soil best adapted to different plants in dry weather and in wet weather.

**Simple Experiments with Dew:**   Summer mornings before the sun is high are the best times to examine the dew. It does not fall, but is formed when the earth cools and the moisture from the warm air condenses on cooler objects. Let the child make dew by adding a little cake coloring to a glass of ice water placed in a warm room. Drops of clear moisture will form on the surface of the glass. Warm air likes moisture, but when the air gets cold, it can no longer carry the moisture, and in this case deposits it on the glass. Some children think that the moisture comes from water inside the glass, but using colored water proves this false.

**Clouds:**   Observe the clouds on a summer day. Children like cumulus ones best, and while they should not be burdened with names, they will soon notice that there are different kinds: some are fluffy like balls of cotton, others are thin and wispy, some are in even layers, while the thunderstorm types are tall, towering and black. Pick out imaginary pictures formed by the clouds. They change so rapidly that a rabbit becomes a dragon in the space of five minutes, and in another five the whole thing may disappear. Most children express a desire to walk in the clouds. They can have their wish by walking in a heavy fog; fog is a cloud resting on the ground.

**Hail:**   If hail falls during the summer, collect some stones and split them open. Notice how they are made up of layers much like an onion. The hail started toward the earth as a drop of water, but it was caught up in an upsurge of air, and carried so high in the atmosphere that it froze. Again it fell, and again came another layer of ice. This process was repeated as many times as there are layers of ice. Speak of the force of such air currents powerful enough to carry anything so far, and discuss the reason pilots avoid thunderstorms.

**Thermometers:**   Watch the thermometer reading on the hottest days. The older child will be interested in an instrument that gives both the temperature and the humidity. In a very short time, he will realize that his comfort really depends as much on the amount of moisture in the air as on the temperature.

**207**

**Water:** No one can become intimately acquainted with rain except by staying out in it; yet too many children are herded inside during summer showers. Water play with a hose is also a merry occasion. Cover part of the nozzle to show the force water has when under pressure. Turn the hose on a grass-covered slope, then on a bare slope, and contrast the amount of soil loosened. What is happening to our soil in areas where erosion is not checked?

**Sunsets:** Too many city children never see a sunrise. It is well worth getting up a few hours early for this experience. Discuss the methods of telling time before clocks were invented. Study the shadow of a tall pole, noticing how its position changes during the morning, noon, afternoon.

Let the child make a simple sundial. Drive a nail in the center of a piece of wood about a foot square. Set it where the sun can strike it all day, and mark the places where the shadow from the nail falls at nine, twelve, three and six o'clock. Make shadow pictures with a flashlight or candle in a dark room. Notice that if one stands behind the candle, the shadow will not form on the same surface. Watch for unusual sunsets and try reproducing some of them with crayon or water colors.

**Droughts:** During an extremely dry period, examine the plants to see what effect lack of moisture has upon them. Notice that some leaves wilt, others curl and, if the drought continues, the whole plant dies. A picnic spoiled because of rain is less a tragedy if the disastrous results of drought to the farmers' living and to our own food supply are understood.

**Farms:** Visit a farm to see food growing in all its stages of maturity. Power machinery has taken away much of the charm of wheat harvesting, but it may be possible to find a farm that still uses a binder and a thresher. Let the child help with as many of the processes as possible. Have him chew some of the wheat grains to get the taste and try grinding some wheat into flour, using the food grinder.

Watch the growing corn and explain what a contribution the Indians gave our new civilization when they introduced corn to the early settlers. Many people think that the colonies could not have survived if it had not been for corn.

Play a game, with one person naming a common domestic food seen on farms, and the other telling how it grows: underground, on vines, trees, stalks or bushes.

**Studying Live Insects:** Insects can be kept for days, if green foliage, food and water are supplied. Grasshoppers eat fruit, lettuce and clover. Crickets and katydids like pulpy fruits and lettuce. Spiders eat flies and insects. A solution of sugar and water tempts butterflies and moths. Any kind of caterpillar should be given the same kind of leaf upon which it was found. There are books that tell how to feed and care for any kind of specimen.

It is diverting to observe many insects in their natural habitat. Break open the nest of a dirt dauber to see all stages of its development. The female makes her nest from mud, then seals food in the passages so there will be an ample supply close at hand when the young hatch.

Because of their incredible skill in web building, spiders are fun to watch. Very few are poisonous, but the child should be taught to look and not touch. Find one building or repairing a web to appreciate the amount of work and perseverance required. Drop a live fly into the web and see what happens. Notice the victims left under the web. The spider does not eat his prey but merely sucks the juices from it.

Point out the good things about different forms of life. The bumblebee fertilizes the red clover and, without its help, we would not have this food for our horses and cows. Spiders destroy flies that carry disease germs. Wasps eat mosquitoes and thus help to prevent malaria. Birds eat thousands of harmful insects. Find out what kinds of snakes in the locality are poisonous and protect the others. They contribute to man by eating insects.

**Toads:** Watch toads on warm summer evenings. They are harmless, they do not cause warts and they are of untold benefit to man because of insects they destroy. Keep one for a few days in a box with damp earth in the bottom. Provide a small dish of water and add live flies. The toad catches them with his long tongue, but the motion is too fast to follow. Notice how well the toad's coloring blends with his surroundings.

**Butterflies:** Older children may want to start a collection of butterflies and insects. A butterfly net is a necessity. Seam a yard of netting down the side and bottom, run a wire hoop through the top and attach it to a broom handle. A fruit jar with a tight lid and a rubber makes an effective killing jar. Put a spoonful of carbon tetrachloride on a piece of cotton, covering the cotton with paper to prevent the specimen's tangling in it. Leave the insect in the killing jar overnight. Cigar boxes lined with corrugated paper in the bottom make good display cases. If the child's interest continues, get a good book on preparing and mounting.

**209**

**Star Gazing:** Winter evenings are especially good for this. Talk about the number, size and brilliance of the stars; point out the Big Dipper, the Little Dipper and the Milky Way. To fix these images firmly, make star maps with blue construction paper and silver gummed stars. Place the stars on the paper in the position of the dippers or any other simple constellations. If there is a telescope in your neighborhood, arrange to take the youngsters for a look through it.

Star study usually results in a multitude of questions about the universe. Use a grapefruit for the sun, an orange for the world, a lemon for the moon and tangerines for the stars. Have your helpers hold them away at varying distances for a concrete demonstration of the solar system.

**Indoor Plants:** Paper narcissus bulbs are a good choice for inside growth. Let the child go to the store to buy them, allow him to examine them leisurely and call his attention to the resemblance between bulbs and onions. Surround the bulbs with an inch of pebbles in a shallow bowl, and cover the pebbles with water. Store the bulbs in a dark closet until they begin to sprout—about a week or ten days—then bring them out and watch the developments carefully.

The sprouted onion from your vegetable bin also has possibilities. Wedge it in a narrow-necked bottle filled with water. The root system develops rapidly and illustrates how much of the plant is below the surface. Sweet potatoes and avocado seeds also make interesting plants, but they are much slower to begin growing.

Lima beans, because of their large size, are good for experimentation. Soak them in water from twelve to sixteen hours, then let the children split some of them open. With a magnifying glass, the tiny baby plant inside can be seen very clearly. Place two of the soaked beans in each of several glasses filled with pebbles and add just enough water to touch the beans. (If they are covered they will rot, but to prove this fact, submerge some entirely.) Leave another glass with no water to demonstrate that the beans will not sprout.

After the roots and leaves have begun to grow, allow the young botanist to examine and experiment upon some of them. Transplant a few to a flower pot with good soil. Postpone final judgments on such questions as "Which will grow better?" by saying, "Let's wait and see." Keep the plants long enough for the experimental evidence to demonstrate that plants do need soil.

When the bean plants have developed a good root system, put one in a glass cup with water to which a little red ink has been added. Say again, "Watch what happens." When the red color seeps up to the top, it will

**210**

illustrate to the child that the plant gets its food through the roots and then carries it up to the leaves.

Because the clear objectivity of science helps to develop logical thinking and accurate perceptions, a parent should use every opportunity to stimulate the inquiring mind.

**Birds:**  Children of all ages are interested in birds. Keep this interest real and vital by putting a feeding station just outside a window. (See our instructions for making one.) Use seeds and bread crumbs for food. On extremely cold days, place a tin of warm water on the feeding tray.

Confirm the fact that birds throw back their heads when they swallow. Talk about the differences in shape, color, size and song of the birds, but don't stress names unless the child wants to know. Even then, instead of saying, "It's a sparrow," say, "Let's look it up." Every home should have a bird book containing the names of those well known in the vicinity.
—*Carmen Stone Allen*

# BUILDING
# A BIRD HOUSE

Bird house building is valuable not only as an outlet for the creative instinct but for the knowledge of birds which it develops.

**Suggestions for Construction.**  To make bird houses safe and comfortable for their occupants, certain principles of construction and design must be observed. A well-built house should be durable, rainproof, cool and readily accessible for cleaning. For making bird houses wood is the best building material. Metal should be avoided because it is a great conductor of heat. Weather boards, rustic cedar, and strips of wood with the bark adhering to them all make excellent material and may easily be cut into proper lengths and nailed together. In the choice of wood an easily workable kind, such as cypress, pine or yellow poplar, is preferable. Some-

**211**

times ready-made boxes of the proper size may be used with a little reinforcement.

In preparing wooden houses, entrance holes should be countersunk from the outside to exclude rain, small holes made in the middle of the floor for drainage, and a row of small holes bored just beneath the edges. Heads of nails and screws should be set rather deeply and covered with putty. Roofs should be made with sufficient pitch to shed water easily, the overhang in the average house being from two to three inches to protect the entrance holes from driving rain.

When placed in trees the houses should be painted a dull shade of green or gray; when mounted on a pole or placed in other exposed positions, white is the best color.

House birds differ decidedly in their requirements for homes. Bluebirds and wrens, for example, are content to build in tomato cans. To make the cans usable and keep them from becoming excessively hot, they should be covered with bark, one end being replaced with a block of wood and an opening of the proper size made in one side of the can. A hollow limb or block of wood hollowed out in the form of a woodpecker's nest is a popular device. Gourds are made acceptable by cutting a hole of the proper size in one side, cleaning them out and drilling a small hole in the bottom to drain out any rain that may leak in.

# ANIMAL HOBBIES

**Pets—A Living and Loving Hobby.** We all know that children love pets. As a parent who has succumbed to some of the pleas for puppies, kittens, ducks, rabbits, birds, mice, hamsters, skunks, monkeys and horses, I have often wondered why I put up with the mess and extra work that go along with them. Basically, I suppose it's because animals have enriched my children's lives in many ways, as well as my own!

When the cat snuggles among her new kittens, her satisfaction as a mother sends forth a reassuring calm that all is well. Animals manage the essentials of birth so easily, that they also help children understand the process

**212**

naturally and unselfconsciously.

Children can learn principals of human growth and development, too, from pets, particularly if a mother animal and her young are kept together for a while. They can see the baby take his first wobbly steps by himself and watch him develop to the point where he can manage on his own.

Animals express their feelings—anger, fear, hunger, attachment and so on—with simple directness. Children are brought up to control their emotions, and control comes hard, so pets provide a kind of safety valve. When Patch snarls and bites, it's something of a relief for Johnny to watch, since he has wanted to do likewise himself at times. But he knows he can't. Blackie, the rabbit, runs in terror and hides when danger approaches. Mary, who has been taught to be a brave girl and face her fears, feels superior to (and comforted by) Blackie who isn't expected to be brave.

Another of the satisfactions is mastery over the animal world. Johnny lords it over his dog, Patch; Mary is the mistress of her rabbit, and it is good for them to be able to feel strong and superior. Many times, in a world ruled by powerful adults, children are made to feel weak and helpless. Parents can do almost everything better than their children can (except stand on their heads or bite their toes), but children can do many things better than their pets can.

Sometimes an animal refuses to obey, particularly when a young master has been cruel, for pets usually reflect the way they are treated.

Thus a child learns such psychological lessons from his pets as: If you want love, you must give it; if you are cruel, you will be hated and feared; if you want obedience, you must be firm and consistent.·

And, although toddlers love their dolls and stuffed toys, they pour out their real adoration on animals which can respond to affection.

Part of this practice in mothering of fathering a pet involves developing responsibility. Young children are too immature to take on all the responsibility of animal care, but they should begin early to feed, train and clean their pets—with their parents' help. As they grow older, youngsters should take over more and more of the job.

So while it's true that animals cost money, ruin the furniture, scratch the floors, scent the house and disturb one's sleep, it's also true that they teach children many critical lessons and enrich their emotions. Let in the pets, therefore, and wait to refurnish the house until the children and the animals have gone their various ways. Even then probably you'll get a new puppy!—*Kate Vickers*

**Acquire an Aquarium.** An aquarium is itself a miniature of the world outside, with its elders and young, its struggle for life space. It shows the child the facts he needs to know about the interchange between living creatures and their surroundings; about the balance between the needs and strengths of one creature and another; about the limits which must be observed if life is to go on. In this glass-enclosed world are moving creatures, some darting and brightly colored, some slow-moving and dull. This is a world of grasses, stones, earth, air and water—all of which a child learns to recognize as interdependent forms of life rather than isolated things.

A child regarding an aquarium discovers something about what makes the larger world go round and how he himself fits into it. He can be a wise protector of his fish, for example, but he cannot compel them to mate or spawn or live—and so he learns responsibility and humility. Whatever the child may some day be and do when he grows up, such an introduction to the kinds of relatedness living creatures have to their environment is vital to his later comprehension of his universe. —*Margaret Mead, Ph.D.*

**An Unusual Aquarium:**  During the spring there are millions of toads' and frogs' eggs along the edges of pools and ponds. Toads' eggs are laid in long jellylike strings while those of frogs are in masses of jelly. Scoop up a few of either kind and bring them home to hatch. Many containers are satisfactory, but a rectangular glass aquarium is perfect. Place a layer of sand in the bottom, set out some water plants, add a few slimy rocks (some of them should project above the water line) and some of the green water scum. Fresh-water snails make good scavengers. After the tadpoles hatch, return all but five or six to the pond. It is absorbing to children to watch the metamorphosis from tadpole to toad. The tadpoles eat the small plant life from the water scum, and new scum should be added from time to time.
—*Carmen Stone Allen*

# HOBBY
# SHOWS

Children love to bring together things they have made or in which they are interested.

Hobby shows may serve a number of purposes:

1. They give recognition and encouragement to the child in his hobby.
2. They provide a meeting place for hobbyists hitherto unknown to each other, with similar interests.
3. They reveal hidden talents and interests.
4. They present a wide variety of leisure-time activities among which a child may find and develop new means or methods of self-expression.

The exhibits should be classified according to some system and grouped by kind. Each exhibit should have a tag stating the owner's name, age and classification of hobby. The following classification covers most of the hobbies likely to be found in the group of young people in a neighborhood.

## I. Creative Activities

### A. Wood Work
1. Construction
   a. Furniture
   b. Bird houses
2. Whittling
3. Toys
4. Miscellaneous

### B. Models
1. Ships
2. Airplanes
3. Miscellaneous

### C. Mechanical devices and inventions
1. Electrical
2. Mechanical

### D. Arts and Crafts
1. Wood carving
2. Clay modeling, soap carving, etc.
3. Paintings
4. Drawings
5. Photographs
6. Leather craft
7. Metal work
8. Sewing—weaving
9. Writing

## II. Collections
A. Stamps
B. Coins
C. Natural Science
D. Antiques and Relics
E. Scrapbooks
F. Miscellaneous

## III. Miscellaneous
A. Kites
B. Paper Construction
C. Pets
D. Other features

Since it is really impossible for parents to judge with exactitude among the displays at a hobby show, and since hobbies are essentially non-competitive, any awards or prizes of little intrinsic value (blue, red, and white ribbons for 1st, 2nd, 3rd place are usually sufficient) should be given in large numbers and should be awarded in each classification. The judging basis is on general merit. Awards may be given for the most unique or the most attractively displayed hobby in the show.

**Pet shows** have become very popular and children enjoy bringing pets of all kinds, to be shown and judged.

In preparing for the show, it is advisable to advertise it well in advance throughout the neighborhood. Appoint a committee of parents as judges. There may also be a committee to take charge of the parade which precedes the show, and another to provide the awards.

A number of towns have adopted the plan of giving talks to the children during the week before the show on the care and kind treatment of animals. Story hours may well be devoted to telling stories of animals.

**Entering the Pets:** Some method of entering the exhibits is important. The children should list the following information:

1. Kind of pet
2. Classification
3. Pet's name
4. Pet's special tricks
5. Owner's name
6. Address
7. Telephone
8. School

**Care of Animals:** Temporary hutches should be provided for the exhibits. These may be made from ordinary boxes covered with wire. Water, changed often, must be provided for the animals. Dogs should be held by leashes. On some playgrounds caretakers are appointed to see that the animals are well cared for. All cats must be in cages.

**Classification:** Animals may be grouped as follows:

1. Birds
2. Cats
3. Dogs
4. Rodents:
   squirrels, rabbits, mice,
   guinea pigs, etc.
5. Cold-blooded animals:
   a. Reptiles
   b. Amphibia, frogs, etc.
   c. Fishes
6. Insects
7. Miscellaneous

**216**

**Judging:** It is difficult to judge a pet show, since each child feels his pet is the finest pet anyone could have, and such a heretogeneous group of mongrel animals defies any really serious judging. The judging should be humorous, the prizes as numerous as possible and of little monetary value. First, second and third place ribbons under each classification are suggested. Judges may select prize winners as follows:

## Birds

1. The fattest chicken
2. Most talkative parrot
3. Best canary

## Cats

1. Longest tail
2. Cutest kitten
3. Cat with most tricks

## Dogs

1. Handsomest
2. Biggest
3. Smallest
4. Longest tail
5. Most tricks
6. Best-cared-for
7. Ugliest
8. Most spots

The other classifications might be judged in a similar vein. Additional prizes might be given for the most unique, the smallest and the most amusingly decorated pet or pet and owner.

The parade offers an opportunity for the expression of much initiative and ingenuity. The animals, in cages, are usually loaded on wagons and drawn along. Doll carriages sometimes serve as floats. The decorating of these conveyances is an opportunity for creative self-expression.

**Mutt Dog Shows:** Mutt Dog Shows have come into favor. These shows are conducted in the same manner as general pet shows, and ribbons may be awarded on the following basis:

1. Dog with the largest number of owners
2. Largest dog
3. Smallest dog
4. Fattest dog
5. Best-cared-for dog
6. Best-decorated dog
7. Ugliest dog
8. Handsomest dog
9. Best-behaved dog
10. Dog with the best tricks
11. Dog pulling or riding a vehicle
12. Prize winners of previous year
13. Plain "dog"

**217**

# HALF-A-DOZEN POPULAR HOBBIES

## Cooking–A Tasty Hobby

**To satisfy appetite and ego.** Cooking is fun! It opens the door to a wonderful new world that uses all of a child's senses—and rewards him with a satisfying feeling of accomplishment.

1. Be sure your child's first cooking venture is a success—at least in her eyes. A successful first builds confidence which a later failure will not destroy; hence, it's important to select a cooking activity within the child's scope. Chocolate pudding made from an instant mix is a good first choice. It's easy, quick and failure proof. Furthermore, it can be sampled soon after it's made—a must for young children.

2. Praise the finished product even though it does not meet adult standards. A child's creative urge is fragile and easily damaged by criticism. You can always find something to commend and then tactfully suggest ways to improve the product next time.

3. Have the food prepared by the beginner form part of a family meal whenever possible. It adds to her feeling of accomplishment to see the family eat her special offerings. But avoid having her prepare just the frills. Desserts and cakes are fine foods but the heart of a meal is the main dish and vegetables.

4. Try to let the child cook or help cook what she wants to, when she wants to. Cooking should be a pleasant experience, not a job assignment.

If you decide to make a real project of teaching your offspring to cook, better set aside a special time in the morning when you are fresh and can approach the job with enthusiasm. It's contagious, you know.

5. Don't push the beginner; let her take cooking at her own speed. Timing varies widely with individual children.

A preschool tot is usually content with helping to stir a batter or cut out cookies. An older child wants to measure, add ingredients and feel the finished product is her very own.

Between the ages of six and nine, children take pleasure in preparing

**218**

simple dishes such as soups, salads, quick breads and easy desserts. They enjoy mixing and shaping foods with their hands, so meat loaf is a popular choice.

A nine to ten-year-old finds preparing and serving a simple meal entirely by herself a challenging and worthwhile experience.

6. Help the child to become increasingly independent by encouraging her to make her own decisions. In the beginning, she will need direction and supervision. Later, after she has learned how to follow a recipe and measure accurately, you should stay out of the picture as much as possible.

7. Accept an occasional failure without fuss. Be sympathetic but matter-of-fact so the child will not be so discouraged she won't want to try again. Tell her you have mishaps, too. Learning to accept failure philosophically when one has done his best is basic to good sportsmanship.

8. See that safety rules are understood and followed. Until a child is experienced enough to know the danger in handling matches and knives, their use should be carefully supervised. Other precautions include instruction in using potholders, setting pots on the range so as to avoid hitting the handles, and selecting proper utensils for the job.

9. Establish reasonable standards of cleanliness and good working habits. A child should learn early that she is expected to wash her hands before handling food, wear an apron while working and help clean up. If a child is taught to wash cooking dishes systematically as she goes along, cleaning up is a challenge rather than a chore.

Agreed, teaching your child to cook requires far more effort in the beginning than doing it yourself. But it pays big dividends as she assumes responsibility, for single foods, first, and then whole meals—and enjoys them all.—*Esther McCormick*

# Ham Radio: A Hobby for the Whole Family

Only recently has ham radio come into its own as a hobby the entire family can share. The popularity of amateur radio is snow balling as thousands of parents and teen-agers discover this most fascinating and democratic of pastimes.

What better way to feel close to people the world around than by speaking together? Voices flashing around the globe in an instant, scorning distance, vaulting political borders. This is actually putting the "One World" concept into everyday use.

There is a magic key which unlocks the doors of international understanding and fellowship. It is the "International Q-Code"—a list of simple three-letter symbols with universal meanings. For instance, "QTH" means "Where do you live?" to a ham Hottentot or Hungarian, Arab or Eskimo, Zulu or Japanese.

The fascination of ham radio to those of mechanical or inventive bent is obvious. Most hams build their own sending sets. The gadget-lover is in seventh heaven while hamming. Radar and television owe their rapid growth to early pioneering by amateur experimenters. Short-wave communication is a ham product.

But how would you go about taking up amateur radio as a family hobby?

**How much does ham radio cost?**  A basic station—receiver, transmitter and antenna—sells from $45 up in build-yourself kits. Factory equipment is priced from $100 to $3,000. The average ham has an investment of around $100 in second-hand gear purchased from a mail-order house or a reliable home-town dealer. Repair costs are negligible on a year-to-year basis. As for boosting the light bill, an amateur radio station draws less current than your electric iron.

**How much space is required?**  A writing desk or bridge table is more than ample room for even an advanced station. In city apartments, whip antennas similar to those on car radios can be installed on a window ledge. On the farm or suburban lot, single-wire roof antennas from 33 to 135 feet are used.

**Is ham radio dangerous for children?**  Any electrical device is potentially lethal if you touch a live wire. High-voltage circuits in ham equipment are inaccessible when the set is in operation. Ham radio gear is no more hazardous than your TV.

**Can a ham station be taken on trips?**  Your license specifies a "fixed" location. However, by signing your call "portable," you can legally operate your station while traveling, on vacation, at school or in a friend's house. By signing "mobile" you can send and receive messages while in an automobile, airplane or boat.

Local civil defense, Red Cross, Boy Scouts or Police Department will be happy to sign you up for emergency duty—especially if you have a miniature transmitter and receiver in your car. FCC records are replete with heroic tales of the roles played by hams during floods, earthquakes, fires, hurricanes, or epidemics.

**220**

**Why be a ham?**  Few experiences in life can equal for thrills and suspense the moment when the mailman brings your "ticket" and you switch in your key or microphone to put your first CQ (calling all stations!) on the air. Who will answer? It may be a movie star in Hollywood or a cowboy on an isolated Arizona ranch.

Fortunately for families on modest incomes, long-distance radio contacts do not depend on high power or fancy equipment. A home-made 20-watt "rig" circles the world as does a deluxe 1,000 watter. The relative unimportance of power, per se, is one of radio's happy paradoxes.

Most cities have Amateur Radio Clubs where local enthusiasts get together. More and more high schools are giving radio courses, graduating pupils as licensed hams.

Doctors recognize ham radio's therapeutic benefits and it is being encouraged in Veterans' hospitals. For the spastic, blind or otherwise handicapped person, radio is a Godsend, since it literally brings the whole world to the shut-in. Polio victims have even operated radio stations from iron lungs! As a deterrent to juvenile delinquency, amateur radio has the enthusiastic endorsement of PTA, churches, social service groups and law-enforcement agencies.

Hamming has long-range benefits. For the young student facing Selective Service, a radio license gives him a tremendous jump over non-hams, since the Armed Forces are hard pressed to find trained communications personnel. And in this scientific age, radio, television, radar and allied fields offer unlimited opportunities.

Just one word of warning: If you expose yourself to ham radio you are lost! Once a ham, always a ham. —*Walker A. Tompkins*

# Photography: for Parents

Photography is a marvelous hobby, giving you pleasure in the picture-taking and then pride in showing them off.

Actually, the only way to take good pictures is to take them. The days do slip by, and there is no way of making up for a picture you missed taking. Why not schedule a minimum of four picture-shooting sessions a year on special occasions?

The two most natural occasions in the world are Christmas and, approximately three months later, Easter. Holidays will probably remind you to take pictures of the children anyway—and of the whole family, for that matter. Then the 4th of July, and vacation time. Be sure not only to photograph the scenery, around home or at vacation spots, but get, too, picture record of the growth of the children.

**221**

Of course, there are other special occasions, anniversaries, parties, special events. But these are likely to be centered around something other than the children. The four holidays mentioned, though, belong to the kids and should be especially earmarked for them.

Chances are, too, that your pictures will increasingly improve as you continue to take snapshots, and as you learn to handle your camera—and your children. — *Don Mohler*

## Photography: for Children

Children are naturals at many things. And in the case of photography, its attraction for the young is that it is fun from the start. Parents who want to encourage their youngsters' interest in picture-taking should remember:

A youngster's desire to film his vision of the world doesn't usually show up strongly till about age eleven. This, then, is a very good time to give your child a camera. He has always loved to look at the pictures of people and places you've taken; now he can select the people, places and time.

Most children have great imagination. Before they even begin to take pictures, they have unconsciously mastered the most important element in photography—the ability to visualize a good picture. All they need is the knowledge of equipment to transfer this image to film. And this is not too hard to gain, since picture-taking has been simplified mechanically with cameras that adjust automatically to lighting conditions and film that provides for a wide margin of error.

Until your child makes friends with his new camera, you'll want to help him along a bit. Or perhaps you'd like to visit your local camera store for a brief demonstration of the correct way to load and unload film, how to hold the camera steady and press the shutter release slowly to prevent jiggled images.

Your dealer will also suggest the proper film. It's best to stick to one kind of film in the beginning. Try to encourage your child to practice clicking pictures around the house, using an unloaded camera. When he can handle the camera easily, it's time for the real thing.

**Subject matter.** Suggest that your youngster look at his subject from different angles before shooting. A child's natural agility and unconcern about dignified posture give him an advantage. Adults usually shoot from a standing position with monotonous regularity, but a child is unabashed at shooting from almost any position.

Everything that interests your child is material for pictures. To a junior high student, subjects might be anything from a pet hamster to a Go-kart race. A simple camera, by the way, can record both subjects; simply add a close-up attachment to the lens for a small subject. If your child wants to take pictures of his friends in motion, explain to him that movement coming toward the photographer can be stopped with a box camera, but action moving across the lens requires a faster shutter speed.

**A parent can help** to sustain a child's interest in picture-taking by seeing that exposed film rolls are promptly sent to be developed. And do provide an inexpensive album for keeping your youngster's pictures. If they are scattered around in bureau drawers and boxes, his enthusiasm may wane. Show interest in his shots, pointing out what's good about each one; the bad points will be obvious to both of you. Remind him to pack his camera when he is taking off for a visit or an outing.

Above all, teach your child the care of his equipment. Explain how dust or fingerprints on the lens will show up on his pictures. Although simple cameras are made to take a beating, a neck strap is a good investment because it minimizes the bumps and jolts a child's camera is apt to suffer.

As your youngster's skill increases, you may consider getting him a more complex camera to allow more versatile shots. If he's interested in natural science, for example, he'll welcome a single lens reflex camera with which he can take the extreme close-ups that fascinate naturalists.

The faster shutter speed such a camera has will also enable him to record athletic events at camp and school and to capture fleeting unposed pictures of family and friends. Suggest that your youngster cut out the directions for exposure that come with the film he uses and tape it to the back of the camera. If he pre-sets his shutter speed, there will only be one adjustment to make—the lens opening.

**Advantages.** Picture-taking is practical, too. One boy used his camera in a series of shots to demonstrate phototropism for his school science fair project. Each shot showed a stage in a bean plant's progressive growth.

A high school youngster can make a real contribution to the school by photographing social and athletic events for year books. He may even find ways to use his camera to earn a little spending money. A local paper might buy good pictures of newsworthy events—particularly school and community functions not covered by a news photographer.

Though youngsters won't become professional photographers, picture-taking is a useful skill for anyone. Above all, it is a means of preserving moments of pleasure. —*Phoebe Dunn*

**223**

# Focus on Home Movies

**Theme** is the first step. Your camera should tell a simple story. Most good home movies are not the product of scripts written in advance but of events photographed as they happen, then put together logically and smoothly. A theme need not be complicated; it can center around simple incidents such as a snowball fight, trimming a Christmas tree, a birthday party, toboganning down a hill or trying out new ice skates. Hold your shooting until you have decided on your theme and worked out its beginning, middle and end. Then start at the beginning.

Let's say you decide to photograph the trimming of your Christmas tree. Your children can bundle up and start their hike into the woods (if you cut your own tree) or to the local tree mart. Then—how to get the tree home? Do you carry it on your back? Does your family line up Indian style, each toting his bit? Now bring in the actual trimming. You might follow with shots of putting the gifts under the tree, friends who drop in, the children shaking a package trying to guess its surprise. And what better ending than the younger ones going to bed in happy anticipation? On a 50-ft. roll of 8 mm film, four minutes of action easily tell a story.

A theme serves several purposes. It gives your film shape—a structure to be filled out with your family's own experience. It is also a way of holding the attention of the audience. But even more important it is a device to get your cast engrossed in doing something rather than awkwardly staring into the camera.

Here's a tip about how to avert self-consciousness among your actors: get out your empty camera and aim it at your fledgelings. Release the shutter and let them get used to the buzzing sound. Then you'll get the spontaneous expressions and uninhibited movement you want.

**Story treatment** is the next consideration. Often, the most disturbing element in amateur movies is the frantic panning or swinging of the camera from right to left in a desperate attempt to get everything on film. The movies flies across the screen like a mad merry-go-round, leaving the audience dizzy. No panning is better than bad panning. Pan only when you are following an action. However, if you feel a need to pan at other times, remember that the eye doesn't zoom but travels from one point to another.

One good opening for a movie is an over-all shot using, if possible, the wide-angle lens. Suppose your theme is a surprise birthday party for the young man in the house. Let the first scene be the kitchen. The camera should run long enough to establish the fact that the women-folk are busy

**224**

and something is about to happen. Catch one child cautiously peeping out the door to see if brother is aware of the unusual activity. Then, with your normal lens, move in for a medium shot of each person—one child adding color to the icing, another wrapping a birthday gift. Then move in for close-ups.

Now you have placed the scene of action for the audience and indicated the working elements of your story, use close-ups to emphasize the action. Next, your actors start into the next room bearing the cake with candles.

**Action and Reaction.** With this we have arrived at the most exciting part of a film for the amateur—the action itself. You may want to set the camera on only the surprised birthday boy and let him monopolize the entire next scene. This is only half the fun. If you record the reactions of the others, you add warmth, richness and personality to your movie. It is fine to record the birthday boy and his surprise, but better still to intersperse quick close-ups of his sisters watching and reacting to him. When he opens a gift, add a quick closeup of his sister who gave him the present. Her concern with whether he'll like it, her pleasure when he does will make the original action doubly memorable.

Keep all this quick and very close—your major interest is in the face. Such a series of short, close inter-reactions will give sparkle to your film.

**Continuity.** As in a good short story, transitions are important. This means that one scene leads naturally to another, carrying the audience smoothly along. Scenes must necessarily start and stop, but with planning, this can be done unobtrusively. In any case, before ending one scene, it helps to have the next in mind.

In most home movies, the continuity is built into the situation, but if you change background, a conscious effort to make the transition smoother may help. If, for instance, you have photographed the family piling into a car, it's a good idea to show them getting out of the car before picking up the next point of action. This allows the audience to imagine the interlude of the trip and the next scene then follows naturally. If you want to change from one location to another, follow the subject walking out of the picture in the first setting. Then pick him up walking into the next scene in the new location—so the scene in the new location holds together logically.

**The running gag.** By violating the foregoing rule completely, it is possible to create one of the easiest spurs to laughter in home movies—the

**225**

running gag. This is a corollary situation you set up early in the unfolding of your story and to which you keep cutting back at intervals.

It can go like this: suppose you have chosen to film your family on a snowy afternoon. You lead off with the children building the base of a snowman—or perhaps the first snowball flies, which, of course, sets off a series of actions. This is your first situation. Meanwhile, back in the driveway, father is patiently plodding through piles of snow with his shovel. We watch father at intervals going from confident enthusiasm to weary half-hearted attempts to finish his chore. Cutting back in this way gives the audience the feeling that he's been at it continuously for days. Of course, this entire cut-back series can be filmed as a single prolonged episode which can later be cut up and spliced in at appropriate intervals.

**Timing.** When you read a short story, you'll notice that it has sentences of varied lengths—long, sweeping ones contrasted with short, pointed ones. That's the way you should pace your scenes. There are no rules—it depends on whether it is a wide shot to establish location or quick reactions, or a running action that should come to some conclusion. As a general rule, a scene shouldn't be shorter than three or four seconds, or longer than fifteen. When the action requires you to shoot a single burst of film longer than fifteen seconds, it is better to do it in a series of brief scenes taken from several different distances and angles. This not only saves film but also gives your movie more visual impact, and so keeps it from dragging.

By choosing simple situations for your theme, you'll involve your audience. After all, anyone would want to reach out to help a boy in his first wobbly attempt on a new bike, or give a toddler a hand as he struggles up a flight of stairs. Once you get your audience sufficiently involved, you can take this a step further and play more freely on their emotions—you can create laughter, anxiety, suspense. When father gets a splash of water in the face while giving baby a bath, the audience will recall similar situations and will end up laughing at father and themselves.

**Pattern and color.** Try to avoid dressing your children in multi-colored patterns or brilliant colors which serve as a target for the eye and detract from their faces. The best color pictures need not have the most color.

**Shooting.** Remember that it is false economy to shoot too little. Over-photographing will give you a selection of shots that will serve you well in your final editing.

**226**

If you follow these few simple suggestions, I think you'll find that your movies improve. Instead of a jumpy series of stiff snapshots, there will be a natural flow of related and meaningful scenes—ones that you will look at with deep pleasure for many years to come. —*Lynn Marett*

## Keeping Them in Stitches

Preteen girls are quite ready to learn to sew. They use their hands well. They appreciate nice things. Unfortunately, their enthusiasm for clothes is often frustrated by their figures, since most preteen shapes are still unsettled. So buying clothes, instead of cheering any female's heart as it normally does, can be quite discouraging.

So it is frequently more convenient and easier on the psyche for the pre-adolescent and her mother to stay home and stitch rather than shop at a nearby store.

How does one go about finding sewing classes? There are several ways. Your public school or recreation center may have an organized group with a competent teacher. Or there may be a professional sewing school nearby. All across the country, many of the big sewing machine companies also run sewing classes.

But for a more informal session for mothers and daughters, try a home-sewing class. Incidentally, if you don't have a machine and can't borrow one, you can probably rent one reasonably from one of the sewing machine companies either by the week or the month.

Developing a new skill gives creative satisfaction, as anyone knows who has ever painted a picture or built a cabinet. With sewing, there is the joy of accomplishment, plus the satisfaction of wearing the creation after it's made. The evening your youngster attends a family dinner clad in her home-sewn clothes can be the height of wear-your-wares pleasure.

Perhaps I should qualify this by saying that even if a child doesn't get the same creative satisfaction out of sewing as an adult, she does get other rewards.

She discovers that sewing, though often hard, means larger wardrobes at smaller cost. She learns, too, that there is greater choice in style and color when she sews for herself. Perhaps she learns something about value, craftsmanship and texture, too.

But in addition, there is the positive experience of working together as mothers and daughters—as women—at an art identified with femininity ever since Minerva wove her first cloth. To work with, to identify with, above all to share enjoyment with her mother, gives a young girl comfortable feelings about herself as a female. —*Jean R. Komaiko*

**227**

# ENTERTAINING THE CONVALESCENT

*MOST MOTHERS seem to have a reserve stock of energy that takes them through the troubled days and sleepless nights of serious illness. But once their sick child is on the road to recovery, his care can become really difficult. He is often cranky and irritable, because he still has to stay in bed, and his weary mother may find her own temper grown short. Actually there are many ways to make this period in bed pass quickly and pleasantly for mother and child. With a little ingenuity and planning, the patient can be kept happy all the day—well, almost.*

# ON THE ROAD
# TO RECOVERY

**Routines Help.**  Regular hours for naps and rest periods, meals, baths and play activities help to break up the day. A child likes to know when it's lunchtime and how long it will be before his rest period is over. Letting him take some responsibility for the medical routines can be a help to Mother and a real source of satisfaction to him. A clock by his bed will enable him to remind Mother when the next dose is due. The child can often take his own medicine. It's a good idea for him to have a time chart on which he can check off each dose he takes.

**Clean, Attractive Surroundings** will cheer the youngster who has to stay in bed. A pretty bedspread, a few flowers, a blooming plant, a gay scarf on the dresser—all help to brighten his room. Pictures hung on walls should be large enough and close enough to see without difficulty. It's fun to change them often. Illustrations can be cut out of magazines and placed in dime store frames, or they can simply be shellacked and mounted on cardboard.

**A Bed Tray,** a raised tray that fits over the child's lap, will make mealtime less hazardous and play easier. Many bed trays can be tipped at different angles making them practical for reading and drawing.

If anyone in the house is handy with tools, a simple but useful bed tray can be made out of plywood mounted on wooden legs. Add a plywood back to the tray and tack half a shoe bag to the back to provide pockets for small toys and other small objects. Covering the tray with a gay piece of oilcloth or a heavy coat of bright paint makes it pretty as well as washable. A narrow edge added to the sides prevents spilling.

A simpler bed tray is constructed by balancing a large board across the bed with a chair at each end. Even a bridge table with two legs folded and resting on the other side of the bed on a telephone book will do. Whatever you use, make sure the tray is steady.

**230**

**For a Long Illness,** a child will be most comfortable in a hospital bed, which can be cranked up to provide a back rest for the patient. Being taller than a regular bed, it makes nursing care much easier on a mother's back muscles. If a hospital bed is not available, you can place a canvas back rest under the pillow.

An old shower curtain or big piece of oilcloth will protect a young patient's bed when he is using paints, clay or other messy materials. If a waste paper basket isn't convenient or would clutter up the room, a large paper bag pinned to the mattress can serve instead.

A bell to ring when he really needs Mother and a small bed lamp that he can turn on if he can't reach the light switch are comforting. A small vacuum bottle will keep fruit juice, milk or water fresh and cool.

**Morale Builders.** Hair ribbons and bed jackets to match the general decor, and even matching bed jackets for her favorite doll, will please a little girl. A small boy may enjoy wearing a new cowboy hat or baseball cap, and a pair of good-looking pajamas will have masculine appeal at any age. A hand mirror or shaving mirror will enable children of both sexes to admire the results when they are all "fixed up."

A rubdown with fragrant cologne after the bath or a bit of perfume to dab behind her ears is a truly feminine delight, but even the sterner sex will probably enjoy a bath with pine-scented soap.

**Plants and Pets.** Miniature gardens and farms, complete with seeds to plant and grow, are available in most toy departments. Carrot or beet tops placed in water with small stones heaped around them make a quick growing garden. Pumpkin, grapefruit or orange seeds, soaked overnight in water and planted in a quarter inch of soil will soon begin to sprout. You can make an attractive terrarium in a mason jar. Cover the bottom with sand, stones and a small piece of charcoal. Add bits of moss and vine and close the jar tightly. Watered daily, it will grow for quite a while.

Terrariums can also be planned to house different varieties of small pets, such as frogs, turtles, lizards, even insects—particularly ants. Tropical fish are colorful and fascinating to watch. A canary, with his bright feathers and gay song, is sure to cheer the invalid.

**Submarine Bouquets** are easy to make and beautiful to see when placed in a sunny window. Tie together two or three medium-sized flowers and a spray of greenery, and attach a heavy stone. Place the bouquet in

**231**

any clear glass jar with a wide mouth. Scatter in bright stones or shells and fill the container with cold water. Then add a tablespoon of salt and seal the jar tightly. The flowers will last a week or longer.

**Treasure Box.** A collection of items not used in everyday play is one excellent insurance against boredom for a sick abed child. Packed away in a convenient spot, and brought out only in cases of illness, this treasure trove will have all the novelty of freshness.

All sorts of items can go into the box. Old greeting cards, worn playing cards, post cards, illustrated calendars, leftover party favors, including candy baskets, fancy place cards, noisemakers, paper hats and party napkins, remnants of cloth, lace and ribbons, feathers, veiling, sequins, artificial flowers and other ornaments from discarded hats and dresses, broken costume jewelry, worn-out watches, loose charms, old earrings, cigar boxes, small boxes of different kinds, ring boxes, watch boxes, kitchen match boxes, wooden cheese boxes, old perfume boxes, the small cloth bags new briar pipes come in, old handbags or gloves, bits of tinsel and discarded, non-breakable Christmas tree ornaments, gift wrappings, seals and ribbon, paper doilies, old coasters, old hand mirrors, pine cones, driftwood and sea shells, empty spools of thread, golf tees, sample books of wallpaper and cloth swatches. In addition, the box might include some "sick" toys—puzzles, games, dolls, cars, and so on, that are especially adaptable for play in bed.

**Mobiles** are always entertaining, and making them can be a family project or an interesting occupation for the sick child. Glittery ones to catch the sunbeams are especially appealing. A string of paper dolls or other cutouts can be made to dance if they are attached to a miniature clothesline stretched across the room. A toy bird or airplane hanging from the window blind will twirl gaily in a slight breeze. Wind bells tinkling outside the window will provide a soothing, delightful sound effect.

It is important to remember that sick children usually prefer much less complicated activities than those that interest them when they are well.

**Collages.** These are pictures or designs made by gluing assorted materials to a flat base such as a piece of cardboard. A child, for example, may make a house and garden. A small, shallow box forms the base for the house. Shredded green paper from the bottom of an Easter basket serves for grass. Small twigs are used for trees.

**Splatter Painting.** A simple design is drawn, then cut out and pinned to a sheet of paper. A piece of wire screen is held about an inch above the paper. A paintbrush first dipped in water colors is run over the screen so that the paint splatters on the paper around the cutout design.

**Small Dolls and Animals** can be made from clothespins, spools, pipe cleaners, colored yarn and cork as well as from oilcloth and stockings. A pair of tweezers, some sea shells and glue are all that is necessary to make all kinds of shell animals.

Boxes of assorted sizes with toothpicks (for bars), poster paints and paste can be transformed into a circus or zoo. Boxes glued together can become a doll house, while a shoe box stood on end makes an excellent apartment or hotel, which can be peopled and furnished with paper, cardboard and imagination. Doll furniture is also made from match boxes, spools, bottle tops and cereal boxes.

**Clay and Fingerpaints.** Clay can be purchased inexpensively in powdered form and prepared by mixing with water. Fingerpaints may be bought or made at home. (Cream one cup of corn starch with a half cup of cold water. Add 1½ cups of boiling water, ½ cup of soap flakes and 1 tablespoon of glycerine. Cool and color the mixture with vegetable coloring or poster paints, then store it in tightly closed jars.) Smooth shelf paper is a good surface for fingerpainting. Unless a child is capable of working without supervision, though, let this kind of messy play be a special treat reserved for times when an older member of the family is around.

**Handwork.** Construction sets for model airplanes, automobiles, trains, and so forth are popular with boys, while girls usually like knitting, or, if they are too young, braiding strips of different colored cloth and stringing beads, spools and macaroni (which they can color with water paint). For a special treat, give a small child a roll of aluminum foil to use in any way he wishes. Piles of old magazines, colored paper, blunt scissors, crayons, paste and the coarse drawing paper used in nursery schools are standbys to keep small fry occupied.

**As for Toys,** they do not have to be elaborate or expensive, nor should they be too complicated for the youngster to handle. The most successful toys are those that can be used in many different ways.

**233**

**Water Play.**  Bubble pipes and bubble solutions, or blowing through a straw into a bowl of soapy water are fun. Sometimes an egg beater in a bowl of suds keeps a youngster happily occupied. Washing a small doll and sailing tiny boats in a pan of water are also enjoyable activities.

**Hobbies and Collections.**  School-aged children like all sorts of hobbies and collections such as coins, stamps, leaves, magic tricks. Planning a project of any sort gives purpose to a sick child's activities and retains his interest whereas he might become bored with flitting from one to another unrelated occupation.

**Books.**  The sick child needs books that are well printed and easy to hold. He will probably want ones that are a little simpler to read than his ordinary fare, and he will enjoy re-reading old favorites. Some libraries have special facilities for the shut-in child and will deliver books to the patient's home. Projected book machines, which reflect on the ceiling the book pages printed on microfilm, are available in hospitals and at some public libraries.

**Radio and Records.**  The radio forms a soothing background to which the child half listens when he doesn't feel like doing anything else. Children's records, too, which can be obtained from some libraries as well as from record shops, provide pleasant, relaxing entertainment.

**Work to Do in Bed.**  Children like to feel that they are being useful even though they are in bed. If they do not have a contagious illness, they can serve as assistant cooks—scraping vegetables, shelling peas or performing similar chores. Arranging Mother's favorite recipes in a file box, tidying up her sewing kit, folding socks, straightening drawers, making jar labels and covers for favorite books, wrapping gifts, re-stringing broken necklaces, are just a few of the many jobs a sick child will take pride in doing.

**School Work.**  The child who is only going to be in bed for a short time is probably better off without any school work. Unless there is a request by the teacher that he keep up with the material being covered in class, it is best not to try to tutor him.

**Time Alone With Mother and Dad.** Time spent with the sick child brings dividends in terms of a closer relationship between parents and children. In a busy family of growing youngsters, this may be one of the few occasions when a child has his parents all to himself.

Most sick children enjoy being read to. They also like playing games with their parents, but here it should be remembered that a child is often a poorer sport when he is sick and less able than usual to tolerate being the loser in a game.

**Back to Normal.** The sick child wants plenty of cuddling and attention, and is certainly entitled to it; but it can be hard to get back to normal once he has recovered. There is often a let-down feeling when he has to return to school, and when he is no longer the recipient of so much attention. But gradually the gratifications of being up and together again with his friends replace the pleasures of his more pampered existence in bed. This tapering-off period is a smoother one if parents are patient and do not expect demanding behavior to disappear overnight. A treat to look forward to—perhaps a family excursion or party—emphasizes the advantages of being well again.

*—Paulette Hartrich*

# FUN

# FOR ADULTS

# ONLY

*SOME OF THE FUN AND GAMES which adults can engage in are obvious—visiting, theatre-going, sight-seeing, etc. Others are suggested here. What should be remembered, however, is that parents are not appendages of their children's lives. They are individuals, with individual needs and interests. They need the opportunity to develop their adult interests, enjoy adult companionship, pursue their own dreams, and take time—away from the children—to play, to laugh, to reflect.*

# FUN
# FOR ADULTS:
# WHY?

Parents must keep on growing, too. Look around, and note which mothers and fathers among your acquaintances seem to be finding satisfaction in life and usually radiate a sense of well-being. It will probably be those who are broadening their interests and sympathies, their knowledge and skill.

The children's well-being comes first, but their well-being doesn't require every moment of your time and effort. To extend the field of your interests, however, may take conscious effort. The important point is that you regard yourself as a person capable of learning, of contributing and of venturing into the unknown. You have to believe, too, that you owe it to yourself and your family not to vegetate.

Actually, what interferes with becoming engaged in study or community service, in politics, the arts or whatever it may be, is sometimes not so much the family's welfare, as it is habit or inertia.

Perhaps it would be helpful to think through the questions: What really matters to me now? What am I doing today that will be valuable to me ten or twenty years from now? What is vital is that you continue to be elastic in your abilities. And as you broaden your interests and activities, you will like yourself better, and so will your family.—*Edith G. Neisser*

# FUN
# FOR ADULTS:
# WHERE?

**The answer: all over town.** Out on Fourth Street, Mrs. Lucile Hult-quist picks up her violin and starts out for the symphony rehearsal. A few blocks away Mrs. Baba Grossman is getting ready to leave her family for an evening ballet lesson. Other parents are busy locating sneakers, packing easels or getting ready to make pottery.

What's going on? Nothing unusual. It's just a typical weekday evening, because of something that is happening in communities all over America. Parents are discovering that fun is a matter of individual taste; it doesn't have to include the whole family.

Mr. Martin Hultquist sums up this trend as he waves goodbye to his wife on her way to rehearsal. "We have an agreement," he says. "I don't have to go to her symphony concerts and she doesn't have to go to my chemical society meetings." Mrs. Baba Grossman expresses it from a mother's point of view, "I'm down to earth all day long with the children, but once a week I can get off the ground in ballet."

**Theater.** Out on the edge of another town, a group of parents is finding a creative outlet in putting on plays. Acting talent isn't necessary for joining such a little theater group, for there are many jobs to do. Betty Lovelace, whose specialty is digging up props, joined because she was at home most of the day with her young children, and she got the feeling she couldn't carry on a conversation above the four-year-old level. "I knew if I joined a bridge group I'd end up talking about my kids. At the theater we were so busy I worked in five plays before anybody even knew I had a family."

Betty is also pleased to have made new friends. "A theater attracts people from all age groups and occupations, with different backgrounds and attitudes," she explained. "It's stimulating to be associated with people outside of business acquaintances or neighborhood friends."

Any town can set up a theater group on a shoestring. One started out in a tent with a stage built from timbers and sheet iron salvaged from an abandoned mine. One night when the tent was threatened by wind, members were hastily summoned from their dinners to help hold it down. The tent has now been replaced by a reasonably priced Quonset type of structure. This theater group is now self-supporting and produces six plays a season. It provides pleasure for the community and for those who participate.

At times, talents emerge. One mother of two little boys has made a name for herself by the moving way she portrays tragic characters. Her husband says it distresses him to go to the theater to see his wife suffer, but she replies sensibly, "It's much better than seeing me suffer at home."

**The opera.** In another city, the Civic Opera calls for all kinds of abilities. Kathryn Stone, a mother of two, is a semi-invalid because of arthritis, but she can still use the sewing machine, and her costumes for many productions have won her the respect of the community. "It's exciting for me to feel I have a part in these musicals," she says, "and my greatest satisfaction comes from making the costumes as authentic as possible."

Choruses in the Civic Opera productions are large, and both singers and dancers are much in demand. "Just as on Broadway, these musicals are expensive," one of the producers points out. To help make ends meet, she advises: "Pick a popular musical. Some of the older ones are great and royalties are lower. Then get some lively publicity to stir up interest."

Publicity work on the shows also provides an outlet for parents interested in writing, illustrating and taking photographs.

A word of encouragement for any community musical group comes from Dr. Antonia Brico, who studied in Finland with Jean Sibelius. "The only difference between professionals and amateurs," she says, "is that the professional plays for money, the amateur for love." A clarinet player explains the love and the lure of creative expression this way, "I joined not only because I missed the music I had majored in at college but also because the night rehearsals meant my husband could do the baby sitting. Then he got so interested he went out and bought a double bass, took lessons and joined the Philharmonic, too!"

**Painting groups** are relatively easy to organize in most communities. Our Art Association meets once a week with each member donating fifty cents toward the model's fee. The group's art works are hung in banks, stores and other buildings all over town, and many an amateur has had the unexpected pleasure of becoming professional with a sale.

There are more informal groups of housewives who meet at a house once a week with a sack lunch and just paint for the fun of it.

**Writing.** Another housewife confessed to finding the same sort of comfort in a writer's group—friends who get together once a week just for the pleasure of expressing themselves on paper. "It may be true that everybody has one good book in him," she said, "but who's going to read it outside of a writing group?" Her skepticism has been proved wrong by several sales made by group members, although most still insist their greatest successes are those which are written simply to offer some thought to an appreciative audience.

Of course, not all fun for parents has to be creative. One member of a walking group said, "My children had explored our area with the Cubs

**240**

and Brownies and Scouts and I was the only member of the family who hadn't gotten outdoors to enjoy the countryside." Her group meets every Tuesday morning, even when it snows. They drive to some designated spot outside town and walk for a couple of hours. Sometimes they invite an expert to identify wild flowers in May or mushrooms in the fall. "But generally we rely on nothing more educational than just plain gossip while we walk," she admits.

**Eating.** Speaking out for the International Cooking Group, a member says, "Our efforts are dedicated more to our stomachs than our brains." Sponsored by the public schools in cooperation with the State Board for Vocational Education, ten sessions cost just nine dollars. The group meets once a week in the home economics room of the high school, and after two hours members eat the results of French, Japanese, Italian, Norwegian and other recipes.

**Dancing.** For husbands and wives who like to dance together, we have the square dancers, 600 strong in our town. Not limited to square dancing alone, one club in town is devoted to round dancing, and the others divide the numbers equally between square and round. "Our group is organized for pure fun and we don't take ourselves too seriously," a member said.

**Other interests.** Parents give remarkable reasons for developing a particular interest. A member of an orchid-growers group revealed, "Raising those glamorous blooms gives me a sense of security. When I've used up the food budget and have to serve corned beef hash for dinner, all I do is pin on an orchid and feel rich." One father, a member of a poker club that meets one evening a week, explained, "We do it for charity." He's not kidding. Twenty-five cents out of every pot goes into a scholarship fund that has already sent several local boys to college. A woman I know has a practical reason for joining the PTA's Tuesday night volley ball games for parents. "I just liked the people in the group and needed the exercise," she said simply. The desire for exercise is the main incentive, too, for parents who join Judo and Jiu-jitsu groups.

**All outside interests.** The point is that fun doesn't have to include the whole family. Many parents stressed the importance of going right ahead and following an interest even if nobody else cared to join in.

The most surprising activity, particularly suited to fathers, I heard about from the owner of a local hobby shop. Of course he told me about ham radio sets and sports cars and then added, "Don't forget to include model trains."

Many communities have a group of enthusiastic fathers who set up their tracks and allow the kids to join in occasionally.

" 'Train nuts,' we call them," one wife explained. Her physician husband is one of the most dedicated railroaders in town. "But even if we are railroad widows, none of us really objects. When our husbands get together in the basement to play with their trains, we know where they are!"

She summed up the importance of this consideration between couples for an unshared interest when she added, "Everybody needs an outlet. My husband is just as tolerant of my bowling as I am about his trains. Perhaps that's because he's a doctor and he knows what happens to people who don't have outside interests."—*Dorothy Van Ark*

# FUN
# FOR ADULTS:
# HOW?

**Develop a hobby**   (See our chapter on Hundreds of Hobbies.).

**Join a club,** a group, an organization. Good friends add much to life. You may meet congenial people with similar interests who can make life more pleasant, more interesting.

**Arrange for some quiet time,** alone, away from the sounds of children. This is not a contradiction to the suggestion for new friends. But fun in life is a balance of many good things (most youngsters get tired of a solid diet of ice cream—eventually) and we need both the stimulation of interesting adult companions and the peace of solitude and silence.

**Plan ahead.**   The children will grow up, and it may be difficult then to start finding things to do to fill the loneliness. A life rich with interests and

**242**

activities, however, only becomes richer when the youngsters have grown and you have more time and energy to devote to the interests you have been nurturing all along.

**Seek recreation.**  Plan short trips without the youngsters to places of historic interest which they're too young to appreciate. Go on a more rugged camping expedition than you had thought possible for the family. Go to lectures, exhibits, art galleries.

**Volunteer your services** . . . to your church, temple, local Y, the PTA, park department, private club. Maybe you can help plan, paint, organize, lead, or just lend a helping hand.

Your local hospital—and other health, welfare, and social agencies—have a great need for volunteers: reading to patients, or writing letters for them, or just talking to them to cheer them; distributing and caring for flowers, books; assisting in the gift shop; helping in community surveys; giving out educational material; fund raising; working as adult leaders for groups of young people. Libraries may need you to help at a children's story hour, or running a book-mobile for bedridden or far-away readers. The list is endless—and so are the satisfactions in volunteering for important, useful community work.—*Pauline Landau*

# FUN
# FOR ADULTS:
# WHEN?

Four-day work weeks? Three-week vacations for everyone? They're in sight. Not coming around the corner, perhaps—but surely just over the horizon. From changes that have already taken place, it seems a certainty that we will soon be blessed with more free time to use as we wish.

**Blessing or burden?**  Could it be, however, that all those amber hours "to do what you want to do" will prove not a blessing, but a burden? Well, look at us. We are indeed the busy-busy generation, our recitative "not enough time . . ." Yet most of us are obliged to put in only seven or eight hours a day to earn our bread. What happens to those other hours that we supposedly use as we wish? A remarkable portion is devoted to scrambling from one "activity" to another, like a disturbed ant colony.

Look again—at those of us who do try—or must try—to use leisure time leisurely. Many of us just can't do it, or we come away from the effort without cheer, vaguely unfulfilled. The overworked businessman under doctor's orders to take it easy, attacks taking it easy as though he were building a new industry—or maybe he gets sicker because he feels so useless when he's not working hard.

**Hobbies.** Older people must be helped to find a hobby, when some time during their lives there must have been a thousand things they'd have liked to do. Hobbies are fine and are certainly to be encouraged, but too often a hobby is a crutch when it should be a wing. Where a hobby should be a welcome chance to fulfill a natural inclination or desire, it is often no more than a filler-in of an apparently frightening vacuum.

**Does time on our hands** make us uneasy? It all suggests strongly that while we dream of hours when we can "do what we want to do," we don't really know what it is we want to do. Or if we do know, we can't do it because we lack the skill or the confidence or both.

**Education.** Obviously, education is important preparation for leisure. A well-designed education teaches people how to spend leisure time, as well as preparing them for particular careers. Schooling should not be designed exclusively toward earning a living, but toward completing one's living. Though vocational instruction is becoming increasingly important, liberal education is in the long run the best preparation for living as a whole. In a technological era, we can return to school for a broad, general, liberal education—for this matters tremendously to both leisure and work.

**What about fun?** Once there was good reason for a fun-is-sin and all-must-be-useful notion. Once, almost every waking hour had to be devoted to labor in order to survive. It was valid early in our nation's history to view idleness as sin—on a frontier, with a continent to be tamed, in a time when how you worked the fields in summer determined whether or

244

not you ate in winter. Though many Americans still have a distressingly low standard of living, however, most of us aren't worried about next week's meals. Are we going to cling to outmoded values?

**Spontaneity.** Usefulness and groupiness are the worms that eat their way through time that should be our own. Both must be bypassed if there is to be room for the true roots of enjoying leisure: creativity and spontaneity and the knowledge of where, for each individual, the most satisfying outlet lies. We should retain the capacity to turn out painting after painting, song after song, hobby after hobby—and throw them all away if we want to. Because we get pleasure from the doing. Because we are not making something that must be permanently useful or in order to please others. We must develop the kind of pleasure that comes of appreciating, too, not necessarily of doing. We should be able, if we wish, to spend three hours at the Louvre—if that's really all we have—gazing only at a single painting or marvelling at a renaissance bronze or losing ourselves in the world of the Egyptian antiquities. Perhaps we will come to feel with William H. Davies that leisure is "time to stand and stare."

It will be very difficult to put into words, should someone ask if we "did" the Louvre, just what it was we did. For what each of us brings away will be part of his soul and it's hard to describe one's soul. But pleasure in its most "useless" sense is most truly useful. It warms the stomach and the heart. It makes for a people that can live without pick-me-up and tone-me-down pills. It makes for people who are content with themselves and therefore inclined to be content with others.

**Affecting the family.** With increased leisure, mothers and fathers will just naturally be doing things with their children because they are together with their children—and time-time-time for activities does not press. A mother surrounded by toil-saving automation wonders may decide that she wants to work on a loom and weave her own cloth—and there will be time for the children to learn, too. (The one who doesn't want to weave can go off and stare out the window and still be together with his family—because no one's in a panic for him to do something useful or considers him "different" or anti-social.)

Leisure time will thus be a fruitful time—and a happier time for us all.

—*Margaret Albrecht*

# INDEX

**246**

**248**